Samuel Beckett as World Literature

Literatures as World Literature

Can the literature of a specific country, author or genre be used to approach the elusive concept of 'world literature'? **Literatures as World Literature** takes a novel approach to world literature by analysing specific constellations – according to language, nation, form or theme – of literary texts and authors in their own world-literary dimensions.

World literature is obviously so vast that any view of it cannot help but be partial; the question then becomes how to reduce the complex task of understanding and describing world literature. Most treatments of world literature so far either have been theoretical and thus abstract or have made broad use of exemplary texts from a variety of languages and epochs. The majority of critical work, the filling in of what has been traced, lies ahead of us. **Literatures as World Literature** fills in the devilish details by allowing scholars to move outwards from their own areas of specialization, fostering scholarly writing that approaches more closely the polyphonic, multiperspectival nature of world literature.

Series Editor
Thomas O. Beebee

Editorial Board
Eduardo Coutinho, Federal University of Rio de Janeiro, Brazil
Hsinya Huang, National Sun-yat Sen University, Taiwan
Meg Samuelson, University of Cape Town, South Africa
Ken Seigneurie, Simon Fraser University, Canada
Mads Rosendahl Thomsen, Aarhus University, Denmark

Volumes in the Series
German Literature as World Literature
Edited by Thomas O. Beebee
Roberto Bolaño as World Literature
Edited by Nicholas Birns and Juan E. De Castro
Crime Fiction as World Literature
Edited by David Damrosch, Theo D'haen, and Louise Nilsson

Danish Literature as World Literature
Edited by Dan Ringgaard and Mads Rosendahl Thomsen

From Paris to Tlön: Surrealism as World Literature
By Delia Ungureanu

American Literature as World Literature
Edited by Jeffrey R. Di Leo

Romanian Literature as World Literature
Edited by Mircea Martin, Christian Moraru, and Andrei Terian

Brazilian Literature as World Literature
Edited by Eduardo F. Coutinho

Dutch and Flemish Literature as World Literature
Edited by Theo D'haen

Afropolitan Literature as World Literature
Edited by James Hodapp

Francophone Literature as World Literature
Edited by Christian Moraru, Nicole Simek, and Bertrand Westphal

Bulgarian Literature as World Literature (forthcoming)
Edited by Mihaela P. Harper and Dimitar Kambourov

Philosophy as World Literature (forthcoming)
Edited by Jeffrey R. Di Leo

Elena Ferrante as World Literature (forthcoming)
By Stiliana Milkova

Modern Indian Literature as World Literature (forthcoming)
Edited by Bhavya Tiwari

Modern Irish Literature as World Literature (forthcoming)
Edited by Christopher Langlois

Persian Literature as World Literature (forthcoming)
Edited by Mostafa Abedinifard, Omid Azadibougar, and Amirhossein Vafa

Samuel Beckett as World Literature

Edited by
Thirthankar Chakraborty and
Juan Luis Toribio Vazquez

BLOOMSBURY ACADEMIC
NEW YORK • LONDON • OXFORD • NEW DELHI • SYDNEY

BLOOMSBURY ACADEMIC
Bloomsbury Publishing Inc
1385 Broadway, New York, NY 10018, USA
50 Bedford Square, London, WC1B 3DP, UK
29 Earlsfort Terrace, Dublin 2, Ireland

BLOOMSBURY, BLOOMSBURY ACADEMIC and the Diana logo
are trademarks of Bloomsbury Publishing Plc

First published in the United States of America 2020
This paperback edition published in 2022

Volume Editor's Part of the Work © Thirthankar
Chakraborty and Juan Luis Toribio Vazquez
Each chapter © Contributors

Cover design by Simon Levy / Levy Associates

For legal purposes the Acknowledgements on p. xviii consistute
an extension of this copyright page.

All rights reserved. No part of this publication may be reproduced or transmitted
in any form or by any means, electronic or mechanical, including photocopying,
recording, or any information storage or retrieval system, without prior
permission in writing from the publishers.

Bloomsbury Publishing Inc does not have any control over, or responsibility for,
any third-party websites referred to or in this book. All internet addresses given
in this book were correct at the time of going to press. The author and publisher
regret any inconvenience caused if addresses have changed or sites have
ceased to exist, but can accept no responsibility for any such changes.

A catalog record for this book is available from the Library of Congress.

Library of Congress Cataloging-in-Publication Data

Names: Chakraborty, Thirthankar, editor. | Vazquez, Juan Luis Toribio, editor.
Title: Samuel Beckett as world literature / edited by Thirthankar
Chakraborty and Juan Luis Toribio Vazquez.
Description: New York: Bloomsbury Academic, 2020. | Series: Literatures as
world literature | Includes bibliographical references and index.
Identifiers: LCCN 2020001964 | ISBN 9781501358807 (hardback) |
ISBN 9781501358821 (pdf) | ISBN 9781501358814 (ebook)
Subjects: LCSH: Beckett, Samuel, 1906-1989–Criticism and interpretation. |
Beckett, Samuel, 1906-1989–Translations. | Beckett, Samuel,
1906-1989–Adaptations. | Beckett, Samuel, 1906-1989–Influence.
Classification: LCC PR6003.E282 Z8174 2020 | DDC 823/.914–dc23
LC record available at https://lccn.loc.gov/2020001964

ISBN: HB: 978-1-5013-5880-7
PB: 978-1-5013-7194-3
ePDF: 978-1-5013-5882-1
eBook: 978-1-5013-5881-4

Series: Literatures as World Literature

Typeset by Integra Software Services Pvt. Ltd.

To find out more about our authors and books visit www.bloomsbury.com
and sign up for our newsletters.

CONTENTS

List of Figures ix
Notes on Contributors x
Foreword xv
Acknowledgements xviii

Introduction: Samuel Beckett as world literature
Thirthankar Chakraborty and Juan Luis Toribio Vazquez 1

PART I Translation

1 Bilingual Beckett *John Fletcher* 17

2 Shifting cultural affinities in *Molloy*: A genetic bilingual approach *Dirk Van Hulle and Pim Verhulst* 29

3 Samuel Beckett and the politics of post-war translation *Thirthankar Chakraborty* 45

4 Unformed and untranslatable: The global applicability of Beckett's theatre of affect *Charlotta Palmstierna Einarsson* 59

5 100% guaranteed Beckett: An intercultural reading of Beckett's *Waiting for Godot* as world literature *Mary O'Byrne and Wei Zheyu* 71

PART II Adaptation

6 Modernism, medium and memory *Mischa Twitchin* 85

7 Knock, knock, who's there? The circulation of *Macbeth*, *Ulysses* and the myth of Echo and Narcissus in *Ohio Impromptu* Laurens De Vos 99

8 Echoes, rags and bones: A few Brazilian Becketts on the way *Fábio de Souza Andrade* 109

9 Samuel Beckett's *Fin de partie* in Hungary: A brief reception history *Anita Rákóczy* 125

10 Tracing Beckett in the avant-garde theatre of mainland China *Liu Aiying* 137

PART III Circulation

11 What goes around comes around: *Godot*'s circularity and world literature *Juan Luis Toribio Vazquez* 153

12 Unworlding world literature: Or how Godot travels from a country road to the world *Arka Chattopadhyay* 167

13 Godot's arrivals: Beckettian and anti-Beckettian discourses in Bulatović's *Godot Has Arrived* and Komanin's *Godot Has Arrived to Collect His Dues* *Snežana Kalinić* 181

14 Waiting for the arrivant: Godot in two poems by Nizār Qabbānī *Hania A. M. Nashef* 191

15 Forgetfulness of the past as revealed in Minoru Betsuyaku's *Godot Has Come*: A play inspired by *Waiting for Godot* *Mariko Hori Tanaka* 203

Index 214

FIGURES

1 Ana Kfouri directed by Isabel Cavalcanti in *Moi lui*, 2014. Dalton Valério 116

2 Yara de Cunto directed by Guimarães Brothers in *Sopro* (d'après *Act without Words I*), Ocupação Sozinhos Juntos, 2015. Ismael Monticelli 120

3 *Quadrado* (d'après *Quad*), *Ocupação Sozinhos Juntos*, directed by Guimarães Brothers, 2015. Ismael Monticelli 120

CONTRIBUTORS

Liu Aiying has a PhD in English Language and Literature from Shanghai International Studies University. She is currently Professor of English at the School of English Language and Literature, Sichuan International Studies University. As Visiting Scholar, she has worked with the Faculty of English at the University of Cambridge, Stanley Gontarski at Florida State University and Stephen Greenblatt at Harvard University. She has published two research monographs entitled *Samuel Beckett: The Body Matters* (2013) and *Interpreting Beckett's Drama* (2012). She has published critical essays in journals such as *Foreign Language and Literature*, *Journal of Sichuan International Studies* and *New History of Foreign Literature*. She has also translated the works of Samuel Beckett, Hugh Honour, Julia Kristeva and Martin Esslin, and several critical works on Beckett by Stanley Gontarski, John Fletcher and Ruby Cohn.

Fábio de Souza Andrade is Professor of Literary Theory and Comparative Literature at the University of São Paulo, Brazil. He has published extensively on Brazilian and European modernism, reviewing regularly fiction and poetry for Brazilian cultural periodicals. His publications on Beckett include *Samuel Beckett: o silêncio possível* (Ateliê 2001), as well as many articles. He has translated *Waiting for Godot*, *Endgame*, *Happy Days*, *Murphy* and *Watt* into Brazilian Portuguese (Cosac Naify) and is presently working on the translation of Beckett's complete dramatic works.

Thirthankar Chakraborty is Assistant Professor in the Department of Liberal Arts at the Indian Institute of Technology (IIT) Bhilai, India. Funded by a 50th Anniversary GTA Scholarship, he holds a PhD in Comparative Literature from the University of Kent. He co-organized the 'Samuel Beckett and World Literature' conference in 2016, which was sponsored by the Centre for Modern European Literature. He won a British Centre for Literary Translation bursary for participating at the Institute of World Literature in 2015 and was recipient of the Samuel Beckett Summer School's international bursary in 2014. His research interests focus around comparative and world literature, modernism and literary theory.

Arka Chattopadhyay is Assistant Professor of Humanities and Social Sciences in IIT Gandhinagar, India. He has been published in books like *Deleuze and Beckett* (2015) and in journals such as *Interventions, Textual Practice, Samuel Beckett Today/Aujourd'hui, The Harold Pinter Review* and *Psychoanalysis, Culture and Society* etc. He has co-edited the book, *Samuel Beckett and the Encounter of Philosophy and Literature* (2013) and is also co-editor of the online journal *Sanglap* (http://sanglap-journal.in/). He has guest-edited the SBT/A issue on *Samuel Beckett and the Extensions of the Mind* (2017). His first monograph, *Beckett, Lacan and the Mathematical Writing of the Real*, was published by Bloomsbury in 2019. Arka is currently editing a volume of essays on and translations of the writer Nabarun Bhattacharya, slated to come out from Bloomsbury in 2020.

Charlotta Palmstierna Einarsson is Senior Lecturer in English at the Mid-Sweden University, Sundsvall. Her research interests include modernist literature, drama and dance studies, aesthetics, reception theory, philosophy and phenomenology. She is the author of *A Theatre of Affect: The Corporeal Turn in Samuel Beckett's Drama* (2017).

John Fletcher is the author, co-author, editor or translator of some twenty books on modern writers including Flaubert, Beckett, Robbe-Grillet, Claude Simon and Iris Murdoch. He recently translated a critical study of Hervé Guibert and is currently working on the novelist and playwright Marie NDiaye. His reviews of recent French publications appear regularly in the *Times Literary Supplement*. He has researched extensively on French film and twentieth-century French history. He is also an authority on twentieth-century poetry in English (especially Wilfred Owen, Philip Larkin, John Hewitt and Bob Dylan).

Snežana Kalinić is Assistant Professor at the Faculty of Philology of the University of Belgrade, Serbia, in the Department of Comparative Literature and Literary Theory. Her research interests focus on comparative literature, theatre and performance studies, utopian studies and gender studies. She is a member of the research project *Knjiženstvo – Theory and History of Women's Writing in Serbian until 1915*. Her recent book is *Sećanje i zaborav u Beketovim dramama* (*Memory and Forgetting in Beckett's Plays*, 2016).

Hania A. M. Nashef is Associate Professor in the Department of Mass Communication at the American University of Sharjah, United Arab Emirates. Her research interests focus on comparative and postcolonial literatures, media studies and film in the Arab world. Her publications include *The Politics of Humiliation in the Novels of J. M. Coetzee* (2009), essays on J. M. Coetzee, José Saramago, Mahmoud Darwish, Raja Shehadeh, and Palestinian literature and film. Her most recent book is *Palestinian Culture and the Nakba: Bearing Witness* (2018).

Mary O'Byrne is a final year PhD candidate in the School of English in Trinity College Dublin. The working title of her research is 'The phenomenology of death and human consciousness and the inner workings of time in the stage plays of Samuel Beckett'. She is researching under the supervision of Professor Chris Morash, Seamus Heaney Professor of Irish Writing. A graduate of University College Dublin (UCD) with a BA in Social Science in 1982, Mary worked in the public service for over twenty years, obtaining a Masters of Public Administration in UCD in 1989. She completed a Masters of Drama and Performance in UCD in 2010. Mary works as a teaching assistant in the School of English and she is the convener of the Beckett Reading Group established in 2014 to the present.

Anita Rákóczy is Lecturer at Károli Gáspár University of the Reformed Church in Hungary. As a dramaturg and theatre critic, she has reviewed several international theatre festivals. She has conducted research on Samuel Beckett's *Fin de partie* at CUNY Graduate Centre New York with Fulbright Scholarship and also in the University of Reading's Samuel Beckett Collection. She has worked for the Hungarian Theatre Museum and Institute and the International Theatre Institute (ITI) Hungarian Centre. Her paper 'Godots That Arrived – The First Budapest Productions before and after 1989' was published in *Samuel Beckett Today/Aujourd'hui* in 2017. Her PhD thesis focuses on the genesis and post-publication creation process of *Fin de partie*. She is co-organizer of the 2017 Budapest IFTR Samuel Beckett Working Group Meeting.

Mariko Hori Tanaka is Professor of English at Aoyama Gakuin University, Tokyo. With Linda Ben-Zvi and Nicholas Johnson, she co-convened the Samuel Beckett Working Group in the International Federation of Theatre Research. She published essays on the reception of Beckett's works in Japan and the influences of haiku on Beckett in *Samuel Beckett Today/Aujourd'hui*. With Yoshiki Tajiri and Michiko Tsushima, she co-edited *Samuel Beckett and Pain* (Rodopi 2013) and *Samuel Beckett and Trauma* (2018). Her recent interest lies in how the Second World War and the Cold War affected Beckett in writing his post-war works. In 2016–17, she published three essays on Beckett in relation to these wars in Japanese collections of essays. Since 2013, she has been supervising Theater X(cai) in Tokyo. Commemorating the sixtieth anniversary of diplomatic relations between Ireland and Japan in 2017, Theater X(cai) and Mouth on Fire co-produced *Waiting for Godot* in Tokyo and Kyoto.

Mischa Twitchin is a lecturer in the Theatre and Performance Department at Goldsmiths, University of London. His book *The Theatre of Death – The Uncanny in Mimesis: Tadeusz Kantor, Aby Warburg and an Iconology of the Actor* (2016) was published by Palgrave Macmillan in their Performance Philosophy series, and examples of his performance and essay films can be seen on Vimeo (http://vimeo.com/user13124826/videos).

Juan Luis Toribio Vazquez received his PhD from the University of Kent in December 2018, where he formerly taught comparative literature from 2015 to 2018. His thesis, *Narrative Circularity in Modern European Literature*, was funded by a Fiftieth Anniversary Scholarship. Juan Luis graduated in English Philology (five-year programme, BA + MA equivalent) from the University of Seville in 2013 and received an MA with distinction and the prize for best dissertation for his research project *The Theatre of Nihilism: Ionesco, Beckett and Adamov*, from the University of Kent at Paris in 2014. He co-organized the Samuel Beckett and World Literature conference in 2016 and has presented papers at various international conferences. His forthcoming publications include 'On a Circular Road: Queneau, Beckett, Arrabal and Robbe-Grillet' in *Wdrodze / On the Road - Perspektywy badawcze* (2019).

Dirk Van Hulle is Professor of Bibliography and Modern Book History at the University of Oxford and director of the Centre for Manuscript Genetics at the University of Antwerp. With Mark Nixon, he is co-director of the Beckett Digital Manuscript Project (www.beckettarchive.org), series editor of the Cambridge University Press series 'Elements in Beckett Studies' and editor-in-chief of the *Journal of Beckett Studies*. His publications include *Textual Awareness* (2004), *Modern Manuscripts* (2014), *Samuel Beckett's Library* (2013, with Mark Nixon), *The New Cambridge Companion to Samuel Beckett* (2015), *James Joyce's Work in Progress* (2016), the *Beckett Digital Library* and a number of volumes in the 'Making of' series (Bloomsbury) and genetic editions in the *Beckett Digital Manuscript Project*, which won the 2019 Prize for a Bibliography, Archive or Digital Project of the Modern Language Association (MLA).

Pim Verhulst is Assistant Professor of English Literature at the University of Antwerp. He has published articles in *SBT/A*, *Variants* and *JOBS*, of which he is assistant editor, and book chapters in *Beckett and Modernism* (also co-edited) and *Pop Beckett* (2019). As an editorial board member of the Samuel Beckett Digital Manuscript Project, he has also co-edited and authored the modules on *Molloy*, *Malone meurt/Malone Dies* and *En Attendant Godot/Waiting for Godot*, which received an MLA Prize in 2018. His monograph, *The Making of Samuel Beckett's Radio Plays*, is forthcoming with Bloomsbury in 2020.

Laurens De Vos is Assistant Professor in Theatre Studies at the University of Amsterdam. He obtained his PhD in 2006 from the University of Ghent. He is the author of *Cruelty and Desire in the Modern Theater. Antonin Artaud, Sarah Kane, and Samuel Beckett* (2011) and the editor of *Sarah Kane in Context* (2010). Together with Mariko Hori Tanaka and Nick Johnson, he is currently working on an edition of essays entitled *Voicing Beckett/ Beckett's Voices*.

Shane Weller is Head of the School of European Culture and Languages and co-director of the Centre for Modern European Literature at the University of Kent. Besides publishing numerous essays on Beckett, Kafka, Nietzsche, Celan, Blanchot, Benjamin and other modern European writers and literary theorists, he has also published several books on Beckett and European modernism, with the last two being *Language and Negativity in European Modernism* (2018) and *The Making of Samuel Beckett's 'Endgame'/'Fin de partie'* (2018), which he co-authored with Dirk Van Hulle. Shane Weller is also one of the general editors of the Palgrave Studies in Modern European Literature book series, and the books he has edited include *Modernist Eroticisms: European Literature after Sexology* (2012) and *Samuel Beckett's* Molloy, published in 2009 by Faber and Faber.

Wei Zheyu is a lecturer of drama at Guangxi Arts University, China. As a Trinity Long Room Hub Fellow (2013–17), Wei received his PhD at Trinity College Dublin in 2017, with his doctorate thesis entitled, 'Post-Cold War Experimental Theatre of China: Staging Globalization and Its Resistance'. He has published several articles on contemporary Chinese theatre, intercultural theatre and studies in intermedial performances. Wei also translates and writes plays for the theatre.

FOREWORD

In the rapidly expanding critical discourse on the concept of world literature, the argument is often made that world literature should not be mistaken for a corpus of works that have simply transcended national literatures by achieving an international readership. Rather, world literature is to be understood as a particular mode of reading or a particular mode of circulation, the latter including acts of translation and adaptation. And yet, notwithstanding this critical caution, not only have anthologies of world literature been published, suggesting a body of works that are adjudged by the editors to have achieved world-literary standing, but certain authors have repeatedly served as touchstones or test cases in arguments both for and, more rarely, against the concept of world literature. Among those authors, one of the most frequently deployed is Samuel Beckett. The reasons for this are not hard to identify. As the present volume demonstrates, since his coming to international attention in the 1950s, Beckett's oeuvre has circulated across the world; it is bilingual in nature; it engages explicitly with questions of translation and untranslatability; and it includes works in a range of genres and media: poetry, prose fiction, drama, radio plays, film and television. And, of course, Beckett's principal themes speak to people across cultures, not least on account of the apparent minimalism or abstraction of his representations. The (failing) attempt to make sense of human existence, dreams of salvation, the struggle with language, and the experience of alienation and homelessness – such themes traverse national, linguistic and cultures borders. While academic research on Beckett's works – with, in recent decades, a particular focus on the extensive archival materials that have come to light – is thriving, the rich literary, philosophical, psychological and political seams in his writing have also appealed to theatregoers across the world.

As for the often-addressed question of the relation between national literatures and world literature, Beckett seems to anticipate many of the critical debates in this area by explicitly resisting compartmentalization within any one national culture. Beyond his various remarks in conversations, interviews and letters to the effect that he never saw himself as an Irish writer, let alone an English one, Beckett's works often thematize the experience of vagabondage or migration. One need only think of the characters in what remains his best-known work, the play *Waiting for Godot*, to appreciate this point. Judging by their names alone, *Godot*'s dramatis personae suggest a world in which no one is at home. His post-war work in particular is populated by figures who might be described as citizens of nowhere, the dark obverse of the cosmopolitan championed by writers such as Voltaire and Goethe. For Beckett, who had witnessed first-hand the impact of rabid nationalism during his time in Nazi Germany in 1936–7, the very idea of one ever belonging to a national culture, and to a national language, is to be challenged, and it is certainly subjected to unremitting pressure in his oeuvre. It was precisely to the attempt to identify the national character of his friend Jack B. Yeats's painting that Beckett objected when, in the late summer of 1945, shortly after the end of the Second World War, he reviewed Thomas McGreevy's book on Yeats. As Beckett put it a decade later, in his short homage to Yeats, 'The artist who stakes his being is from nowhere, has no kith.' There is, for Beckett, no such thing as a great artist who belongs fully to any national culture. Art and nationalism are, for him, quite simply incompatible. In that sense, genuine art as Beckett conceives is always already beyond the possessive grip of nationalism. And yet he is no less critical of the Enlightenment idea of the cosmopolitan who is at home everywhere. Beckett's figures are at home nowhere and thus belong within neither a national nor an international sphere. Their place is always elsewhere, and this has significant implications for the attempt to coordinate Beckett in relation to the concept of world literature.

What, then, of Beckett's oeuvre as a whole in relation to world literature? An important point when considering this question is the trajectory of Beckett's own career as a writer. For over two decades – that is, from 1929, when his first short story was published, to 1953, when *Godot* was first performed on the stage – Beckett's readership was very limited indeed. Readers' reports on his work repeatedly comment upon the absence of any market for it. His first published novel, *Murphy* (1938), sold very poorly, the many unsold copies being destroyed by a fire during the Blitz. By 1950, when he had already written the three novels, *Molloy*, *Malone Dies* and *The Unnamable*, as well as *Waiting for Godot*, Beckett had not even published a book since 1938. As is well known, the international success of *Godot* in the 1950s transformed Beckett's fortunes as a writer, and it was not long before his entire oeuvre was in print. In 1969, he was awarded the Nobel Prize in Literature, following the award of the International Publishers' Formentor Prize in 1961 – this latter being shared with the Argentinian writer Jorge Luis Borges. The first two decades of Beckett's writing life resemble in many respects that of another twentieth-century European writer whose readership remained extremely limited during his lifetime, only for his posthumous success to project him into the canon of world literature. The writer in question is, of course, Franz Kafka.

It would seem, then, that Beckett's place is, like Kafka's, secure for the foreseeable future in the canon of world literature. When one reflects further on that world-literary status, however, it almost immediately becomes clear that it rests for the most part on very few works and indeed largely on Beckett's dramatic works. While Beckett the novelist has undoubtedly influenced some of today's most highly regarded writers, including Nobel Prize winners such as J. M. Coetzee, it is the major plays that have circulated most widely, and that have been most transformative of artistic practice. The world-literary Beckett is the author of *Waiting for Godot*, *Endgame*, *Krapp's Last Tape*, *Happy Days* and *Not I*. The question then becomes what it is about those plays in particular that has secured Beckett the position he currently holds within the world-literary canon. In January 1827, Goethe famously declared, in conversation with Johann Peter Eckermann, that the epoch of world literature was at hand. It would be fair to say that the time for an exploration of Beckett's place within – and his transformative impact upon the concept of – world literature is itself now at hand. The present volume constitutes a valuable contribution to that exploration, exploring as it does the world-literary nature of his works and addressing important questions regarding translation, adaptation and circulation. In so doing, it testifies to Beckett's enduring relevance in an age when globalization is showing its dark side as much as its light.

Shane Weller
University of Kent

ACKNOWLEDGEMENTS

As editors of this volume, we wish to thank Professor Shane Weller, for his invaluable insights and guidance throughout the last several years. We are thankful to the Centre for Modern European Literature of the University of Kent for funding the 'Samuel Beckett and World Literature' conference held in the spring of 2016, together with the various departments in the School of European Culture and Languages, including Comparative Literature, Modern Languages, Asian Studies and the School of English. We are also grateful to Katherine De Chant, Rachel Walker and Viswasirasini, for their patience and assistance throughout the entire publication process, to Professor Thomas O. Beebee and the Bloomsbury Academic team for taking us on board for this project and for the encouragement we have received along the way. Finally, a very special thanks to our volume's contributors for their cooperation and insightful essays, to Michael Dean-White for his helpful feedback, and to Sofia and Suhasini for their unconditional love and support.

Introduction: Samuel Beckett as world literature

Thirthankar Chakraborty and Juan Luis Toribio Vazquez

> HAMM: *Take me for a little turn. [CLOV goes behind the chair and pushes it forward.] Not too fast! [CLOV pushes chair.] Right round the world! [CLOV pushes chair.] Hug the walls, then back to the centre again.*
>
> BECKETT 2006A: 104

In the decade leading up to the Second World War, Samuel Beckett was frequently left dejected by his repeated failure to secure publication for his work. Following his resignation from a lectureship at Trinity College Dublin in early 1931, and periods spent in Germany, France and England, Beckett ran out of money and was forced to return to his parents with his 'tail between his legs' (Knowlson 1997: 163). While Charles Prentice of Chatto and Windus was among the first to recognize his potential, with the publication of *Proust* (1931) and *More Pricks Than Kicks* (1934), Prentice also rejected Beckett's first novel, *Dream of Fair to Middling Women*, written in 1931–2 but published posthumously in 1992. Moreover, his second novel, *Murphy* (1938), went almost unnoticed and sold very poorly once it finally found a publisher. It was only after the war that Beckett was finally able to find his style and footing, writing in French rather than English and casting off the remaining traces of James Joyce's influence. The generic shift from prose and poetry to drama was the final leap, enabling him to pass from obscurity into the limelight: first Paris and then the world with the publication and staging of *En Attendant Godot* in 1952–3.

Since then, Beckett has grown to be one of the foremost literary figures of the twentieth century. Tracing the reception of his works during his lifetime and then through the decades since his death in 1989 is akin to charting the rapid spread of a religion, with Godot taking the place of God. From his earliest novels to his later dramaticules, Beckett's works have travelled across cultures, continents and religions, breaking language barriers and reaching various communities suffering from social exclusion. Not only has his work drawn responses from prominent European intellectuals such as Theodor W. Adorno, Roland Barthes and Slavoj Žižek, among many others, but it has also penetrated prison walls and found its place among those living on the fringes of society, starting with the famous San Francisco Actors' Workshop at the San Quentin Penitentiary in 1957.[1] Lawrence Graver notes that *Godot*, for instance, has been performed as a political parable for independence, as a solution to the destitution of peasants, as the wanderings of 'no-hopers', and as a means of connecting with life in prison (see 2004: 82). Accordingly, the play is today widely regarded as being among the greatest achievements of modern drama, expressing as it does 'the most vital of contemporary and universal concerns' (Graver 2004: 85).

Along with his theatrical work, Beckett's prose work has also enjoyed very considerable success, having been translated and studied in innumerable languages (see Knowlson 1997: 545). Outgrowing the context in which they were first produced, Beckett's writings have gone beyond boundaries of English, French, Irish, European and even modernist literature to secure their place in recent compilations of world literature, such as the Norton and Longman anthologies. His works have also crossed genre and media borders, for even during his lifetime Beckett received numerous requests for permission to adapt his works for film or television. Despite his disinclination to permit such adaptations, today his works are not only included in countless international syllabi in theatre and literary studies, but they are also simultaneously performed at theatre, dance and music events and adapted into films across the world: both in their original language and form and in translation.

Beyond that, Beckett's name has exceeded even the boundaries of art and literature: the Samuel Beckett Bridge over the River Liffey has linked the north and south sides of Dublin since 2009, his portrait has been printed on Irish passports since October 2013 and the University of Reading (which holds the world's largest Beckett archive) made the international news after purchasing the manuscript of Beckett's first published novel, *Murphy*, for £962,500 in July 2013. What is more, although on a less extravagant scale, the Swiss tennis player Stanislas Wawrinka also caught media attention in September of the same year for sporting a tattoo on his left arm reading: 'Ever tried. Ever Failed. No matter. Try again. Fail again. Fail better' from *Worstward Ho* (1983), and in November 2013, the Irish Naval Service launched a patrol vessel named LÉ *Samuel Beckett*, which has since been used in the Mediterranean for migrant rescue missions.

So not only has Beckett been read across cultures and languages, but he has become a global phenomenon and a point of geographic, academic, economic and sociopolitical reference. On New Year's Day in 2014, Ion Jinga, the Romanian ambassador to Britain, compared British MPs and journalists to Beckett's tragicomic couple from *Godot*, since, following the reinstatement of the permission to live and work in the UK, they waited, and were left waiting, for the falsely anticipated flood of Romanian and Bulgarian immigrants (see Syal 2014: n.p.; and Simons 2014: n.p.). Furthermore, Terry Eagleton cited Beckett's *Molloy* (1951) for its 'uncertainties and ambiguities' when explaining the 'crisis' of Brexit in 2016 (see Lucas, Mason, Meek, and Orbach 2016: n.p.). Thus, the question to be addressed in the light of Beckett's global presence is not so much whether Beckett is part of a world literary canon, but what it *means* for Beckett to be part of world literature: how does one read Beckett in the context of world literature?

Before attempting to answer this question, however, it is crucial to consider the significance of this ostensibly tautological concept, since, as Damrosch remarks, 'A category from which nothing can be excluded is essentially useless' (2003: 110).[2] So in order to formulate a working definition or the conceptual framework of world literature for this volume, it is worth briefly taking on board its historical evolution. While August Schlözer was one of the first to use the term *Weltliteratur* in the eighteenth century (see Tihanov 2011: 142–3), the conceptual framework commonly associated with world literature is built around Goethe's conversation with Eckermann in 1827. In this frequently cited exchange, Goethe remarks, 'National literature means little now, the age of *Weltliteratur* has begun; and everyone should further its course' (D'haen, Domínguez, and Thomsen 2013: 11). He later writes in his Introduction to Thomas Carlyle's *Life of Schiller* (1825):

> General world literature can only develop when nations get to know all the relations among all the nations. The inevitable result will be that they will find in each other something likeable and something repulsive, something to be imitated and something to be rejected.
>
> (D'haen, Domínguez, and Thomsen 2013: 14–15)

In elaborating his views, Goethe thus proposes the idea of a space where literary works from a national literature would circulate beyond local and national boundaries, entering into intercultural dialogue. Far from being exempt from *Weltliteratur*, national literatures form an integral part of Goethe's conception of world literature, in contrast to Herder's understanding of national literatures as both distinct and independent from one another. In this light, the cosmopolitan Beckett, who read, studied and occasionally translated French, Italian, German, Mexican and English literatures while also delving into art, music and philosophy from various parts of the world, fits well with what Goethe had in mind.

Two decades after Goethe's conversations with Eckermann, in *The Communist Manifesto* (1848), Marx and Engels argue that in an increasingly globalized market '[n]ational one-sidedness and narrow-mindedness become more and more impossible' (2000: 249). In this new context, both the form and the content of the literary work will be affected if it is to find its place within the 'universal interdependence of nations' (2000: 249). It remains unclear, however, whether this is an argument for 'world literature' commodified as commercial transaction or against world literature as part of the 'gigantic means of production and of exchange' that modern bourgeois society has conjured up and is 'no longer able to control' (2000: 250).

This ambiguity opens up a space for the critical backlash that world literature faced following the two world wars, particularly when we map sociopolitically the processes of exclusion and inclusion in determining a world canon. Looking back at the publication history of 'world' classics reveals the many biases of literary value, while critics even today continue to delineate or to denounce centres and peripheries within the literary world. Historically, the very notion of a canon has been largely determined by American, European or Russian academics, a problem that Erich Auerbach identifies in 1952 when he states, 'All human activity is being concentrated either into European-American or into Russian-Bolshevist patterns' (1969: 2–3). This, according to Auerbach, explains both the process and the dangers of standardization: a levelling of the immense variety of literary traditions into 'a single literary culture, only a few literary languages, and perhaps even a single literary language' (1969: 3). As Auerbach observes, '[H]erewith the notion of *Weltliteratur* would be at once realized and destroyed' (1969: 3).

Soon after Auerbach's critique, Beckett was involved in a UNESCO project, translating Mexican poetry into English, under the editorship of Octavio Paz. He was thus well aware of the impact on literary works of both editorial selection, or anthologization, and translation, under an increasingly institutionalized NGO set upon determining literary and cultural value and then marketing national canons. Auerbach's emphasis upon the need for an historicist-philological approach to world literature is an attack on precisely these attempts at determining a literary standard controlled by one or more nations and regulated at the expense of cultural diversity. However, working as a translator, and, subsequently, as a self-translator, Beckett grew to possess a keen sense of ambivalence towards any one linguistic field and came in his own work to reside in no one single language (see Weller 2006: 78). When asked if he was English, Beckett famously replied, 'au contraire', and when asked why he wrote in French instead of the 'Irish language', he said, 'If there is one [language] that is really foreign to me, it is Gaelic' (2011: 464).

In recent decades, the critical discourse for or against world literature has grown increasingly prolific. With the publication of *La République mondiale des lettres* (1999), in which an alternative to world literature is proposed, Pascale Casanova argued that 'nothing is more international than a national state: it is constructed solely in relation to other states, and often in opposition to them' (2004: 36). The same would be true of a national literature. From Casanova's point of view, the literary revolutions achieved by Kafka, Joyce and Beckett, among others, are 'often the product of emerging national spaces' within an irrefutably Gallocentric world republic of letters (2011: 131). In contrast, while David Damrosch's *What Is World Literature?* (2003) also pays close attention to the differences between literary cultures, his threefold definition of world literature is built upon the principles of encounter and exchange. His three main criteria are:

1 World literature is an elliptical refraction of national literatures.
2 World literature is writing that gains in translation.
3 World literature is not a set canon of texts but a mode of reading: a form of detached engagement with worlds beyond our own place and time.

(Damrosch 2003: 281)

From Damrosch's standpoint, Beckett's dramatic works and particularly his three novels belong to world literature, given their circulation across numerous foreign cultures in translation and their innumerable adaptations for the stage, television, film, and the World Wide Web.

A decade later, Emily Apter echoes Auerbach in her seminal book *Against World Literature* (2013), when she suggests that one must harbour 'serious reservations about tendencies in World Literature toward reflexive endorsement of cultural equivalence and substitutability' (2013: 2). Instead, Apter proposes 'untranslatability as a deflationary gesture toward the expansionism and gargantuan scale of world-literary endeavors' (2013: 3). From this point of view, she refers to Beckett's 'aberrant translation' of Rimbaud's French poem 'Le Bateau ivre' ('The Drunken Boat') and defends him on the basis of *'translating untranslatably* [sic]', namely, 'using a kind of over-translation that embraces wild infidelity to the original and pushes the envelope of translatability' (Apter 2013: 146–7). Beckett thus finds a prominent place in arguments both for and against world literature.

As another case in point, when compiling *The Random House Book of Twentieth-Century French Poetry* (1984), the editor Paul Auster asked for Beckett's permission to translate those poems in French that Beckett himself had not translated. Beckett refused to grant the requested permission on the grounds that '[o]nly he could do the translations – and he didn't feel up to the task' (Beckett 2006b: vii). Later admitting his incapacity to translate Beckett, Paul Auster adds, 'Beckett's renderings of his own works are never literal, word-by-word transcriptions. They are free, highly inventive adaptations of the original text – or, perhaps more accurately, "repatriations" from one language to the other, from one culture to the other' (Beckett 2006b: viii). When it comes to Beckett today, his translations and self-translations have led to further adaptations and appropriations into cultures and languages other than English and French, notwithstanding his adamant opposition to the smallest alteration to his texts. These new modes of transfer, typically from literature into various visual, filmic and digital media, have redefined Beckett, no more a modernist or a postmodernist writer, but one whose work is sui generis. This Beckettian element that both resists any single medium or language, while simultaneously crossing over into far removed cultures, necessitates a model of world literature that goes beyond the critical concepts of influence and reception.

One of the means by which writers' oeuvres have been adjudged to belong to world literature has been through the awarding of international prizes and, most notably, the Nobel Prize in Literature. As Pascale Casanova observes, 'The Nobel Prize is today one of the few truly international literary consecrations, a unique laboratory for the designation and definition of what is universal in literature' (2005: 74). In his article on 'The Nobel Experience', Horace Engdahl, a member of the Swedish Academy, argues that 'the prize-winning author should have contributed to humanity's improvement ("conferred the greatest benefit to mankind"), and that the prize should not 'flatter the self-esteem of one or other human herd'' (D'haen, Domínguez, and Thomsen 2013: 318). In 1969, Samuel Beckett was awarded the Nobel Prize 'for his writing, which – in new forms for the novel and drama – in the destitution of modern man acquires its elevation' (The Nobel Foundation 2014). The paradox here is striking: Beckett's work achieves an elevation of the human through its destitution. Moreover, it is not easy to identify how Beckett's work may have contributed to 'humanity's improvement', given that it seems to exhibit a general disinclination towards any form of philanthropic ambition.[3] Rather, as Theodor Adorno asserts, Beckett's works

> enjoy what is today the only form of respectable fame: everyone shudders at them, and yet no-one can persuade himself that these eccentric plays

and novels are not about what everyone knows but no one will admit. [...] Beckett's *Ecce Homo* is what human beings have become. As though with eyes drained of tears, they stare silently out of his sentences.

(Walder 2004: 112)

Whether, in presenting such a vision of the human, Beckett elevates mankind surely remains debatable. What can be asserted, however, is that, far from flattering his self-esteem, the Nobel Prize made Beckett acutely aware of the disruption that celebrity status brings not only to the personal life but also to the work. After receiving a telegram from his French publisher, Jérôme Lindon, advising him to go into hiding, Beckett checked into one hotel after another under a false name and, instead of attending the ceremony, asked his publisher to represent him 'on that Nobloodybeldamday' (Knowlson 1997: 571). He sought to remove himself entirely from the public eye, in accordance with the principle that achieving a worldwide reputation for a literature of impotence was itself a failure or what his wife Suzanne Dechevaux-Dumesnil called a 'catastrophe' (Knowlson 1997: 570–2).

It is amusing to find Beckett using his wife's verdict on the award later as the title to the play that he dedicated to the then imprisoned Czechoslovakian writer and political dissident Václav Havel: *Catastrophe* (1982). The distant storm of applause at the end of the play, which fades as the lifeless Protagonist (P) fixes his gaze on the audience, suggests that Beckett may be satirizing the (mis)fortunes of public recognition (the Nobel Prize or, in Havel's case, the results of dissenting with the government), particularly if P is considered to relate back to the artist through the self-reflexive situation into which he is forced (see also Knowlson 1997: 679–80). Furthermore, to return to Engdahl's essay:

> The Nobel Prize guarantees an entry in encyclopaedias if not a presence in the living memory of literature. The Catholic system of sainthood incorporates a lower rank, where a person is not *sanctus* (sainted) but *beatus* (beatified). Let us say that Nobel prize-winners in relation to actual canonicity achieve something analogous: immortality of the second grade.
>
> (D'haen, Domínguez, and Thomsen 2013: 325)

Perhaps, then, Beckett is staging the effects of achieving an 'immortality of the second grade' through the Protagonist's zombie-like portrayal of a loss of identity and character. The artist, not the artist's art, is thrust into the spotlight 'that gleams an instant, then it's night once more' (Beckett 2006a: 83). Be that as it may, evaluating Beckett based on the rapid growth in his international reputation immediately following the Nobel Prize is not the key to exploring his place in world literature.

If those whose works belong to world literature are not merely the authors who win international awards – and there are numerous Nobel Prize-winning authors who are today all but forgotten – then what are the criteria by which such a critical judgement can be made? Horace Engdahl reverses the question, arguing that '"World literature" shifts from a descriptive term to something of a performative. Rather than designating the bulk of literary works existing worldwide, it signifies a context into which we hope to bring the winning *oeuvre*' (D'haen, Domínguez, and Thomsen 2013: 327). So, the question, in Franco Moretti's words, is no longer '*what* we should do – the question is *how*. What does it mean, studying world literature? How do we do it?' (Moretti 2000: 54–5). In other words, we must identify a common ground upon which to build a discourse that is acceptable worldwide, especially once we have recognized the fallibility of any conception of world literature shaped by Western powers.

Notwithstanding the difficulties in determining what exactly world literature is or how it should be done, and precisely owing to Beckett's peculiar status as a 'divided' author (as an Irish-born exilic writer who published across literary genres in French, self-translated into English and English self-translated into French), one could hardly think of a better candidate to examine in relation to the frameworks of world literature. Beckett's increasingly minimalist style, both in prose and in drama, seems to render his texts inherently resistant to any single sociopolitical bent, geographic milieu or fixed identity. It is, in part, for this very reason that his work has been adapted so extensively, translated into numerous languages and has exerted a considerable influence upon art, literature and film across the world. Marjorie Perloff's 2006 presidential address to the Modern Language Association highlights this extraordinary dissemination very clearly: referring to eighteen cities in fourteen different countries (Argentina, Brazil, Bulgaria, France, Germany, Ireland, Israel, Japan, New Zealand, Russia, Spain, Switzerland, the UK and the United States) where Beckett was performed in 2006 (the centenary of his birth), the speech stresses his unrelenting international status to the extent that one is encouraged to ask, as does Perloff: 'Who, indeed, [is] more global an artist than Beckett?' (2007: 652).

In the analysis of Beckett's work, the prevailing critical tendencies have been to consider him either as a writer of impotence or as an absurdist. In contrast with many other modern authors, there also lies a politics of failure at the heart of his oeuvre: 'you must go on, I can't go on, I'll go on' are the final words of *The Unnamable* (1953); 'Fail again. Fail better' says the narrator in *Worstward Ho* (1983). This commitment to 'impotence', 'ignorance' and 'impoverishment' takes on a new meaning in the light of his global dissemination. Similarly, although Beckett's importance in establishing the Absurdist movement is undeniable (*Godot* being among the central texts leading Martin Esslin to delineate the trend), the way in which the play appears to be intrinsically resistant to a specific meaning, and its consequent vibrant afterlives, has led the work to transcend such a narrow classification. Thus, despite the tendency to characterize Beckett as a writer of failure, or as an absurdist, his texts resist being circumscribed by any single literary or aesthetic category and, perhaps also for this reason, call for a multicultural response.

Consequently, this volume provides alternative readings to prevailing modes of approaching Beckett's oeuvre through labels such as 'minimalism', 'absurdism' or even 'modernism' and 'postmodernism'. Bringing together a selection of readings of Beckett's texts by scholars from Belgium, Brazil, China, Hungary, India, Ireland, Japan, Netherlands, Serbia, Spain, Sweden, the UK and the United Arab Emirates, the volume aims to serve as a wide-ranging introduction to the author from the perspective of world literature. The underlying purpose of the collection is thus to show how and why Beckett's texts are particularly resistant to any 'contemporary pigeon-hole' by exploring those aspects which are central in establishing Beckett as an author of global status. Accordingly, the volume examines Beckett as a cosmopolitan author; the ways in which the idea of nation and nationality figure in his writings; whether his work gains or 'fails better' as a result of his bilingual ability; whether he is lost in further translation or found anew; and how and why his work has been culturally reciprocated, refracted and circulated globally. The essays also consider a number of vital issues arising from Beckett's global status, such as his place within the literary field and other relevant cultural industries. They pay particular attention to the sociopolitical repercussions of his theatre as performed or cinematized around the world, in an effort to determine whether, and, if so, to what extent, his texts resist the very globalization to which they are themselves subjected.

To this end, the collection is divided into three parts, each considering Beckett's work from a unique methodological perspective in contribution to contemporary discussions, both in world literature and in Beckett studies. The three-part division corresponds to the conventional critical approaches within the field, and they reflect upon the methods and criteria used to determine the international status of an author. Part I considers Beckett's early translations, self-translations, the translation of his texts into other languages and untranslatability. Part II examines the adaptation of his texts into different mediums and across countries, as well as Beckett's own adaptation of classical myths. Part III assesses the intercontinental circulation, transnational appropriation and cultural reciprocation of his oeuvre, both in literature and in art.

In Part I, on translation, John Fletcher discusses the importance of Beckett's early career as a translator, which helped shape his bilingual dexterity when it came to writing his most famous works. Pim Verhulst and Dirk Van Hulle examine the various strategies that Beckett employed to achieve his atmosphere of cultural destabilization, through a genetic approach comparing the textual variants in the French and English manuscripts. Thirthankar Chakraborty examines the political dimensions of Beckett's role as a translator during the Second World War and later for UNESCO, with the suggestion that Beckett is a key player when it comes to the recent discourse of world literature, particularly dealing with issues of translation. Charlotta Palmstierna Einarsson shows how the cosmopolitanism of Beckett's drama is intrinsically linked to it being a theatre of affect, where the audience's process of meaning-making transcends language, thus inviting an international audience through its unformed and untranslatable nature. Mary O'Byrne and Wei Zheyu dwell upon the (im)possibility of 'translating' Beckett, proposing a model of interdisciplinary, collaborative, intercultural translation to engage with his works through performance and to reflect upon the issues raised in the context of translation/reception theory and world literature studies.

Part II, on adaptation, opens with Mischa Twitchin's comparison of Beckett's 1985 television production of his last play *What Where* (1983) with the version made for the prize-winning *Beckett on Film* project (2001), in order to consider his sense of 'lessness' as key to transposing his works intermedially. Laurens de Vos' chapter studies intertextuality and the adaptation of the myth of Echo in Beckett's writings, revealing the interconnectedness of the mythological and the Beckettian worlds. Fábio de Souza Andrade presents an overview of the twenty-first-century reception of Beckett in Brazil, paying particular attention to three recent productions of his work: Isabel Teixeira's *Fim de jogo* (*Endgame*), Isabel Cavalcanti's *Moi lui* (based on *Molloy*) and Fernando and Adriano Guimarães's *Ocupação Sozinhos Juntos*, treating all three as examples of the challenges involved in staging Beckett in a Brazilian cultural context. Anita Rákóczy traces the history of Hungarian theatre productions of *Endgame* (1957), offering insights into the play's translations, its TV and stage premieres, and its adaptation as an opera by the Hungarian composer György Kurtág. Liu Aiying examines an array of Chinese productions of Beckett's *Godot*, highlighting the ways in which the drama has been appropriated to suit the sociopolitical developments of mainland China.

In Part III, on circulation, Juan Luis Toribio puts to test the claim that Beckett's minimalist poetics are key to decontextualizing his works and allowing them to transcend national and even continental frontiers. To this end, the chapter focuses specifically on the analysis of *Waiting for Godot* and its circular narrative structure. Arka Chattopadhyay's chapter offers a close study of how *Godot* went from a minor play to an international phenomenon by looking at the circulation and intermeshing of multiple worlds between *Godot* and the Bengali plays *Nayan Kabirer Pala* (1968) and *Tepantor* (2012), while also discussing the Indian cinematographer Ashish Avikunthak's film *Kalkimanthankatha* (2015), a re-creation of *Godot* at the Maha Kumbh festival set in India. Hania A. M. Nashef examines Nizar Qabbani's poems in relation to *Godot*, in order to illustrate how the Beckettian wait is a familiar trope to many Arab writers and poets and how the mythical 'Arab' Godot evolves into the only hope available to several generations of Arabs. This is followed by Snežana Kalinić's mapping of the 'effective life' of *Godot* through two key rewritings of his play in a Serbian context: Miodrag Bulatović's *Godot Has Arrived* (1965) and Žarko Komanin's *Godot Has Arrived to Collect His Dues* (2002). In the final chapter, Mariko Hori Tanaka discusses Beckett's reception in a postmodernist Japanese context, highlighting the amnesia of post-war Japan.

Through this ternary approach, the volume addresses the ironic transformation of a writer of 'impotence' and 'failure' whose works have gained a universal currency. The essays propose a new way of reading Beckett, as well as of understanding world literature, by examining his works through some of the major topics in Samuel Beckett and also in world literature studies. This is the first volume to bring together this threefold combination of chapters that collate a rigorously academic, cultural, political, epistolary and part-historicist reading of Beckett's works, which have moved widely into the fields of theatre practice and pedagogy, translation practice and theory, poetry, and cinematography. The chapters provide a way into Beckett's cosmopolitan work, while its translation, adaptation and circulation open up new modes of enquiry into the international, inter-linguistic and intercultural dimensions of the iconic writer, who is perhaps to be understood less in terms of globalization than in those of a spirit of belonging, paradoxically, at once 'everywhere' and 'nowhere'.

Notes

1 See, for example, the Introduction to Esslin (2001).
2 So in Beckett's case, although one might avoid forcing his works 'into a contemporary pigeon-hole' (Beckett 1984: 19), there is the risk of losing them within the amorphous space of a volatile canon.
3 More recently though, across universities in the UK, there have been AHRC-funded projects using Beckett's works 'to interrogate current concepts of mental disorder', with the object of providing 'an intellectual framework to the intuition of many clinicians that literature offers a means to understand challenging mental and neurological conditions' (Barry n.d.). While certainly a step away from Harold Pinter's remarks commending Beckett for 'grinding

my nose in the shit' and 'not flogging me a remedy or a path or a revelation or a basinful of breadcrumbs' (Graver and Federman 2005: 12) these and similar projects appear to be concerned above all with establishing a value beyond the aesthetic, indeed an instrumental value, for literature, and thereby to secure funding that is targeted at research that can be shown to have a positive impact upon society.

Works cited

Apter, E. (2013), *Against World Literature: On the Politics of Untranslatability*, London: Verso.
Auerbach, E. (1969), 'Philology and *Weltliteratur*', trans. E. Said and M. Said, *The Centennial Review*, 13 (1): 1–17.
Barry, E. (n.d.), 'Beckett and Brain Science', *University of Warwick Website*. Available online: http://www2.Warwick.Ac.uk/fac/arts/english/research/currentprojects/beckettandthebrain (accessed 13 Febrary 2019).
Beckett, S. (1984), *Disjecta: Miscellaneous Writings and a Dramatic Fragment*, New York: Grove Press.
Beckett, S. (2006a), *The Complete Dramatic Works*, London: Faber and Faber.
Beckett, S. (2006b), *The Grove Centenary Edition, Vol. I, Novels*, ed. P. Auster, Colm Tóibín (intro), New York: Grove Press.
Beckett, S. (2011), *The Letters of Samuel Beckett, Vol. 2*, eds. G. Craig, M. D. Fehsenfeld, D. Gunn, and L. M. Overbeck, Cambridge: Cambridge University Press.
Casanova, P. (2004), *The World Republic of Letters*, trans. M. B. DeBevoise, Cambridge: Harvard University Press.
Casanova, P. (2005), 'Literature as World', *New Left Review*, 31: 71–90.
Casanova, P. (2011), 'Combative Literatures', *New Left Review*, 72: 123–34.
D'haen, T., C. Domínguez, and M. R. Thomsen, eds. (2013), *World Literature: A Reader*, London: Routledge.
Damrosch, D. (2003), *What Is World Literature?* Princeton: Princeton University Press.
Esslin, M. (2001), *The Theatre of the Absurd*, London: Methuen.
Graver, L. (2004), *Samuel Beckett, Waiting for Godot*, Cambridge: Cambridge University Press.
Graver, L. and R. Federman, eds. (2005), *Samuel Beckett: The Critical Heritage*, London: Routledge.
Knowlson, J. (1997), *Damned to Fame: The Life of Samuel Beckett*, Paperback Ed., London: Bloomsbury.
Lucas, C., P. Mason, J. Meek, and S. Orbach (2016), '"Inspiration in Dark Times": Books to Make Sense of Brexit', *The Guardian*, 16 July. Available online: https://www.theguardian.com/books/2016/jul/16/inspiration-in-dark-times-books-to-make-sense-of-brexit (accessed 13 October 2015).
Marx, K. (2000), *Selected Writings*, ed. David McLellan, Oxford: Oxford University Press.

Moretti, F. (2000), 'Conjectures on World Literature', *New Left Review*, 1: 54–68.
Nobel Foundation (2014), 'The Nobel Prize in Literature 1969', *Nobelprize.org*, Nobel Media AB. Available online: http://www.nobelprize.org/nobel_prizes/literature/laureates/1969/ (accessed 8 March 2015).
Perloff, M. (2007), 'Presidential Address 2006: It Must Change', *PMLA*, 122 (3): 652–62.
Simons, N. (2014), 'Romanian Ambassador Attacks "Insulting and Alarmist" Campaign against Immigration', *The Huffington Post: Huffpost Politics*, 2 January. Available online: https://www.huffingtonpost.co.uk/2014/01/02/romania-immigration-ambassador_n_4530366.html (accessed 10 September 2016).
Syal, R. (2014), 'Romanian Ambassador Mocks MPs and Media Waiting for Immigrants', *The Guardian*, 2 January. Available online: https://www.theguardian.com/uk-news/2014/jan/02/romania-ambassador-jinga-mps-migrants-airports-godot (accessed 10 January 2014).
Tihanov, G. (2011), 'Cosmopolitanism in the Discursive Landscape of Modernity: Two Enlightenment Articulations', in D. Adams and G. Tihanov (eds.), *Enlightenment Cosmopolitanism*, 133–52, London: Legenda.
Walder, D., ed. (2004), *Literature in the Modern World: Critical Essays and Documents*, Oxford: Oxford University Press.
Weller, S. (2006), *Beckett, Literature, and the Ethics of Alterity*, New York: Palgrave Macmillan.

PART I

Translation

1

Bilingual Beckett

John Fletcher

If his novels and plays had failed to find an audience, Samuel Beckett would still be remembered as a literary translator. His career as a translator began, as it does for most people, by chance. In accordance with the terms of an exchange agreement between Trinity College Dublin (TCD) and the École Normale Supérieure (ÉNS), Samuel Beckett was appointed to serve for two years as *lecteur d'anglais* at the prestigious *Grande École*. He arrived in Paris in the autumn of 1928, aged 22. He was soon introduced to fellow-Dubliner James Joyce, who asked him to translate into French 'Anna Livia Plurabelle' (usually abbreviated ALP), a section of 'Work in Progress', the forerunner of Joyce's magnum opus *Finnegans Wake* (1939); ALP was later incorporated as the book's eighth chapter.

Beckett asked his friend Alfred Péron, who had served for two years as the ÉNS *lecteur* at TCD, to collaborate with him on the translation. They were the perfect team: both were bilingual and both were totally familiar with Dublin and its river, the Liffey, of which Anna Livia, as her name implies, is the embodiment. But when the galleys of their translation arrived Joyce blocked publication and decided to seek the opinion of others in his circle, chiefly Eugene Jolas and Adrienne Monnier. His reasons for what amounted

---

This chapter is a translation and an expanded version of 'Écrivain bilingue' which the author published in *Samuel Beckett: Cahier de l'Herne, no. 31* (see Fletcher 1976). It was revised and translated by Thirthankar Chakraborty and Juan Luis Toribio Vazquez in 2019 in close collaboration with John Fletcher. In his PhD dissertation written in Toulouse in 1964 John Fletcher included a section on Beckett's French. He later translated this into English as 'Samuel Beckett's French'. It forms chapter 6 in his 1967 book *Samuel Beckett's Art*.

to a slight to Beckett (with whom he had coincidently quarrelled over a personal matter, the infatuation – not reciprocated – felt by his mentally ill daughter Lucia for the young Irishman) are unclear, but it would seem that Joyce, having become interested in the practice of translation, chose to coordinate a team of translators himself. 'Work in Progress' was after all a kind of metatranslation, so Joyce's action, morally dubious though it was, had some logic. The irony is that the version published in 1931 in the *Nouvelle Revue Française* differs little from the Beckett/Péron version: as every translator is aware, it is easy to criticize the work of others, but hard to improve on it.

Over the years critics have begun studying Beckett's verse increasingly closely (the verse translations less so), beginning with my article 'Beckett's Verse: Influences and Parallels' (1964) and continuing with Lawrence E. Harvey's *Samuel Beckett: Poet and Critic* (1970). The poems were reissued from time to time in volume form by John Calder Publications with, invariably, numerous misprints, so a scholarly, textually impeccable edition was badly needed. In 2012 Faber and Faber published *The Collected Poems of Samuel Beckett: A Critical Edition* by Seán Lawlor and John Pilling. This monumental work of scholarship rendered superfluous all previous editions of Beckett's poetry and verse translations. Unlike earlier critics, Lawlor and Pilling devote many pages to the verse translations, which they rate highly. And rightly so: critics have noted how exceptional is Beckett's capacity to disrobe his own voice and come to the work of the writer being translated.

The same qualities that were shown in occasional pieces of self-translation, undertaken selflessly to oblige a scholar or literary critic, are all evident in Beckett's renderings of other writers, especially poets, and above all in his versions of a dozen poems by Paul Éluard (1895–1952). Two poems in particular stand out: 'À peine défigurée' ('Scarcely Disfigured') with its haunting second line 'Bonjour tristesse' (later adopted by a modish young novelist for the book that made her rich) and 'L'Amoureuse' ('Lady Love'), one of the greatest love lyrics in the French language. Beckett does full justice to both poems: in each case he turned a French chef-d'œuvre into an English masterpiece.

Unsurprisingly perhaps, Beckett was a great translator, not only of Joyce but of many texts from the 1930s to the late 1950s. To begin with, Samuel Putnam's *This Quarter* published a special edition dedicated to Italian writers with three translations by 'S. B. Beckett'. Two years later, in the same journal, Beckett published verse translations of André Breton, René Crevel and Paul Éluard. One of the most interesting among these is his translation of Guillaume Apollinaire's *Zone*. Confronting the delicate issues of translating Apollinaire, Beckett chose to translate his works as literally as possible so that we cannot reproach him for being unfaithful in his versions. He also undertook various commissions for Jolas's *Transition*,

Nancy Cunard's *Negro Anthology* (1934), E. L. T. Mesens's *London Bulletin* and UNESCO's *Anthology of Mexican Poetry* (1958). Beckett's French was of native standard, he was fluent in Italian and German, and his Spanish was good.

The fact that Beckett undertook literary translation to keep the wolf from the door until the royalties from *Godot* poured in and the Nobel Prize made him rich (although nearly all that money was given away) does not detract from the fact that he was a master of the art. He was modest about it, never departing from his conviction that translation was impossible (*traduttore, traditore*). Fortunately that did not stop him translating his French works into English and vice versa. In this task, in the early days, he worked with a collaborator but soon decided that no one could do the job as well as himself, so there were limits to his modesty. In writing my books on Beckett I would ask him to check my translations of quotations from his work. He never demurred; on the other hand my drafts came back heavily emended. He did the same with John Spurling's quotations from *Éleuthéria* in our book *Beckett: A Study of His Plays* (1972), where his emendations were extensive. In addition to correcting the odd misreading, he edited Spurling's drafts by cutting out words which he deemed unnecessary so that his texts are invariably shorter than Spurling's. He also struck out Spurling's more elaborate readings, opting in one case for a literal translation: 'It seemed to me that these were the things that held me prisoner' became 'these were my prisons' (Fletcher and Spurling 1972: 54). In one instance he completely rewrote Spurling's draft:

> All right, let's keep quiet, so sorry, goodnight, let's go to bed, sorry we dared speak, we philistines, about anything except the price of margarine. Oh yes, I quite understand your music. I quite understand that you were all glassy-eyed with the stuff.

is revised as:

> So silence please, at least that decency, good night all and happy dreams. We were mad but it's over, mad to dare speak of anything higher than the price of margarine. Oh I can hear it from here, your music. You were all tight naturally.

Being a well-known playwright, it comes as a surprise that Spurling's version is less speakable than Beckett's.

From 1945 onwards, Beckett's apprenticeship as translator served him well when it came to his adopting the French language as a medium for literary expression. Beckett once tried explaining, in bad French, as a joke, why he changed his language (*'pour faire remarquer moi...'*). He told Niklaus Gessner: '[I]n French, it is easier to write without style' (Gessner

1957: 32), but on the contrary, as shown later in this chapter, his French is far from lacking style. He told Israel Shenker that after returning to his flat in Paris after the Liberation, he chose to write in French quite simply because 'I just felt like it' (Shenker 2005: 161), but this too fails to explain the profound reasons of his choice, for there can be no doubt that he *did* have a choice. To understand his reasons, we are left with closely examining his oeuvres, particularly from 1942 to 1946, which was a period of transition in Beckett's early career.

To begin with, although Beckett's case is rare, it is not unique. The English writer William Beckford, for instance, wrote his strange novel *Vathek* (1786) in French towards the end of the eighteenth century, his reasons being that the French public would better appreciate his ironic oriental fantasy when compared to the English who were less familiar with the then popular genre in France. Almost two centuries later, the young American Bruce Lowery wrote his novel *La Cicatrice* (1960) first in French and subsequently translated it to English. Beckett's bilingualism is thus not unprecedented, albeit he must be the only writer to exploit all its possibilities: he writes his texts either in French or in English and then translates them into the other language on numerous occasions.

However, Beckett did not turn to French without, little by little, having his reasons. Besides the poems he had written in French before 1937, he translated *Murphy* in 1939 with the help of Alfred Péron. By the time we get to *Watt*, written during the Occupation while Beckett was in hiding in Vaucluse, deprived of all contact with people who spoke his mother tongue, we find instances of Gallicisms that Beckett unwittingly included in his English text. Here are some examples:

- 'I do not rise, not having *the force*' (*la force*).
- 'I was not found *under a cabbage*' (cf. *dans un chou*).
- 'But does the penny fare end here, at a merely *facultative stop*' (*arrêt facultatif*).
- 'Certain fish, in order to *support* the lower depths [...]' (*supporter*).
- 'He quoted *as well* from his ancestors' experience (*aussi bien*) as (*que*) from his own'.
- 'We should ever have *embraced*, and never on the mouth' (*embrasser*).
- 'Dives from a dreadful height, before a *numerous public*' (*public nombreux*).
- 'That old put' (*putain*).

(Beckett 2006: 173, 178, 182, 265, 284, 292, 350, 366)

Several of these Gallicisms, particularly the last one, were voluntarily comic. They were attributable to the fact that Beckett was listening to French throughout the day, despite it not being his mother tongue so that translations such as 'facultative stop' would have appeared no doubt amusing. But the other examples, such as 'as well... as' are results of an assimilated unconscious mental habit. This is definitely the case when he writes 'to support' with its French meaning, which is repeated several times in the novel.

Despite his Gallicisms, Beckett dedicated some of his time to writing a pure French, free from reminiscences of his mother tongue. We find in 'Suite' (1946) Gallicisms that Beckett took care to eliminate when revising the text for a 1955 re-edition of the short story, entitled 'La Fin'. The following are some examples:

1946:

- Je vous suis *très obligé pour* ces vêtements.
- Un petit garçon demanda à sa mère *la cause de cela*.
- Il *offrit* d'envoyer chercher un taxi.
- les longs mois de calme, *oblitérés* en un instant.
- il était très *amical et hospitalier* (friendly and hospitable).

1955:

- Je vous suis *reconnaissant*.
- Un petit garçon demanda à sa mère *comment cela était possible*.
- Il *proposa* d'envoyer chercher un taxi.
- les longs mois de calme, *anéantis* en un instant.
- il était *bon*.

Likewise, when translating *Murphy*, Beckett let instances of Anglicism into his text. For example, the translation of 'eight sixes forty eight' (2006: 40) becomes 'huit six quarante-huit' (2013: 65) – where it should have been 'huit fois six quarante-huit'. In *Godot*, he had written 'l'une de trois choses' and then changed it to 'de deux choses l'une' only when the director Roger Blin remarked that the phrasing was not French. Furthermore, we also find instances of Anglicism in *Malone meurt* ('Songe aussi que la chair n'est pas tout, spécialement à notre âge') and in *L'Innommable* ('il ne faut pas faire attention aux apparences' is translated as 'pay no attention to appearances'). If we look further, we would no doubt find more such instances.[1]

In addition to clear instances of Anglicism, because Beckett strove to retain his style, we find that the French version of *Murphy* retained much of its Englishness. Here is one example:

> She stormed away from the callbox, accompanied delightedly by her hips, etc.
>
> (2006: 9)

> Elle quitta le kiosque en coup de vent, voluptueusement suivie de ses hanches, etc.
>
> (2013: 15)

Verbal humour resides mainly in the way words are used; it is a comic genre that cannot be easily translated from one language to another. Nonetheless, Beckett did his best to translate as many of his wordplays as possible. He was obliged to remove the ones he wasn't able to translate, adding elsewhere adjustments in their place. The pun in *Murphy*, for instance, 'Why did the barmaid champagne? – Because the stout porter bitter' (Beckett 2006: 85), and all its lengthy development is omitted and replaced with the brief phrase: 'il fit une plaisanterie de fort mauvais goût' (2013: 139). The translation is all the more strange considering the joke is not in bad taste at all. Similarly, an entire paragraph describing Murphy's pleasure in traveling on bus number eleven during peak hours (between Walham Green and Liverpool Street) is removed, clearly since it was too difficult to convey this in a Parisian context. A few words spoken as an aside by the author are added instead, as if in compensation: for example, we are told that Neary curses the night of his birth, by adding, 'car il avait toujours été un fils respectueux' (2013: 50).

When it comes to his short prose, Beckett does not attempt to write in the manner of *Murphy* and adopts from the start a more French personality. As he masters the French language, he restrains his initially immense inclination to indulge in popular puns and wordplay. For popular language was to Beckett a revelation since the time he arrived in France following his extensive studies in the literary language. His fascination with the riches of this language has left traces throughout his oeuvre; when translating *Murphy*, for instance, we find a language that is more colloquial than the text in the English original:

> My God, how I hate the char Venus and her sausage and mash sex [...] How can I care what you DO?
>
> (2006: 26)

> Putain de putain, ce que ça m'emmerde, la Vénus de chambre et son Eros comme chez grand-mère [...] Qu'est-ce que ça peut me foutre, ce que tu FAIS?
>
> (2013: 41)

Much the same way, in the essay entitled 'Le Monde et le Pantalon' (1945), we encounter inappropriate language that a native French speaker would never use in a text of this nature; we find words such as 'emmerder', 'déconner' and 'foutre la paix' throughout this critical study. We find here a Beckett who, dazzled by the discovery of a popular and unexpected linguistic universe, cannot resist using slang language even where it does not suit his purpose.

This transition period did not last for long. Beckett quickly learned to tame this tendency, so much so that the obscenities, through being less frequent, carry an added force:

> Il faisant cette étrange lumière qui clôt une journée de pluie persistante, lorsque le soleil paraît et que le ciel s'éclaircit trop tard pour pouvoir servir. La terre fait un bruit comme de soupirs et les dernières gouttes tombent du ciel vidé et sans nuage. Un petit garçon, tendant les mains et levant la tête vers le ciel bleu, demanda à sa mère comment cela était possible. Fous-nous la paix, dit-elle.
>
> (2014: 57)

The movement in this passage is characteristic of Beckett's method and his modesty before emotion; much like his theatre, all drift into sentimentality is cut off by a final vulgarity: 'fous-nous la paix'.

Beckett often uses French obscenity to establish a contrast between his protagonists and their tormentors. The former use polite expressions, while the latter use crude language:

> Je fus arrêté par un second agent [...]. Il me fit remarquer que le trottoir était à tout le monde [...]. Désireriez-vous, dis-je, sans penser un seul instant à Héraclite, que je descende dans le ruisseau? [...] Si vous n'êtes pas foutu de circuler comme tout le monde, dit-il, vous feriez mieux de rester chez vous. [...] Qu'il m'attribuât un chez moi n'avait pas de quoi me déplaire.
>
> (2014: 17)

We have the opportunity to enjoy this genre of humour on another occasion, when Molloy complains about the interrogating commissioner's tone:

> Il écouta le rapport de son subordonné, puis se mit à m'interroger sur un ton qui, du point de vue de la correction, laissait de plus en plus à souhaiter, à mon idée.
>
> (2012: 29)

The effect is striking when the Beckettian hero loses patience and is obliged to use angry and spiteful words:

On ne lynche jamais les enfants [...]. Moi je les lyncherais avec délices.

(2014: 16)

Nonetheless, when it comes to verbal humour, Beckett's French characters display far more restraint than his English counterparts. They can barely exploit paradoxes ('une espérance accablante') and decompose ready-made phrases in an absurd manner ('si j'ose dire, et j'ose'). But if verbal games are largely excluded by Beckett from the French version, the characters find their compensation through situations that are much more satiric and ironic, as shown earlier in this chapter.

There have been several attempts at explaining why Beckett chose the French language. Critics have suggested, for instance, that he was reacting against Ireland or Irish culture, but the fact that he wrote several works in English proves the opposite. Mrs Jolas has suggested that Beckett, influenced by Joyce's Francophilia, wished to address a more intelligent public than the one which had shunned *Proust*, *More Pricks Than Kicks* and *Murphy* between 1931 and the war. This explanation is not entirely convincing. Finally, in his study *The Theatre of the Absurd*, Martin Esslin affirms that Beckett chose French as a way of asceticism and discipline, but Esslin insists too much on the difficulties involved in changing one's language of expression. Let us not forget that Beckett had already lived a number of years before 1945 in a place that was entirely French. Let us also bear in mind that he had exceptional linguistic talent, especially when taking into account his brilliant exam results at Trinity College, Dublin. It does not appear that he would have experienced many problems writing in French. It is thus difficult to accept Esslin's hypothesis for, in speaking of discipline, it presupposes that Beckett had, like Joseph Conrad, to struggle with words in expressing himself in a foreign language.

A more probable explanation for his adoption of French is perhaps what this chapter outlines. Based on his translation of *Murphy* (completed *before* the war), based on the poems he wrote directly in French between 1937 and 1939, and based also on the instances of Gallicism that slipped into his English texts, no matter with or without his knowing, by the time we get to *Watt* Beckett would already have been attracted by the French language as a medium of literary expression. As he told Israel Shenker, 'It was a different experience from writing in English. It was more exciting for me – writing in French' (2005: 161). French would, moreover, have offered him a way to express himself more directly, less subject to the stylistic artifice that always seduced him in English, more sober and more relevant to the subjects that were closer to his heart following his experiences with the Resistance during the Occupation. Moreover, as he tells himself, it was more 'amusing' to write in French: having exhausted the resources of English in *Watt*, it was now time for him to try something else, and anyone who reads the dialogues of the clowns in *Waiting for Godot* would no doubt agree with that view. French was for him a new point of departure, a way of relaunching his oeuvre following the war, but having arrived in 1950 in French at yet another impasse with 'Texts for Nothing', it was only too natural for Beckett to return to English. Henceforward circumstances tended to dictate the linguistic choices Samuel Beckett made. When he was asked to write a play for New York, he wrote in English, and when l'ORTF asked him for a text for radio, he wrote in French. It appears then that adopting French in 1945 was not for Beckett a way of looking for difficulties, as it has been argued, nor was it to target another audience, but it was to conquer a new terrain where he might use his talents in a new manner. 'It was more exciting' – these are the words of a man who discovers a world whose existence he had not suspected and who remains one captivated by its riches.

Around 1947, Beckett became a master of his chosen language. It is seldom possible, for those who read *Waiting for Godot* or *Molloy*, to guess that it is a foreigner who wrote them. Only the rhythm is personal, owing nothing to contemporary French writers, whatever Ruby Cohn may say when suggesting that Beckett was influenced by Céline. While the latter created characters who speak in a popular manner, even using slang, Beckett's heroes, as we saw earlier, express themselves in a pure, archaic and even pedantic French (consider Vladimir's 'où allez-vous de ce pas?' in *En Attendant Godot* (1952: 125)). The correctness of language constitutes a source of humour that Louis-Ferdinand Céline did not seek to exploit in his works.

The particular rhythm of the Beckettian prose comes in first place from his habit of employing words like 'oh' to intersect his phrases, as well as from the use of the comma, which is an important element in his style. There is also a tendency to add at the end of a phrase three or four additional words that elongate the meaning and make the echo reverberate:

> Oui, la nuit tombait, mais l'homme était innocent, d'une grande innocence, il ne craignait rien, si, il craignait, mais il n'avait besoin de rien craindre, on ne pouvait rien contre lui, ou si peu.
>
> (2012: 9)

Another of Beckett's habits is to repeat a noun, or to replace it by a pronoun, in order to avoid a phrase that would be too long without the 'breathing pause' that the comma represents:

> Le silence qui suivit ces aimables paroles, je l'employai à me tourner vers la fenêtre, sans rien voir vraiment, car j'avais fermé les yeux.
>
> (2012: 30)

In this phrase, Beckett avoids writing: 'J'employai le silence qui suivit ces aimables paroles à me tourner vers la fenêtre, sans rien voir vraiment' because it has a rhythm that he does not like and that forces the speaker to hold his breath for too long. Here is another example from the same novel:

> Cet étrange instrument, je l'ai encore quelque part je crois, n'ayant jamais pu me résoudre à le monnayer.
>
> (2012: 101)

This particular rhythm of Beckett's prose therefore seems to be the result of the combination of several factors: the repetition of simple words ('mon crâne tout ride et crevassé et brûlant, brûlant' (2012: 97)); the use of a great number of commas; the repetition of a word that has been used previously or its replacement for a pronoun; and finally, the addition, at the end of the phrase, of a supplementary element. All this forms a characteristic whole.

Is Beckett truly a French writer or did he remain an Irishman who, for personal reasons, often expressed himself in French?[2] The issue is not an easy one to resolve because his works, while impregnated by the atmosphere of his native country, also owe a lot to France, and the elements of Irish and French origin are so intertwined that one would not know how to separate them. To take an example: at the end of *Malone Dies*, Macmann finds himself in an Irish asylum. Beckett translates its name literally, House of Saint John of God (*maison Saint-Jean-de-Dieu*). But in this house the residents speak French, because one of them, who expresses himself in English at times, is so noticeable that he is given the nickname 'the Englishman' even though he is far from being so (p. 215). Having chosen an asylum that exists near Dublin, Beckett did not want to go all the way but proceeded with his story as if the house existed in France even if the surrounding landscape is of county Dublin, as we can tell from the numerous indications provided in the text. Everything happens as if Beckett operated simultaneously on two planes, Irish and French.

Nevertheless, Beckett would be the last one to deny his origins, to pretend to be of a nationality not his own; especially for one who always travelled with a passport delivered by the authorities of the Irish Republic and who received with pleasure his fellow-countrymen when they visited Paris. He remains truly Irish in his humour as well as in the joy he finds in jokes in bad taste, in scatology and in obscenity. Roger Blin expressed his astonishment and admiration seeing some Irish comedians perform *Waiting for Godot*: 'C'étaient des blagues à l'irlandaise', he affirms. It seems therefore that Beckett is really a son of this remarkable country which has already given European literature and culture so many geniuses – a son who is not always respectful, true, but who bears his motherland in the depths of his soul. At the same time he is a skilled writer who has given France a number of great works that have enriched and made a permanent mark on its literature.

Notes

1 In his account of *Molloy* (in *Cahiers du Sud*, no. 307), Paul Gadenne notes, among other things, the slip of the tongue 'différemment que' instead of 'autrement que' (*Molloy*: 73).
2 See 'Elle les écartait de ses flancs, je dirais brandissais si *j'ignorais encore mieux le génie de votre langue*' (my italics) (Beckett 2004: 51).

Works cited

Beckett, S. (1952), *En Attendant Godot*, Paris: Les Éditions de Minuit.
Beckett, S. (2004), *Malone Meurt*, Paris: Les Éditions de Minuit.
Beckett, S. (2006), *The Grove Centenary Edition, Vol. II, Novels*, ed. Paul Auster, New York: Grove.
Beckett, S. (2012), *Molloy*, Paris: Les Éditions de Minuit.
Beckett, S. (2013), *Murphy*, Paris: Les Éditions de Minuit.
Beckett, S. (2014), *Nouvelles et Textes*, Paris: Les Éditions de Minuit.
Fletcher, J. (1964), 'Beckett's Verse: Influences and Parallels', *French Review*, 37: 320–31.
Fletcher, J. (1967), *Samuel Beckett's Art*, London: Chatto & Windus.
Fletcher, J. (1976), 'Écrivain bilingue', in T. Bishop and R. Federman (eds.), *Samuel Beckett. Cahier de l'Herne, no. 31*, 212–18, Paris: Klincksieck.
Fletcher, J., and J. Spurling (1972), *Beckett: A Study of His Plays*, London: Eyre Methuen.
Gessner, N. (1957), *Die Unzulänglichkeit der Sprache: eine Untersuchung über Formzufall und Beziehungslosigkeit bei Samuel Beckett*, Zürich: Junis Verlag.
Harvey, L. E. (1970), *Samuel Beckett: Poet and Critic*, Princeton: New Jersey.
Shenker, I. (2005), 'An Interview with Beckett', in L. Graver and R. Federman (eds.), *Samuel Beckett: The Critical Heritage*, 160–3, London: Routledge.

2

Shifting cultural affinities in *Molloy*: A genetic bilingual approach

Dirk Van Hulle and Pim Verhulst

Introduction

For a work of fiction to have 'an *effective* life as world literature', according to David Damrosch, it needs to be 'actively present within a literary system beyond that of its original culture' (2003: 4). At first glance, Beckett's work seems to amply meet that requirement, having reached a wide readership and elicited a critical response beyond English, French and German – i.e. the three main languages in which he regularly wrote or translated his work, sometimes with the help of third parties. But what exactly is its 'culture of origin'? In the beginning of Beckett's career, one might argue it was Ireland, even though he turned his back on its literary and cultural life in the late 1930s, after travelling to Italy, France, England and Germany. However, was Irish still the 'culture of origin' for Beckett's work by the end of his life in 1989, when he had actually spent more years living in the city of Paris and his country house in Ussy-sur-Marne than in his native Dublin suburb of Foxrock? Did the one supplant the other, or had they established a form of coexistence over the intervening decades? These questions are especially pertinent with regard to Beckett's so-called 'trilogy' of novels.

Molloy, *Malone meurt*/*Malone Dies* and *L'Innommable*/*The Unnamable* were written in French between 1947 and 1950, just after the Second World War and Beckett's return to Paris from Rousillon by way of Saint-Lô, in what he described to his biographer, James Knowlson, as the 'siege in the room' or the 'frenzy of writing'. He then translated the novels into English – *Molloy* with the help of Patrick Bowles, on and off between 1950 and 1958.[1] This decade marked a transitional period in Beckett's literary career, during which he first switched to an adopted language, only to reconnect with his mother tongue later on by way of self-translation as well as original composition. That Beckett himself was unsure as to how long his linguistic exile would last is clear from a bio that he drafted at the back of the second notebook containing the original French manuscript of *Molloy*. After listing some poems, a book of stories (*More Pricks Than Kicks*) and a novel (*Murphy*), he ends by saying that he has been writing in French since 1945, tellingly crossing out the word 'exclusively': 'Depuis 1945 écrit en français. ~~exclusivement~~' (BDMP4: FN2, 144v).[2] This same sense of indetermination also affected the prose that he was literally in the middle of writing.

For Leslie Hill, the trilogy exudes an 'unmistakable sense of unbelonging' that lends it a 'hybrid status': 'Though composed in one language, French, the novels gesture towards another, Anglo-Irish' (1990: 40). As Emilie Morin points out, this observation is not limited to the original text but also pertains to the translation, since 'comparing English and French versions forbids a straightforward alignment with an Irish setting and Irish origins' (2009: 61). Sinéad Mooney describes the cross-cultural identity of the trilogy as a 'Babel-like in-betweenness': 'It is caught [...] between France and Ireland, and the demands of "source" and "target" languages and cultures, although it is never plain which role of the two French and English play' (2011: 123). Because Beckett first wrote the novels in the language of Molière, they 'present a savagely reduced world that always already feels like an eccentric translation into French from some non-existent Hiberno-English original' (134), which only came into being *post factum*. For the purpose of this chapter, we wish to limit our focus to *Molloy*, in both French and English. In addition to being more grounded in external reality than *Malone meurt*/*Malone Dies*, *L'Innommable*/*The Unnamable*, it was the first instalment of a larger-scale project that forced Beckett to examine his position as an Irish author in a French literary field, while at the same time it exposed him to an international market via translation.

Whereas the culturally divided status of *Molloy* has already been acknowledged, our purpose is to explore what genetic criticism can add to its understanding and to the study of world literature in general.[3] According to Pierre-Marc de Biasi, the task of *critique génétique* is twofold: (1) to classify, transcribe and make public all the available pre-publication material of a literary work (notes, manuscripts, typescripts, proofs etc.); (2) to reconstruct the creative dynamics of the writing process from a particular critical vantage point (2004: 42). By analysing the extant manuscripts of *Molloy* from the perspective of world literature, 'in the making' so to speak, it becomes possible to understand how Beckett crafted this famous effect of cultural displacement, in French and in English, after careful revision and shifting cultural affinities. Additionally, our genetic bilingual analysis of *Molloy* will reveal that the referential framework of the novel extends well beyond the Irish-French dichotomy to which it is often confined and that it also includes British, German and American culture, especially in translation, but already in the original.

The French *Molloy*

While the setting of the French *Molloy* has widely been recognized as vaguely Anglo-Irish, the published text never identifies it as such in explicit geographical terms. The manuscript was quite different in this respect. For example, Molloy cannot remember the name of his town, thinking it starts with 'un D', as in Dublin (BDMP4: FN2, 07r), whereas the published version replaces the letter 'D' with 'un B' or 'un P' (1951: 45), which undoes the reference. Something similar happens when Moran dispatches his son, Jacques, to get a bicycle from the nearest village. In the manuscript, it is not called 'Hole' but 'Carrick' or 'Carrig' (BDMP4: FN3, 90r, 94r), a common place name resembling Carrickmines, the suburb south of Dublin between Dalkey and Bray where Beckett used to play golf. However, another revision to the text invokes Dublin again, albeit in a more opaque fashion. In the manuscript, Molloy finds himself near a canal – 'me voilà [...] aux bords du canal' (BDMP4: FN1, 69r) – but Beckett adds on a second one for the published text: 'il y en a même deux' (1951: 38). This revision strengthens the suggestion that the setting might be Dublin after all, with its Royal and Grand Canals, but many other cities share this characteristic so that it becomes a playful allusion opening up the text to multiple possibilities rather than pinpointing it to one exact location.

It is not just references to Ireland that undergo this treatment in the writing process. When Moran is attempting to describe the size of his region and explains that 'in modern countries this is what I think is called a commune, or a canton' (2009a: 139), Beckett used France as a point of comparison in the manuscript, be it after a few false starts: 'C'était ce qu'on appelle en Fra ce que les Français appellent une commune on appelle en une com En France on appelle ça une commune' (BDMP4: FN3, 63r). In the published version of *Molloy*, this explicit invocation was generalized to 'les pays évolués' (1951: 207), thus contrasting a by now vaguely hinted Ireland with any foreign country more advanced. The phrase differs conspicuously from the one printed on Professor Suk's sheet in *Murphy*: 'Famous throughout

Civilised World and Irish Free State' (2009b: 22). For an English-language novel about the marginalized position of Irishmen in London (see Bixby 2010; Davies 2017) such frankness makes sense, but for his Anglo-Irish novel in French Beckett adopted a different approach. In the revised version of the sentence, Moran aligns himself neither against the Irish Free State – as in *Murphy* – nor with the French Republic – as in the drafts of *Molloy* – settling instead for the middle ground of a cultural no man's land.

The passage discussed above is one of the rare instances where Beckett uses the word 'pays' or 'country' to denote a nation or state. Another example is when Lousse tells Molloy she has no other means of support than the pension of her departed husband, who has 'fallen in defence of a country that called itself his and from which in his lifetime he never derived the smallest benefit, but only insults and vexations' (2009a: 30–1). While this comment may be construed as 'an allusion to Irish involvement in the Great War under the British flag' (Morin 2009: 91–2), it is nondescript enough to represent a general 'alienation of citizens from states' (Harrington 1991: 164). Still, the word 'patrie' in the original French – 'une patrie qui se disait la sienne et dont de son vivant il ne retira jamais le moindre avantage, mais seulement des affronts et des bâtons dans les roues' (1951: 48) – underlines the patriotic or nationalist connotations of the remark, which Beckett is careful not to overuse in other sections of the novel. When Molloy explains that where he comes from, the word 'da' is used to mean 'father', as in Ireland, he originally refers to the place as 'ma putain de patrie' (BDMP4: FN1, 36r) – 'my fucking country' – before rephrasing it as 'ma région' (1951: 23) – 'my region' – in the published text. In translation, this even becomes 'my part of the world' (2009a: 50), situating it on the global map rather than enclosing it within national or regional borders.

Roughly the same phrase is used when Molloy describes the weather 'in that part of the world' (2009a: 28) – 'dans cette région' (1951: 44), 'ce pays' in the manuscript (BDMP4: FN2, 05r) – as sunny till noon, rainy the whole day, followed by a brief glimpse of sunlight before darkness descends, which is again characteristic of Ireland. A crucial difference is that Molloy has now put a distance between himself and his place of origin, by means of the determiner 'that' in English and 'cette' in French. This becomes a pattern in the later stages of the genesis, when Beckett adds various phrases to hint that Molloy is now in a different, undisclosed location. About the blandness of the weather, he now remarks, 'Ça a peut-être changé depuis' (1951: 76) – 'Perhaps things have changed since then' (2009a: 50). Apart from obscuring the name of Molloy's home country and further removing him from it physically, Beckett also subdues a potential disclosure of the character's ethnicity. Confessing that he fears the 'far whisper' in his head, Molloy goes on in the manuscript: 'à l'égal [...] des anglo-saxons' (BDMP4: FN2, 25r). This is another remark that might have identified him as Irish-Celtic, which would have given him good reason, historically speaking, to be wary of Anglo-Saxons, not long after the Easter Rising of 1916, with its violent build-up and bloody aftermath.

Up to a certain point in the novel's genesis, it seems that Beckett considered mixing elements of Anglo-Irish with French culture to destabilize the frame of reference. A case in point is a longer episode omitted from the published text but still present in the manuscript and typescript of *Molloy*. It occurred when Moran states, 'What then was the source of Ballyba's prosperity? I'll tell you', at which point a lengthy but amusing digression on the subject followed, which Beckett simply cut and replaced with 'No, I'll tell you nothing. Nothing' (2009a: 140). On the one hand, this passage detailing the particulars of Ballyba's agrarian economy centred on human excrement has been read by Adam Winstanley as a Swiftian critique of '[Éamon] de Valera's vision of a self-sufficient Ireland' (2014: 97), when the Irish Free State elected to pursue a policy of economic protectionism and to build an 'indigenous' industry, 'producing primarily for the home market' (Neary and Ó Gráda 1991: 250). On the other hand, references to French culture delocalize and broaden this complex satire. Moran mentions a character called Colbert, who amassed a fortune simply by eating, defecating and selling his excess faeces to the needy. Given the commercial context of the episode, a name like 'Colbert' could easily refer to Jean-Baptiste Colbert, the Minister of Finances under Louis XIV, who reformed the domestic economy, introduced a fairer tax system and improved the mode of collection in France. An interesting detail is that he suffered frequent stomach aches, which limited his meals to bread soaked in broth. The fictional Colbert is so revered by the poor that he deserves a statue, and according to Moran the sitting posture would be most fitting: 'Assis j'espère' (BDMP4: FT, 222r). Not coincidentally, perhaps, the historical figure of Jean-Baptiste Colbert is honoured with a statue in front of the Assemblée nationale in Paris, depicting him seated with left hand raised.

Another curious example of cultural intermingling is the way Beckett uses distances in the drafts of the novel. When Molloy explains that he has never put more than '10 ou 15 kilomètres' (BDMP4: FN2, 06r) – '10 or 15 kilometres' – between himself and the town where he was born, this later becomes 'quinze ou vingt milles' (1951: 44) – 'ten or fifteen miles' (2009a: 28). What appears to be a simple conversion from the Franco-European metric system to Anglo-Irish imperial measurements in the first part of *Molloy* is complicated by the use of distances in the second part. Moran, expressing the size of the area he inhabits, already does so in square miles in the manuscript, not in kilometres: '5 ou 6 milles carrés' (BDMP4: FN3, 63r). However, they still occur every now and then, when he estimates the distance to the nearest town at '15 kilomètres' (BDMP4: FN3, 91r), not changed until the published text to 'quinze milles' (1951: 218) – 'fifteen miles' (2009a: 147). This suggests that Beckett had decided on switching to the imperial system by the time he reached Part II in the manuscript, occasionally relapsing into his old habits from the Molloy part and normalizing everything later. However, if we look at the way currencies occur in the drafts, it is possible that Beckett at least considered using different cultural frames of reference for Molloy and Moran, with the miles in the second part suggesting not an Anglo-Irish but an American setting.

Molloy never mentions money except in the vaguest of terms, contrary to Moran's part. The value of young Jacques's Timor stamp is given at '40 cents' (BDMP4: FN3, 15r) in the manuscripts, later revised to 'un florin' (1951: 246) – 'a florin' (2009a: 113). It is not an American stamp, as his pocket money – 'chaque cent qu'il recevait' (BDMP4: FN3, 57r) – is also expressed in that monetary unit, later becoming 'chaque penny' (1951: 202) – 'every penny he received' (2009a: 136). As with distances, Beckett eventually transposes everything to the currencies of Ireland and England. Yet one major difference is that the original values in the manuscript are not French, which uses 'centime' as the decimal unit, not 'cent'. So much is borne out by the larger amounts that occur in the drafts. The weekly wages of Gaber and Moran amount to '40 dollars' and '32' dollars (BDMP4: FN3, 11r), which, after exchange, become 'huit livres' and 'six et demie' (1951: 165) – 'eight pounds' and 'six pounds ten' (2009a: 111). They are not getting their money from abroad, because Moran also sets the maximum price of the bicycle that his son is to buy at '40 dollars' in the manuscript (BDMP4: FN3, 90r), later revised to 'cinq livres' (1951: 218) – 'five pounds' (2009a: 147). So, rather than inscribing *Molloy* as a novel within a unified cultural context from the outset, simply swapping the Franco-European setting with an Anglo-Irish one further in the writing process, Beckett sought to destabilize straightforward identifications between the two parts, even using a currency as foreign as American dollars to maximize that effect. While the published French version, after revision, eventually shows 'an adherence to anglophone norms of measurement' (Morin 2009: 60), this was certainly not yet the case in the manuscripts.

The overall adjustment of the measurements and currencies to Anglo-Irish norms was a late change, as the partially surviving typescript of *Molloy* reveals. References to American money had been removed by this stage, as the value of shit per weight in the aforementioned 'Ballyba' episode was still given as 'douze à quinze cents le kilog brut' in the manuscript (BDMP4: FN3, 67r-68r) but changed to 'onze cinq à sept pence le kilog brut' (BDMP4: FT, 215r) – 'five to seven pence per gross kilogramme'– in the typescript. While the passage was eventually removed in its entirety, the fact that metric units had not yet been changed to imperial pounds confirms that Beckett continued revising them over a longer period of time, here allowing the Anglo-Irish currency – still American in the drafts – to coexist with a Franco-European unit of mass in the selfsame sentence. As we will see in the following section, this process of cultural destabilization continued in the English translation.

The English *Molloy*

The eventual adoption of Anglo-Irish measurements and currencies in French seems to have briefly inspired its expansion into other areas of the novel in English, for example beverages. Molloy's 'cinq ou six pots de bière' (1951: 81) at first became 'five or six Imperial pints of porter' (BDMP4: ET1, 63r), a measurement equal to 1/8th of an imperial gallon that is only used in the UK and Ireland. Beckett downplays the Anglo-Irish reference again to 'mugs of beer' (BDMP4: ET2, 63r) on the second typescript, yet in other cases he replaces general French terms with English equivalents that emphasize the Anglo-Saxon setting of the novel, slightly heightening its Britishness in Moran's part. His 'pommier', for example, becomes an 'apple tree' ^Beauty of Bath' (BDMP4: ET2, 02r), a popular dessert apple no longer commercially grown because it bruises easily, but which is still a common garden variety. Another instance occurs when Moran refers to his 'carpette' (BDMP4: FN3, 15v) in French, later changed to his 'moquette' (1951: 168) for the published text, possibly to pun on the expression 'fumer la moquette' ('to talk nonsense'). The English translation hesitates between the brand names 'Axminster' ^Wilton' (BDMP4: ET2, 22r), types of carpet manufactured in Devon and Wiltshire, eventually settling for the latter.

The reverse also occurs, when a specific brand name in the French version is replaced with a more neutral term in the translation. One interesting example is 'baume Bengué' (1951: 87), an ointment to soothe muscle pains that Molloy administers to Edith's rump. In English, Beckett doubted between 'wintergreen'^cream' (BDMP4: ET2, 67r), the first being a blanket term for oil extracted from the Gaultheria plant, which is used as a folk remedy for arthritis, poor blood circulation, rheumatism, inflammation or tendinitis, and the latter a general term for ointments with a similar function. The term 'baume Bengué' stands out in the original *Molloy* because the story is vaguely set in an Anglo-Irish context, where a French brand name would seem exotic. Beckett also used the term in Part II, when Moran feels a sharp pain in his knee and asks his son Jacques to bring him 'du Baume Bengué' ^de l'iodex' (BDMP4: FN3, 86r), an English brand unknown to a French readership. So what originally established symmetry between the novel's two parts was subsequently used to disrupt the cultural unity of *Molloy*, similar to what the different currencies effectuated in the manuscript, one character using a French brand, the other an English one to remedy ailments. By opting for 'wintercream' and 'iodex' in the English version, Beckett smooths over the dissimilarity, but he destabilizes the cultural context elsewhere in the translation.

When Moran's sore knee plays up again in the story, he shrugs it off as a touch of neuralgia and reminds himself to procure 'une boîte de thermogène, avec le joli démon dessus' (1951: 215). The phrase refers to a brand of thermogenic cotton, produced in France, which became very popular after 1909 thanks to a successful marketing campaign using artwork by French-Italian designer Leonetto Cappiello. As William H. Helfand explains, the colourful image of a 'fire-eating circus performer holding the product close to his chest [...] has become an icon of creative advertising imagery' (1991: 34). Though common in France, the product was little used in Ireland, the UK or the United States, so Moran's reference to 'a packet of thermogenic^e wool, with the pretty demon on the outside' (BDMP4: ET2, 57r) must have been foreign to Irish-English and American readers alike. It not only disturbs the Anglo-Saxon context of the story, strengthened by some of the brand names mentioned above, but it also harks back to the novel's French origin, which is further emphasized by Beckett's preference for the unusual Gallic spelling of 'thermogene' over 'thermogenic' in the typescript.

In this respect, it is important to keep in mind that Beckett was translating *Molloy* into English for an audience more diversified and global than that of the French text. He had a contract with Maurice Girodias of Olympia Press, who ran an English-language publishing house out of Paris. Although Girodias was mostly known for putting out 'dirty books' or 'DBs' (de St Jorre 2009: 96), he also had a more respectable list including the 'Collection Merlin', which consisted of translations commissioned by the editors of the eponymous literary magazine. One of those titles was *Molloy*, converted into English by Beckett with assistance from the South African writer-translator Patrick Bowles. When the American publisher Barney Rosset, who had already taken on *Waiting for Godot* by this time, caught wind of Olympia and Merlin's plans for *Molloy*, he also signed a contract with them for its distribution in the United States. As a result, Beckett was translating for a number of international markets, encompassing more than one variety of the English language: America, the sizeable expat community in France, the UK and its Commonwealth territories. His awareness of this peculiar situation clearly impacted the translation process, as we learn from Beckett's correspondence with Grove Press. On 4 August 1953, having read the first specimen by Beckett and Bowles, Rosset made a critical comment which he referred to as 'a mention of words':

> Those such as skivvy and cutty are unknown here, and when used they give the writing a most definite British stamp. That is perfectly all right if it is the effect you desire. If you are desirous for a little more vagueness as to where the scene is set it would be better to use substitutes which are of common usage both here and in Britain.
>
> (Rosset 2016: 72)

While he sympathized with Rosset's reservations, Beckett also noted the complexity of the matter in his reply of 1 September 1953:

I understand your point about the Anglicisms and shall be glad to consider whatever suggestions you have to make in this connexion. But the problem involved here is a far-reaching one. Bowles's text as revised by me is bound to be quite unamerican in rhythm and atmosphere and the mere substitution here and there of the American for the English term is hardly likely to improve matters, on the contrary. We can of course avoid those words which are incomprehensible to the American reader, such as skivvy and cutty, and it will be a help to have them pointed out to us.

(2011: 397–8)

The word 'skivvy' (BDMP4: Sp1-3, 02r) – 'boniche' in French (1951: 8) – was eventually replaced with the more neutral term 'chambermaid' (2009a: 3), but 'cutty' (2009a: 8) – a short tobacco pipe – was retained. A playful nudge to the American public is the expletive 'fuck the son of a bitch', which Bowles suggested adding to the repertoire of Lousse's parrot (Bowles 1994: 33), prompting Molloy to conclude that the bird 'must have belonged to an American sailor' (2009a: 35). At the same time, many more decidedly un-American words were added to the English version during the translation process. Molloy, who admits that he 'began at the beginning, like an old fool, can you imagine that' (BDMP4: Sp1-3, 02r) in the early drafts, refers to himself with the more Irish-British term 'ballocks' in the second typescript (BDMP4: ET2, 02r). Other later-stage revisions to the novel's opening sequence give the narrator a more distinctive Anglo-Irish tone. 'It was he who told me I'd begun all wrong' (BDMP4: Sp1-3, 02r) – referring to the man who collects Molloy's pages every Sunday – was altered to 'It was he told me I'd begun all wrong' (BDMP4: ET1 02r). This same type of revision occurs further on in the text, where Molloy speaks of Lousse's dead dog, 'her Teddy ~~whom~~ she had loved like ~~her own~~ an only child' (BDMP4: ET2, 42r). In both cases the pronoun is deleted, which is a typical characteristic of Hiberno-English.

Beckett's stress on 'Bowles's text as revised by me' in his letter to Rosset suggests that they deliberately enhanced its un-American flavour, while making a few concessions. At the same time, they destandardized the language by making it sound less 'English' or, perhaps more correctly, less 'British'. This notion of substandard English relates to a comment that Beckett made in a letter to Cyril Lucas of 4 January 1956, namely that he was still able to write 'the queer kind of English' that his 'queer French' deserved (2011: 591–2). As several critics have noted (Fletcher 1967; Morin 2009; Mooney 2011), Beckett's use of French in *Molloy* often deviates from the norm, infused as it is with Irish inflexions. Hiberno-English traits appear to fulfil a similar destabilizing function in the English version, but this is not to say that Beckett naturalized *Molloy* into an Irish novel. Although he did introduce a few outspokenly Hiberno-English traits in the earlier drafts of the translation, he removed some of these again later. As a result, the 'queer' Anglo-Irish flavour of the novel remains as subtle as the 'queer' ambiance of his non-native French, which is just slightly off-standard and conjures up a sense of Irishness while not embracing it wholeheartedly.

One of the most interesting examples in this regard is the word 'puckaun' (BDMP4: ET1, 31r), which Beckett employed in an early version of the translation for 'le bouc' (1951: 41) but later replaced with the more neutral 'buck-goat' (BDMP4: ET2, 31r). He had also used the word in *Watt* (1953), in the scene where 'a goat emerged, dragging its pale and chain' and Mr Nolan complains: 'Riley's puckaun again [...], I can smell him from here' (2009c: 213). 'Puckaun' is a markedly Hiberno-English word, derived from the Irish *pocán*, the diminutive form of the male goat *poc*. This provenance may explain why the term was problematic in a deliberately bi-cultural, Anglo-French text such as *Molloy*, but not in a more openly Anglo-Irish novel like *Watt*, which was inscribing itself deliberately into the 'Big House' tradition (Harrington 1981). According to the *OED*, the earliest use of the word 'puckaun' is encountered in Jonathan Swift, more precisely in his 'Dialogue in Hibernian Style between A and B'. In volume VII of *The Works of Jonathan Swift*, edited by Walter Scott, this burlesque is introduced as a 'specimen of Irishisms, or what Swift condemned as such [...] taken from an unfinished copy in the Dean's handwriting, found among Mr Lyon's papers' – a clergyman attending to him during his last years (Swift 1824: 156). Swift packs a great many examples of Irish words, phrases and syntax into a twenty-four-line conversation between two characters Beckettianly named A and B, ending with the question:

A   Do you make good cheese and butter?
B   Yes, when we can get milk; but our cows will never keep a drop of milk without a Puckaun.

(Swift 1824: 157)

Swift uses the word differently, meaning a bull instead of a male goat, so it may not be the (only) source of Beckett's 'puckaun', but the fact that it functions there as a specimen of Hiberno-English is relevant for *Molloy* and may explain why it was eventually replaced – evoking an Irish context all too strongly. As Molloy himself admits, he is not an expert on the Irish language, claiming as much ignorance about this subject as about the meaning of tears and laughter: 'they are so much Gaelic to me' (2009a: 35). This was a late addition, probably on the proofs, as both surviving typescripts still read 'Hebrew' (BDMP4: ET1, ET2, 42r) for the French 'je m'y connais guère' (1951: 54). Some of its most outstanding features having been removed from the text by this stage, or mixed in with other cultural references, Molloy's disavowal of Irishness seems very appropriate indeed.

The German *Molloy*

In addition to the Irish, British and American elements which have been discussed until now, German culture also features significantly in the drafts of the English *Molloy*. This may have been triggered by Beckett's assistance of Erich Franzen with the German *Molloy* in January and February of 1954, when he was yet to begin translating the second part of the novel into English with Patrick Bowles. One of the issues that Beckett and Franzen disagreed about was the word 'coenaesthesis' in Molloy's claim: 'coenaesthetically speaking of course, I felt more or less the same as usual' (2009a: 53). As Beckett told Franzen, quoting from the *OED* in his defence, the term denoted 'the general sense of existence arising from the sum of bodily impressions', giving Wilhelm Wundt's 'Gemeinempfindung' as a roughly equivalent German philosophical concept, together with 'Coenesthesis' and 'Gemeingefühl'. Franzen, however, did not find Beckett's suggestions acceptable, explaining that 'Hitler's propaganda monopolized the term': 'if such terms which you intend to bear a special meaning, but which to Germans indicate something general (Hitler's Gemeingefühl), are used, the blame will be on the translator' (Beckett and Franzen 1984: 29). It seems that Beckett did yield to German sensitivities, as the published translation opts for a paraphrase instead, but the incident will have reminded him of his own time in Germany from 1936 to 1937, where he witnessed first-hand the appropriation of everyday language by Nazi Socialism. One of those arrogated words was 'Eintopf'.

A German stew typically consisting of a broth with vegetables, potatoes and meat, it comes in a number of varieties and denotes the method of cooking the ingredients in one pot rather than a specific recipe. Beckett recorded the term several times in his so-called German diaries (UoR MS 2901), frequently complaining of the dish's ubiquitousness and unpalatability. He also mentions the 'Eintopf-Sonntage', a propagandist initiative by the Nazi government ordering citizens and restaurants to eat or serve only cheap stew dishes on every first Sunday of the month from October to March, to support the idea of one nation eating from one pot ('Beckett's Blick' 2005: 152). According to James McNaughton, Beckett is taking issue with this type of nationalist propaganda when he introduces the word in the typescript of *Watt* and describes Mr Knott's pot as 'an invariable Eintopf' (McNaughton 2018: 13). Even though Beckett removed it again later, it still resonates in the following passage: 'It resembled a pot, it was almost a pot, but it was not a pot of which one could say, Pot, pot, and be comforted' (2009c: 67). Expanding on the nominalist interpretation that is usually given to this sentence, McNaughton argues that '[t]he pot is not merely, or not only, some abstract noun, but, more compellingly, an everyday object and meal supersaturated with ideological investment: specific propaganda has made it difficult to call a pot simply a pot' (2018:

14). In the drafts of the English *Molloy*, the word 'Eintopf' shared a similar function – and, eventually, fate.

In the Edith episode, Molloy states that what little he ate, he devoured voraciously: 'I flung myself at the mess, gulped down the half or the quarter of it in two mouthfuls without chewing (with what would I have chewed?), then pushed it from me with loathing' (2009a: 53). In the first English typescript, Beckett still used the word 'Eintopf' (BDMP4: ET1, 63r), which did not get replaced with the more general 'mess' until the second typescript (BDMP4: ET2, 63r). Being a translation of what in the French version is still called a 'plat unique' (1951: 81) or 'single-course meal', it acts as a parallel to the scene in the second part of the novel where Martha has cooked a meal for Moran, who inspects it as follows: 'I peered into the pots. Irish stew. A nourishing and economical dish, if a little indigestible. All honour to the land it has brought before the world' (2009a: 101). Moran's high-flown rhetoric is strikingly similar to the Nazi propaganda Beckett mocked when defining 'Eintopf' in his German vocabulary notebook as 'arish stew = neues nationalgericht der deutschen [new German national dish]' (cited in Nixon 2011: 206n6). By connecting 'Eintopf' to Irish stew in the typescripts of the English *Molloy*, through a pun on Irish/arisch in his German diaries – similar to the one on Aryan/Eireann that occurs in *Malone Dies* (2010: 95–6; see Mooney 2011: 153) – Beckett at least considered associating the nationalism of the Irish Free State with that of Nazi Socialism, both using food as '*lieux de mémoire*' (Morin 2005: 229) to fabricate a sense of patriotic unity. Perhaps a word such as 'Eintopf' inserted all too explicitly a notion of politics into the novel, especially since other authors like Victor Klemperer, whose diaries became public in 1947, had already written about it (McNaughton 2018: 13, 171n89). Still, its temporary (re-)occurrence reveals that Beckett continued to draw on different cultures, even in translation, to further shift the cultural affinities of *Molloy* and deepen its hybridity.

Conclusion

As our discussion of some genetic variants from the French and English drafts of *Molloy* has tried to show, the sense of cultural displacement or unbelonging that readers and critics have commonly associated with the novel was only arrived at after a long and careful process of revision. This was marked by considerable hesitation, mirrored in Beckett's acute self-awareness of his dubious position as an Irish expat author wanting to make a literary career for himself in France, from there to attract a global English readership abroad. On the one hand, the genesis of both language versions reveals the resulting bilingual work to be more wordly, perhaps, than it appears in print. On the other hand, one might contend that it remains, after all, embedded primarily in a Eurocentric or, if we include the American frame of reference, Western outlook. Still, following Damrosch's distinction of 'world literature from a notional "global literature" that might be read solely in airline terminals, unaffected by any specific context whatever' (2003: 25), it is not necessary for literary works to be so diluted that they become generic, rid of all nationality. On the contrary, as Vilashini Cooppan states, a work of world literature should at once be 'locally inflected and translocally mobile' (cited in Damrosch 2003: 22), regardless of the culture(s) in which it is embedded. Reading *Molloy* against the Irish-French background from which it emerged, compounded with its forays into English, German and American culture, certainly enriches the experience for readers who are both inclined and equipped to do so. At the same time, Beckett seems to have understood very well that works which 'remain largely within their local or national context, never [achieve] an effective life as world literature' (Damrosch 2003: 289). Delocalizing the novel through its successive draft stages only increased its sense of alienation, which Hill associates with Freud and the *umheimlich* (1990: 40). This is a feeling that any reader can relate to, allowing the novel to take on a rich variety of meanings in national contexts far beyond its own, which may already be multiple rather than singular.

Notes

1 For more information on the translation process of *Molloy*, *Malone Dies* and *The Unnamable*, see O'Reilly, Van Hulle and Verhulst (2017), Van Hulle and Verhulst (2017), and Van Hulle and Weller (2014).
2 This notation refers to the online genetic bilingual edition of *Molloy* in the Beckett Digital Manuscript Project (www.beckettarchive.org). The reference to the volume (no. 4, edited by Édouard Magessa O'Reilly, Vincent Neyt, Dirk Van Hulle and Pim Verhulst) is followed by the abbreviation of the document in the catalogue (e.g. FN2 is the second French notebook) and the page number.
3 In *The Routledge Companion to World Literature* (2011), Theo D'haen, David Damrosch and Djelal Kadir list various disciplines and theoretical fields from which world literature can be analysed, including philology, comparative literature, translation studies, postmodernism and postcolonialism, but genetic criticism or manuscript studies is not one of them.

Works cited

Beckett, S. (1951), *Molloy*, Paris: Les Éditions de Minuit.
Beckett, S. (2009a), *Molloy*, London: Faber and Faber.

Beckett, S. (2009b), *Murphy*, London: Faber and Faber.
Beckett, S. (2009c), *Watt*, London: Faber and Faber.
Beckett, S. (2010), *Malone Dies*, London: Faber and Faber.
Beckett, S. (2011), *The Letters of Samuel Beckett, Vol 2: 1941–1956*, eds. George Craig, Martha Dow Fehsenfeld, Dan Gunn, and Lois More Overbeck, Cambridge: Cambridge University Press.
Beckett, S. (2016), *Molloy: A Digital Genetic Edition*, (Series 'The Beckett Digital Manuscript Project', module 4), eds. Magessa O'Reilly, Dirk Van Hulle, Pim Verhulst and Vincent Neyt, Brussels: University Press Antwerp (ASP/UPA), http://www.beckettarchive.org (accessed 29 March 2020).
Beckett, S., and E. Franzen (1984), 'Correspondence on Translating *Molloy*', *Babel*, 3: 21–35.
'Becketts Blick auf Berlin' (2005), *Der Spiegel*, 51: 152.
Bixby, P. (2010), 'Beckett at the GPO: *Murphy*, Ireland, and the "Unhomely"', in S. Kennedy (ed.), *Beckett and Ireland*, 78–95, Cambridge: Cambridge University Press.
Bowles, P. (1994), 'How to Fail: Notes on Talks with Samuel Beckett', *The PN Review 96*, 20 (4): 24–38.
Damrosch, D. (2003), *What Is World Literature?* Princeton and Oxford: Princeton University Press.
Davies, W. (2017), '"Home and Visiting Temperaments": Beckett's Diasporic Encounters', in M. Bariselli, N. M. Bowe, and W. Davies (eds.), *Samuel Beckett and Europe*, 55–76, Newcastle upon Tyne: Cambridge Scholars Publishing.
de Biasi, P-M. (2004), *La génétique des textes*, Paris: Nathan.
de St Jorre, J. (2009), *The Good Ship Venus: The Erotic Voyage of Maurice Girodias and the Olympia Press*, London: Faber and Faber.
D'haen, T., D. Damrosch, and D. Kadir, eds. (2014), *The Routledge Companion to World Literature*, London and New York: Routledge.
Fletcher, J. (1967), *Samuel Beckett's Art*, London: Chatto & Windus.
Harrington, J. P. (1981), 'The Irish Landscape of Samuel Beckett's *Watt*', *The Journal of Narrative Technique*, 11 (1): 1–11.
Harrington, J. P. (1991), *The Irish Beckett*, Syracuse, NY: Syracuse University Press.
Helfand, W. (1991), *The Picture of Health: Images of Medicine and Pharmacy from the William H. Helfand Collection*, Philadelphia: University of Pennsylvania Press.
Hill, L. (1990), *Beckett's Fiction: In Different Words*, Cambridge: Cambridge University Press.
Knowlson, J. (1997), *Damned to Fame: The Life of Samuel Beckett*, London: Bloomsbury.
McNaughton, J. (2018), *Samuel Beckett and the Politics of Aftermath*, Cambridge: Cambridge University Press.
Mooney, S. (2011), *A Tongue Not Mine: Beckett and Translation*, Oxford: Oxford University Press.
Morin, E. (2005), '"But to Hell with All This Fucking Scenery": Ireland in Translation in Samuel Beckett's *Molloy* & *Malone Meurt / Malone Dies*', in O. Pilný and C. Wallace (eds.), *Global Ireland: Irish Literatures for the New Millennium*, 222–34, Prague: Litteraria Pragensia.

Morin, E. (2009), *Samuel Beckett and the Problem of Irishness*, Basingstoke: Palgrave Macmillan.
Neary, J. P., and C. Ó Gráda (1991), 'Protection, Economic War and Structural Change: The 1930s in Ireland', *Irish Historical Studies*, 27 (107): 250–66.
Nixon, M. (2011), *Samuel Beckett's German Diaries 1936–1937*, London: Continuum.
O'Reilly, É. M., D. Van Hulle, and P. Verhulst (2017), *The Making of Samuel Beckett's 'Molloy'*, Antwerp and London: University Press Antwerp and Bloomsbury.
Rosset, B. (2016), *Dear Mr. Beckett: Letters from the Publisher. The Samuel Beckett File*, ed. L. Oppenheim, New York: Opus.
Swift, J. (1824), 'A Dialogue in Hybernian Style between A and B', in Sir W. Scott (ed.), *The Works of Jonathan Swift*, Vol. VIII, 156–7, Edinburgh: Ballantyne.
Van Hulle, D., and P. Verhulst (2017), *The Making of Samuel Beckett's 'Malone meurt' / 'Malone Dies'*, Antwerp and London: University Press Antwerp and Bloomsbury.
Van Hulle, D., and S. Weller (2014), *The Making of Samuel Beckett's 'L'Innommable' / 'The Unnamable'*, Antwerp and London: University Press Antwerp and Bloomsbury.
Winstanley, A. (2014), '"Grâce aux excréments des citoyens": Beckett, Swift and the Coprophagic Economy of Ballyba', *Samuel Beckett Today / Aujourd'hui*, 26: 91–105.

3

Samuel Beckett and the politics of post-war translation

Thirthankar Chakraborty

> *The mistake, the weakness at any rate, is perhaps to want to know what one is talking about. In defining literature, to one's satisfaction, even brief, where is the gain, even brief? Armour, all that stuff, for a loathsome combat.*
>
> BECKETT 2011: 98

The once reclusive writer, adamant in maintaining his privacy and refusing almost all proposals to adapt his works, is today one of the most widely read, performed and appropriated literary figures of the twentieth century. The untranslatable Godot is now almost a cliché, while quotations from his texts abound in the most unexpected places. And yet Beckett's 'world-making' fiction must stem from somewhere within his oeuvre, even if that somewhere is the 'nowhere' Beckett speaks of when discussing Jack B. Yeats's paintings. This essay begins by exploring Beckett's role as a translator in Paris before and during the Second World War. It then examines his responsibilities under UNESCO, shortly after the war, when he translated Octavio Paz's selection of Mexican poetry into English, later published as *An Anthology of Mexican Poetry* (1958). These two biographical instances provide the basis on which to assess Beckett's cosmopolitanism, bilingualism and self-translated works. The chapter then posits that with the outbreak and the culmination of the Second World War, the experience of world literature lies in the deeper significance of translation, as seen in Beckett, with the realization that meaning cannot be trusted to one linguistic field or the other.

Prior to the Second World War, Beckett spent several years translating poems and short stories from French to English and English to French, and he was also well versed in Spanish, Italian (through his knowledge of Dante) and German (as seen in his 1937 letter to Axel Kaun[1]). In her contentious book *Against World Literature: On the Politics of Untranslatability* (2013), Emily Apter considers Beckett's 1932 translation of Arthur Rimbaud's 'The Drunken Boat' (1871) as an example of *'translating untranslatably'* (2013: 147).[2] However, besides giving the example of two stanzas that support her case, Apter does not engage with the translated poem in depth and neither does she relate it to Beckett's later bilingual work. Looking at the last but one stanza of Beckett's translation of Rimbaud, it is in fact possible to find the early operations of a writer who is aware of the linguistic divide between English and French. The stanza in Rimbaud's original French reads:

> Si je désire une eau d'Europe, c'est la flache
> Noire et froide où vers le crépuscule embaumé
> Un enfant accroupi, plein de tristesse, lâche
> Un bateau frêle comme un papillon de mai.
>
> (2005: 134)

Beckett translates this as follows:

> I want none of Europe's waters unless it be
> The cold black puddle where a child, full of sadness,
> Squatting, looses a boat as frail
> As a moth into the fragrant evening.
>
> (1977: 105)

The sceptical nature of Beckett's translation distances the speaker (the drunken boat) from the Continent, overshadowing the obstinate romantic desire for a cold and darkened European pond in the French original. Unhindered by the rhyme scheme and the alexandrine meter of Rimbaud's poem, Beckett infuses his English translation with a greater bathos than the French original. The experience of disillusionment may appear to be common, but while the French *bateau* has yet a final desire to be in the same pond as the child's frail paper boat before giving up, the English boat has seen enough of Europe already, even as the child sets his boat free. The phonetic aspect of the word 'looses' (not 'releases' or 'lets go of') adds the suggestion of the boy 'losing' his boat to the 'fragrant evening', a wordplay that is not present in the French original. The homonym thus entails a sense of youthful loss and impotence in the translated text, with echoes of Beckett's later aesthetic of failure; also, the May butterfly becomes a moth, in keeping with the evening context, but also evoking Percy Bysshe Shelley's 'The desire of the moth for the star' that is likewise doomed to failure (Shelley 2002: 525). If the boy's paper boat is a self-referential metaphor for the poet's boat (also crafted on paper), the translated poet is as much a Beckett as he is Rimbaud: the last glimmer of hope predestined to failure and misery in a disenchanted Europe.

As recorded in James Knowlson's biography, Beckett joined the Resistance on 1 September 1941, recruited by his friend Alfred Péron, following the arrest of James Joyce's friend Paul Léon during the second mass round-up of Jews in Paris (1997: 304). Beckett was increasingly distraught by the Nazi and Vichy regimes and Hitler's racist ideology. Gloria SMH, the cell of which Beckett was a part, functioned under the British Special Operations Executive, and it soon grew into an information network. The cell's mission was to help British airmen escape from the occupied zone when their planes were shot down (1997: 305). Regarding Beckett's role, Andrew Gibson writes, 'His job was to process information provided for him by agents, putting it in order, condensing and translating it so that it could then be miniaturized and sent on to London' (2010: 102). Beckett's skill as a translator was thus already well recognized by the time of the Second World War, as was his skill at 'condensing' and 'miniaturizing' pieces of significant information to be transmitted across the Channel.

The secrecy and anonymity associated with Beckett's task, when seen in light of the principle *'traduttore, traditore'* (translator, traitor), lends this sixteenth-century Italian adage a new meaning. At its inception in 1539, the alliterative proverb referred to the incompetent translator, who, instead of translating the source text interlingually, played a traitor's role of blinding those who were incapable of reading the original by presenting them with misinformation (see Venuti 2019: 94–5). Around the same time, the Italian saying also suggested untranslatability, where the act of betrayal was associated not so much with the translator but with the impossibility of translating (Venuti 2019: 100–2). However, in Beckett's case, working from within the Vichy regime in translating information for the allies made him quite literally a traitor. Considering the wartime scenario in relation to Emily Apter's view that 'War *is* [...] a condition of nontranslatability or translation failure at its most violent peak' (2006: 16), Beckett was among those who trespassed the borders of the combative languages of the period (including German) through the secretive act of translating classified information. He was thus what Thomas Beebee has described as a 'transtraitor' (2010: 310).

Beckett's awareness of working against the Vichy regime in war-torn Europe was most acute when he had to flee Paris and go into hiding in Roussillon, only narrowly escaping the Gestapo, who nonetheless arrested several of his co-workers, including his close friend and fellow-translator Alfred Péron (Knowlson 1997: 315). While in Roussillon between 1942 and 1945, Beckett took up manual labour in a farm, and although he wrote his second novel, *Watt*, the war largely interrupted Beckett's early writing and translation career. For instance, in his letter to George and Gwynedd Reavey in 1940, Beckett writes about the French translation of *Murphy* and reviews by Anatole Rivoallan as going 'down the drain for the moment' (Beckett 2009: 680). However, this interruption was crucial for Beckett's development as a writer of world literature.

Following Germany's defeat and after visiting his mother in Ireland, Beckett applied for work as an ambulance driver in order to gain entry back into France; he writes to the Reaveys, 'I am returning to France as (tenez-vous bien) interpreter-storekeeper to the Irish Red Cross Hospital Unit in Normandy' (Beckett 2011: 15). The feeling of alienation was all too present when the Irish staff helped the Red Cross set up their hospital in Saint-Lô. This is shown through Beckett's letter to Thomas MacGreevy on 19 August 1945: 'We have the impression that the locals would like the stuff, but don't want us (very reasonable attitude) and that the French Red X, for reasons not clear, insist on an Irish staff' (Beckett 2011: 18). As an Irish expatriate, Beckett was conscious of the sense of distrust that engulfed post-war France, particularly towards any foreign body, but rather than using his estranged state to denounce the ingratitude of the French, he embraces the cross-cultural differences as reasonable, much the same way he navigated the linguistic divide when translating Rimbaud. This consciousness of being an English-speaking outsider is also present in *Waiting for Godot*, as shown later in this chapter.

In her seminal and widely contested work *The World Republic of Letters* (1999), Pascale Casanova places Beckett at what she calls the meridian of world literature: Paris in the 1950s (see Casanova 2004: 87–103). She argues that it is Paris's centrality in the literary world that provides Beckett with the autonomy to reject past traditions and break from James Joyce's grip (Casanova 2004). However, any such simplistic understanding of Beckett's choice of living in Paris and writing in French can be misleading, for as Casanova herself writes in her earlier book on Beckett:

> [W]e cannot understand the full implications of Beckett's option for bilingualism unless we take into account all the debates peculiar to Ireland, the violent relations with England, Yeats's choice of English, Joyce's polyglottic solutions [...], and the literary dead end Beckett found himself in.
>
> (Casanova 2006: 96)

From Beckett's letters, moreover, one learns more about the discomforts and obstacles faced when living in Paris rather than its benefits. For instance, Beckett writes to George Reavey, 'Life in Paris is pretty well impossible, except for millionaires' (Beckett 2011: 24). And even considering his increase of earnings in France, Beckett's wealth was subject to the immense fluctuations of the French franc: 'The ten or fifteen thousand francs advance, when they are taken, last about a fortnight', writes Beckett to Thomas Macgreevy (Beckett 2011: 72). The editors of Beckett's letters add the informative footnote: 'In December 1945, the French franc had been devalued from 200 to 480 francs to the British pound: in the face of low wages, rising prices, and the need to be competitive in world markets, the French franc was devalued again on 26 January 1948, from 480 to 864 francs to the British pound' (Beckett 2011: 74). Such drastic fluctuations would make anyone living in France regret their position, especially when earning a writer's wages.

Notwithstanding the post-war precariousness of the French economy and the depreciation of the French franc, theorists of world literature such as Damrosch, Casanova, Sapiro and Moretti have remarked that in order to be published and to reach an international audience, the trajectory that literary works usually take is through key cities of publication, which have for a long time remained Paris, London and New York (see Damrosch 2009: 106). Recently, however, the publishing industry and global organizations such as UNESCO have attempted to expand this localization, recognizing various 'international' cities of literature, with their criteria being the city's inclusion of 'foreign literature' (see UNESCO, Nottingham City of Literature n.d.). The evident Eurocentrism even in the more recent selection of cities can only be understood when one takes account of the political context in which the formation of UNESCO took place in 1945.

Following the two world wars that concerned almost all the European nations, the United States, the Soviet Union and the rest of the world agreed on the need for peace. But simultaneously, there were major differences that arose between the two superpowers that led to the Cold War: the capitalist United States and the communist USSR. Europe was divided between the two, between NATO and the Eastern bloc. It was in this context that the notion of the 'Third' or the rest of the unaligned world was first formulated, with the United States and its allies considered as 'First' and the Soviet Union with Eastern Europe forming the 'Second' worlds.[3] But 'Third World', moving away from Alfred Sauvy's Marxist notion of 'Tiers Monde' (see Solarz 2012: 1561–4), within the next two decades came to designate underdeveloped and developing countries that were former colonies. Following their independence, these countries had yet to establish their own cultural, economic and political presence in a world driven increasingly by America-centric capitalism (see Kiely and Marfleet 2004: 6–9).

At this juncture, organizations such as UNESCO, funded by the 'First' and 'Second' worlds, affirmed a sense of Western hegemony by lending monetary and cultural assistance to its international member states, in the form of 'holistic policies that are capable of addressing the social, environmental and economic dimensions of sustainable development' (UNESCO n.d.). Even today, when the denomination of a 'Third World' has been scrapped and replaced by the Global South, the so-called literary capitals have largely remained within the 'First' world when seen from a Western academic's perspective, notwithstanding the flourishing of literary cultures across the planet.

When seen in this light, Moretti's *'law of literary evolution'* also makes sense, despite now being considered largely outdated (Moretti 2000: 58). Writing specifically about the rise and spread of the novel genre, he suggests that it is Western influence on peripheral cultures that produces a compromise between foreign form and local material (Moretti 2000). In this light, Beckett's bilingualism and the fact that he published the majority of his works while living in Paris already place him within one of the world's major literary centres so that he has no need to affect a compromise: there is no 'foreign' form, or the foreign form is in Beckett's case local material. The texts he writes during a period that Knowlson calls a 'frenzy of writing' (i.e. the years 1946–53) are entirely *sui generis*, a literary form in themselves. Yet a supposition as uncomplicated as this simplifies Beckett to the extreme, seeing that he was not solely a European novelist but also a bilingual (if not multilingual) genius who worked across literary genres and languages.

Besides translating French poets such as Rimbaud, Paul Éluard and Guillaume Apollinaire, Beckett also worked for UNESCO, 'that inexhaustible cheese' (Beckett 2011: 206). He translated Octavio Paz's selection of Latin American poetry, first published as *An Anthology of Mexican Poetry* (1958) and republished as *Mexican Poetry: An Anthology* (1985). At first glance, this puts Beckett at the heart of a European panoptic enterprise and linguistic neo-colonization, for which English has secured a bad name due to its Orientalizing tendencies since the Romantic period. As a matter of fact, when discussing his translations in a letter during the publication process, Beckett reveals to Georges Duthuit: 'I had unwittingly missed out lines, stanzas, and even whole poems! And the little Spanish that I had then has well and truly gone. If their practitioners of the plastic arts bear even a remote resemblance to their poets, I shall let myself off going to see them' (Beckett 2011: 200). In other words, Beckett appears to entirely forgo the authorial intentions of the originals and focus instead on bringing the Mexican writers towards the Anglophone reader. However, he remains sceptical about his position, and his frustration at being drawn into this project is most apparent when he writes again to Duthuit:

> And then the Mexicans. I am going green over them. A third of the way down the great river, Señor Paz changed his mind, cutting twenty or so poems (a dozen of which I had already translated) and adding on as many. My young Normalien, who already has a highly developed sense of equity, got up on his low horse like the future distinguished philologist that he is, declaring that it was not in his bond. Result: I have to get through the new ones on my own.
>
> (Beckett 2011: 181)

As Patricia Novillo-Corvalán points out, there is also at play here 'the politics of inclusion/exclusion of Mexican authors', which involved Jaime Torres Bodet, the director general of UNESCO, who advocated a traditional canonical approach in the selection of Mexican writers and rejected lesser-known contemporaries, to Paz's infuriation (2017: 79–80). While Beckett's fellow translator remains unidentified, Paz has also written that he was well aware of the fact that Beckett did not speak Spanish but was well versed in Latin, and he wrote the translations in consultation with a friend (see Beckett 2011: 184). But although Beckett took up this project, he was not an advocate of the hegemonizing tendencies of the global organization. On the contrary, much like Paz, he is highly critical of its motives, as seen in his letter to George Reavey in 1946 where he refers to UNESCO when writing, 'They haven't got going here at all yet and don't seem to know what they intend to do' (Beckett 2011: 49). In another 1948 letter to MacGreevy, Beckett writes, 'I have been reduced to applying for employment to UNESCO' (Beckett 2011: 72), as if excusing himself for his job, which was mainly due to his financial troubles. Later, he adds, 'There is an atmosphere of futility & incredulity there that is overwhelming. I don't think it will last very long, or in a very modified form' (75). Notwithstanding his dislike for UNESCO, Beckett worked meticulously on the translated poems, as Novillo-Corvalán explains, and his Spanish was not half as bad as he suggests in his letters (2017: 84–5). The book sales, moreover, have relied not so much on UNESCO's globalizing mission as they have on the fame of the two great writers printed on the cover (see 2017: 83).

Wai Chee Dimock remarks:

> Not stuck in one national context – and saying predictable things in that context – a literary text becomes a new semantic template, a new form of the legible, each time it crosses a national border. Global transit extends, triangulates, and transforms its meaning.
>
> (2001: 177)

While it may be empirically evidenced that literature is marketed from or via the centre, what distinguishes a work of world literature is its potential to speak to a global public in 'the new semantic template(s)' and 'the new form(s)'. In order to achieve this, the work fits with an evolving Zeitgeist determined by the prominent writers of the period and, more importantly, by living off the sociopolitical upheavals in the national 'branches' and having its supposed roots concealed beneath layers of interpretation. As Jacques Derrida puts it, every interpretation is a translation so that the very stability or the roots of a text is questionable (Derrida 2009: 336). Applying this to the case of *Mexican Poetry*, we find not only a transformation of some of the poems into English, but also a glimpse into predominant themes of Beckett's later world-making fiction, which Beckett interprets from the

Mexican poems. While Novillo-Corvalán discusses a number of poems that thematize death, and compares them with Beckett's own preoccupation with death, another case in point is Amado Nervo's poem 'Y tú esperando...' (Acereda and Alarcón 2011: 68), which Beckett translates as 'And Thou, Expectant...'. While Nervo repeats the verb *pasar* in his first three lines, where he refers to the starry night, dazzling days, the rain and the clouds, Beckett modifies the verb to 'Fraught with stars the dark nights come and go / and come and go the dazzling coral days / and the grey [...]' (Paz and Beckett 1985: 149). Beckett's modification of the original becomes the title for his English dramaticule *Come and Go* (1965), which ends with a flourish of introspective questions similar to that in Nervo's poem: 'when shall we behold the open rose!' (Paz and Beckett 1985: 150). The use of ellipses in the title and in the fourth line – 'the fleeting clouds/...' – also predates Beckett's own play for television ... *but the clouds* ... (1977), which is also an allusion to a line from W. B. Yeats's 'The Tower' (1928). In contrast to these instances, while Beckett translates '*esperando*' as 'expectant' throughout the poem, the more literal translation of 'waiting' or '*attendant*' becomes the predominant theme of *Waiting for Godot*. The theological element of the final stanza, 'Eternal God, thou never makest haste, / but man is anxious, being ephemeral', also anticipates the theological underpinnings of *Waiting for Godot*, where the two male protagonists frantically question where and when they are to meet Godot (Beckett 2010: 28–37). Hence, Beckett is not merely translating a relatively unknown literature in the Western world into a global language but digging deep into poetic significance and absorbing literary themes and techniques in the process. As George Steiner writes, 'To understand is to decipher. To hear significance is to translate' (1992: xii), and in this sense Beckett was a translator par excellence during his stint as translator of Mexican poetry.

One of the most common ways that Beckett's *Godot* has been interpreted around the world is from a theological perspective, in spite of Beckett's own comment to the actor Sir Ralph Richardson that, 'if by Godot I had meant God, I would [have] said God, and not Godot' (Beckett 2011: 507). In fact, the few reflections about God and Christianity in Beckett's tragicomedy are mostly agnostic in their outlook, endorsing neither theism nor atheism. For even when Vladimir undermines Christian faith in the Bible with his story about the two thieves, Estragon deliberately turns a deaf ear ('Je n'écoute pas' in French, but omitted in English) (Beckett 2010: 22–3). It is obvious that the word 'Godot' has no phonetic link to '*dieu*' in French, and the description of Godot's house in the French text (omitted in the English), where Vladimir looks forward to spending the evening, makes the French Godot less of a spectral being (Beckett 2010: 56–7). However, as Lawrence Graver points out, theological allusions are present throughout the English as well as the French versions (2004: 72–3). For instance, the theological connotations of 'connaissance' in French when referring to Godot are greater than the English 'acquaintance' (Beckett 2010: 70–1). Likewise, Pozzo's purpose of selling Lucky at the 'fair' is not as theologically inclined as wishing to sell him at the 'marché de Saint-Sauveur' (100–1). The protagonists' agnostic attitude is made clear at the start of the French text but omitted in the English, when Vladimir asks Estragon about whether he read the Bible '*A l'école sans Dieu?*', and Estragon replies, '*Sais pas si elle était sans ou avec*' (Beckett 2010: 20–1). In contrast, when the role of the sufferer is reversed as Pozzo groans, 'clutching his head', Vladimir rebukes Lucky for crucifying his master, with the word 'crucify' missing in the French text (Beckett 2010: 106–7). However, as Graver also observes, the directness of this English allusion in considering Pozzo not only as God, the punisher, but also as Jesus, the sufferer, makes an allegorical reading seemingly absurd rather than serious, particularly when taking into account Beckett's trenchant sense of humour (see Graver 2004: 73).

Furthermore, the relationship between Pozzo and Lucky is clearly one of master and slave, yet the distinction between '*homme de peine*' and 'slave' adds to the French a cultural variance when compared to the English, although, in both cases, Pozzo announces his wish to sell him off. The labourer or the proletariat[4] of the French is the colonial slave in the English, notwithstanding the fact that both countries participated in the slave trade in their colonial past, with France abolishing slavery in 1794 and England in 1833. Yet a demand for hard work that kills the proletariat is not the same as the exploitation of a slave who suffers through perpetual enslavement. This plural interpretation of the pair's relationship has been variously construed across the world. While Rónán McDonald claims that Pozzo could be regarded as a rich Englishman (McDonald 2008: 153), Paul Lawley suggests that he could be anything from Cain to a Nazi overlord, an Irish Victorian landlord, or a Hegelian Master (see 2008: 91), while a Marxist reading places him as 'an effete and pretentious member of the bourgeoisie' (Hutchings 2005: 65).

This is also where the complexity of Beckett's English becomes apparent. If 'Ours is an age of translation and also an era of retranslation' (Damrosch 2003: 187), it is also a world where accents and pronunciations abound, where global English is not so much a homogenized single entity, but where contrasting Englishes either complement or distinguish themselves from one another. In *Waiting for Godot*, for instance, Estragon draws a distinction between his pronunciation of the word 'calme' and the way it is pronounced by the English: 'Les Anglais disent câââm. Ce sont des gens câââms', which is partly retained even in the English version: 'The English say cawm' (2010: 38–9). As an Irish citizen living in France, Beckett thus differentiates Estragon's English from French but also from British English, and this resonates well with the multiplicity of Englishes spoken by people across the postcolonial world of today, outnumbering speakers of the received pronunciation (RP). Moreover, when Beckett's *Godot* was performed in the United States, the script varied not just from the original French, but also from the translated English, and these differences were evident in the editions published by Grove and Faber and Faber, as noted in *The Theatrical Notebooks of Samuel Beckett, Volume 1: Waiting for Godot*.

Harold Bloom famously places Beckett as a shelf-bracket to his canon in *The Western Canon* (1994), and Beckett's works have been included in various English and world literature anthologies. The question remains, however, do Beckett and his works champion canonicity? This essay has so far shown that it is neither Beckett's pursuance of one canonical course or another nor a desperation to enter the French theatrical scene, which brought him to post-war Paris. He did not start writing in French in the 1940s because Paris was the dominant literary capital and that a French version of his works would boost sales and theatrical productions across the planet. While he did employ a French publisher to market his books, he was well aware even when he was living in France that literature and livelihood do not go together: 'if we absolutely must earn money, we do it elsewhere' (Beckett 2009: 517). More than that, Beckett suffered from the difficult position he occupied as an Irishman working in France. For, when Roger Blin expressed his interest in staging *Godot* in 1950, Beckett wrote to Georges Duthuit, 'My nationality complicates things, apparently, foreign plays can only be put on at the rate of one for every three French plays' (Beckett 2011: 182). Hence, writing first in French made matters all the more difficult for Beckett.

Translation has increasingly become a part of a literary text's passage into world literature, and this translation is usually into English. However, Beckett does not translate his works into English in order for them to achieve canonicity; instead, as he suggests in his letter to Axel Kaun in 1937, he does it to 'violate' his own language (Beckett 2009: 520). Translation for Beckett becomes a means to escape the constrictions of the English language, in which Joyce achieved 'an apotheosis of the word' (Beckett 2009: 519). In a letter to Georges Duthuit, a few months after he finished writing *Godot*, Beckett comments in French on his as yet incomplete 'Three Dialogues', which was to be published in *transition*: 'It is perhaps the fact of writing directly in English which is knotting me up. Horrible language, which I still know too well' (Beckett 2011: 170). This makes Beckett's reluctance to write in English all too obvious.

In *The Gay Science* (1882), Friedrich Nietzsche remarks, 'The degree of the historical sense of any age may be inferred from the manner in which this age makes *translations* and tries to absorb former ages and books' (cited in Venuti 2012: 67). He gives the example of the French assimilating Roman art and culture and the Romans drawing from the Ancient Greeks. However, following the revelation he experienced at the end of the Second World War, we find in Beckett an increasing awareness that rather than translating any one culture or language into another, he must translate a deeper significance that lies behind the translated body into the languages he worked with. As a result, his works are placed in between languages: not just French and English, but also Spanish, German, Italian and Latin.

This sense of in-betweenness is tied to the Beckettian idea of failure, which establishes his pervasive presence through further diversification while undermining the politics of hierarchy and centralized authority behind the formation of canons. The sacrosanct literary body and this body's cannibalizing influence on 'minor' literatures are switched off at the creative kernel of Beckett's world, where we find a fuzzy movement that rests neither in French and English nor in any other language. And this state of in-betweenness is increasingly apparent following the Second World War, where Beckett stops self-translating his works from English to French (as he had for *Murphy*) so that he may be published in France but uses French as his primary language for being '*mal armé*': 'ill equipped' but also 'poorly armed' (see Beckett 2011: 462).

It is evident from Beckett's letters regarding organizations such as UNESCO that he resisted globalizing enterprises, almost as much as he resisted the Nazi regime. While writing from Paris in the mid-twentieth century may have secured Beckett a wider readership, the continued interest in his works has less to do with the centrality of the 'First World' than with his ability to write in between languages. And this ability could only have been mastered by someone who, having witnessed the massive destruction of war and the animosity of humankind, took it upon himself to stand apart from any side taking up arms against another: literally and linguistically. Thus, in Beckett's case there is no self-translation from a minor to a major literature or even vice versa. Instead, his primary language of choice becomes one of his tools for being 'ill equipped', and self-translation is a further process of refining this state. From working as a translator during the war, where secret messages were transmitted to better equip one side against the other, Beckett's role as a self-translator is reversed in order to do away with the propensities of language and linguistic tradition, in favour of a literature 'without style' (Knowlson 1997: 324). From being a 'transtraitor', Beckett learnt the art of writing without empowering any one linguistic culture. His work is an appeal against a globalization of the literary world that levels cultural and linguistic difference or replaces them outright with the dominating languages of today, where the writer's only mantra is 'you must go on, I can't go on, I'll go on' (Beckett 2006: 407). To conclude with a letter in French to Georges Duthuit that discloses Beckett's views about the deeper function of translation, which has a bearing upon the Stoic hopelessness found in *Godot* and *The Unnamable*:

Send me texts for translation, of yours as far as possible. I don't know whether we'll be able to do anything. I am not good at fighting. Perhaps we can do something by not fighting. After all, that is a widely shared talent.

(Beckett 2011: 92)

Notes

1 In this letter, Beckett makes several comments regarding his need to break free from the restrictions imposed upon him by the English language: 'It is indeed getting more and more difficult, even pointless, for me to write in formal English. And more and more my language appears to me lie a veil which one has to tear apart in order to get to those things (or the nothingness) lying behind it' (Beckett 2009: 518).
2 Apter explains this as a form of 'over-translation that embraces wild infidelity to the original and pushes the envelope of translatability' (2013: 147).
3 See, for example, Dirlik (1997: 72).
4 See Graver (2004: 17) where he refers to Henry Hewes's interpretation of Lucky as a 'labour-proletariat'.

Works cited

Acereda, A., and J. S. Alarcón (2011), *Del Modernismo A Nuestros Días: Antología Literaria Hispanoamericana*, New York: Lulu Press.
Apter, E. (2006), *The Translation Zone: A New Comparative Literature*, Princeton: Princeton University Press.
Apter, E. (2013), *Against World Literature: On the Politics of Untranslatability*, London: Verso.
Beckett, S. (1977), *Collected Poems in English and French*, New York: Grove.
Beckett, S. (2006), *The Grove Centenary Edition, Vol. II, Novels*, ed. Paul Auster, New York: Grove.
Beckett, S. (2009), *The Letters of Samuel Beckett, Vol. 1*, eds. Martha Dow Fehsenfeld and Lois More Overbeck, Cambridge: Cambridge University Press.
Beckett, S. (2010), *Waiting for Godot/En Attendant Godot: A Bilingual Edition*, New York: Grove.
Beckett, S. (2011), *The Letters of Samuel Beckett, Vol. 2*, eds. George Craig et al., Cambridge: Cambridge University Press.
Beebee, T. (2014), 'Shoot the Transtraitor!' *The Translator*, 16 (2): 295–313.
Casanova, P. (2004), *The World Republic of Letters*, trans. M. B. DeBevoise, Cambridge: Harvard University Press.
Casanova, P. (2006), *Samuel Beckett: Anatomy of a Literary Revolution*, trans. Gregory Elliott, London: Verso.
Damrosch, D. (2003), *What Is World Literature?* Princeton: Princeton University Press.

Damrosch, D. (2009), *How to Read World Literature*, Chichester: Wiley-Blackwell.
Derrida, J. (2009), *The Beast and the Sovereign*, trans. Geoffrey Bennington, Chicago: University of Chicago Press.
Dimock, W. C. (2001), 'Literature for the Planet', *PMLA*, 116 (1): 173–88. Available online: http://www.jstor.org/stable/463649 (accessed 19 April 2014).
Dirlik, A. (1997), *The Postcolonial Aura: Third World Criticism in the Age of Global Capitalism*, Boulder: Westview Press [Ebook]. Available online: http://hdl.handle.net/2027/heb.31020.0001.001 (accessed 23 August 2016).
Gibson, A. (2010), *Samuel Beckett*, London: Reaktion Books.
Graver, L. (2004), *Samuel Beckett: Waiting for Godot*, Cambridge: Cambridge University Press.
Hutchings, W. (2005), *Samuel Beckett's Waiting for Godot: A Reference Guide*, Westport: Greenwood Publishing.
Kiely, R., and P. Marfleet (2004), *Globalisation and the Third World*, Abingdon: Taylor and Francis.
Knowlson, J. (1997), *Damned to Fame: The Life of Samuel Beckett*, Paperback Ed. London: Bloomsbury.
Lawley, P. (2008), *Waiting for Godot: Character Studies*, London: Bloomsbury.
McDonald, R. (2008), '*Waiting for Godot*', in H. Bloom (ed.), *Samuel Beckett's Waiting for Godot, New Edition: Bloom's Modern Critical Interpretations* 143–56, New York: Infobase Publishing.
Moretti, F. (2000), 'Conjectures on World Literature', *New Left Review*, 1: 54–68.
Novillo-Corvalán, P. (2017), *Modernism and Latin America: Transnational Networks of Literary Exchange*, New York: Routledge.
Paz, O., ed. and S. Beckett, trans. (1985), *Mexican Poetry: An Anthology*, New York: Grove Press.
Rimbaud, A. (2005), *Complete Works, Selected Letters: A Bilingual Edition*, trans. Wallace Fowlie, Chicago: The University of Chicago Press.
Shelley, P. B. (2002), *The Selected Poetry and Prose of Shelley*, Ware: Wordsworth Editions.
Solarz, M. W. (2012), '"Third World": The 60th anniversary of a concept that changed history', *Third World Quarterly*, 33 (9): 1561–73.
Steiner, G. (1992), *After Babel: Aspects of Language and Translation*, 2nd ed., Oxford: Oxford University Press.
Venuti, L., ed. (2012), *The Translation Studies Reader*, 3rd ed., London: Routledge.
Venuti, L. (2019), *Contra Instrumentalism: A Translation Polemic*, Lincoln: University of Nebraska Press.
UNESCO: Nottingham City of Literature (n.d.), 'About UNESCO Cities of Literature'. Available online: https://nottinghamcityofliterature.com/about/unesco-cities-of-literature (accessed 30 September 2019).

4

Unformed and untranslatable: The global applicability of Beckett's theatre of affect

Charlotta Palmstierna Einarsson

'For what is that coloured plane, that was not there before. I don't know what it is, having never seen anything like it before.'
– SAMUEL BECKETT

This chapter seeks to address Samuel Beckett's theatre as world literature by looking at and analysing affect. A key element in Beckett's drama, affect intervenes into spectators' meaning-making processes in unpredictable ways (see Einarsson 2017, 1). In *The Singularity of Literature* (2004), Derek Attridge notes that 'to experience something is to encounter or undergo it, to be exposed to and transformed by it, without necessarily registering it – or all of it – as an emotional and physical event' (2004: 19). This description of experience resonates well with the perspective on affect applied here. An invitation to experience, affect in Beckett's theatre does not correspond to predetermined or even conscious meanings, nor does it depend on preconceived knowledge of historical or cultural facts. Rather, by means of affect, Beckett's theatre calls its audience to surrender their claim to knowledge in favour of an opportunity of seeing the world afresh. In so doing, it is both subversive and liberating yet, more importantly, it has the power to touch audiences across time and space.

The wide circulation of Beckett's drama testifies to its applicability in various contexts. Since the premiere of *Waiting for Godot* in 1953, Beckett's creative works have been 'received, translated, read, and performed in Europe and beyond' (Nixon and Feldman 2009: 4).[1] Directors, actors and scholars have probed the material for points of entry that would allow them to connect the situation in a play to a given cultural context. As Mark Nixon and Matthew Feldman point out, exploring the global reception of Beckett's work provides valuable insights into the national, cultural and/or historical contexts in which it has been produced (see Nixon and Feldman 2009: 6) – even if it is virtually impossible to do more than merely 'scratch the surface of Beckett's immensely diffuse global reception' (Nixon and Feldman 2009: 5).[2] Yet while looking at the reception of Beckett's creative work in different contexts is no doubt illuminating with respect to the specific circumstances that have framed these productions, the plays themselves also offer other conduits to address their global application. Past years have therefore seen an increased interest in the affective dimension of Beckett's work, and both the prose and the dramas have been approached from the perspective of their capacity to affect audiences beyond the realms of culture or language.[3]

Among the most influential scholars to explore affect in Beckett's work is S. E. Gontarski, whose long-standing and insightful concern with affect has produced a range of perspectives on Beckett's dramas.[4] According to Gontarski, Beckett's theatre is 'a theatre of perpetual movement or flow, all comings and goings, a pulse that creates affect' (2015: 167). Moreover, Gontarski explains, Beckett's manner of organizing his stage images leads to a situation where his theatre is 'perpetually creating new worlds' (Gontarski 2015: 167). Of course, Beckett's dramas are not oriented towards the world as we know it. Rather, the strong emphasis on aesthetic elements prompts spectators to experience formal qualities without necessarily being able to come to terms with their meaning, thereby setting the stage for a different relationship between spectator and work: one that does not seek to abolish interpretation but rather seeks to invite audiences to experience works beyond trying to grasp their meanings.[5] In light of this, it is worth noticing, with Eric Hayot, that 'the world-oriented force of any given work of art, is an aesthetic effect that emerges only at certain scales of the work itself' (2012, 49) and that the degree to which a work of art is 'world-oriented' as well as the notion of 'a world oriented aesthetic' offers an analytic perspective that 'allows us to describe new kinds of difference and similarity' (Hayot 2012: 46).[6] That is to say, according to Hayot, '[w]orldedness emerges... as the establishing framework for the unmentioned rules that constitute the work as a total whole' (2012: 54), and the aesthetic qualities that comprise this whole may therefore be approached as 'variables or mechanisms of world-production' (2012). Taking the cue both from Gontarski and from Hayot's *On Literary Worlds*

(2012), this chapter therefore proposes that affect in Beckett's theatre is a world-constituting force, emerging on a scale of (aesthetic) experience.

Importantly, however, 'worldedness' in Beckett's theatre of affect is not merely a matter of the work *as* world (content), it is also a function of experience (form).[7] To experience Beckett's theatre of affect is to experience a crisis of representation. Yet, the theatre of affect also invites spectators into the event of performance: a situation that ultimately demands an openness and a willingness on behalf of the spectator to engage with the presentation. Beckett's theatre of affect asks spectators to reconfigure their place vis-à-vis the artwork through a radical acceptance of ignorance, and in so doing it gestures towards an ethics of communication. Beyond presenting epistemological enigmas, therefore, Beckett's theatre of affect prompts spectators to reconfigure their sense of belonging to the aesthetic world emerging in performance.

To illustrate this point, I will refer to a 'singular experience' of watching *Footfalls* (1975), one evening at the Royal Dramatic Theatre in Stockholm in 2004. The notion of singularity is borrowed from Derek Attridge, who invites us to rethink of the most important potential of literature (see Attridge 2004: 5). Admittedly, my memory of the event has since been overlaid with various other memories of performances (and readings), and the description is therefore merely an interpretation of a memory-rendered fiction. Yet my aim is not to extrapolate on the accuracy of this memory but to illustrate how the ambiguity derived from the formal organization of aesthetic experience in Beckett's theatre of affect could, at least in part, account for its global applicability.

Footfalls, originally published in 1976, revolves around the presence of a woman, May, walking a thinly lit strip on the floor. In the *Theatrical Notebooks IV* (1999) Beckett describes her as a 'faint tangle of grey tatters' (283); the stage directions specify that her pacing should start *'with right foot* (r), *from right* (R) *to left* (L), *with left foot* (l) *from* L *to* R' and that the steps should mark a *'clearly audible rhythmic thread... length {nine} steps'* (*TN IV* 1999: 275). According to Beckett, the 'walking up and down is the central image' and the play is 'built around this picture' (cited in Brater 1978: 36). Throughout the play, May continues to pace the stage alone, intermittently stopping to ask the voice of her mother (V) if she needs anything (Brater 1978). Although V never appears on stage, she repeatedly replies in a monotone voice, 'Yes, but it's too soon' (Brater 1978). The moment V begins to talk about May marks the beginning of the second part of the play (*TN IV* 1999: 284). Through V the audience learns that May has been walking like this since she was a child, yet in the third part of the play May momentarily stops walking to tell the story of Amy, who also slips out 'at nightfall and into the little church by the {north} door, always locked at that hour, and walk, up and down, up and down' (*TN IV* 1999: 276). As the stage lights dim out in the last scene, May continues to walk from left to right, and from right to left until *'[a]ll in darkness. Pause. Chime even a little fainter still. Pause for echoes. Fade up to even a little less still on strip.*

No trace of MAY. Hold {*ten*}*seconds. Fade out* [*, including B.*]. CURTAIN' (*TN IV* 1999: 279–80).

These meticulous stage directions reveal Beckett's close attention to the formal structure of the dramatic presentation, yet they also speak to the difficulties that spectators ostensibly face in the process of making sense of the drama. The play demands a responsive attitude on behalf of a spectator faced with the task of trying to interpret the variety of modalities appearing in the context of performance. Enoch Brater confirms that '*Footfalls* is a constant becoming, a work which can never be abandoned through definition because the enigma of its being on stage is its only essence' (1978: 40).

Watching the play, I recall watching the woman walking. I remember listening to the sound of her feet. Her solitary walking existed in my body as a pulse, intermittently interrupted by pauses that beckoned a continuation. I seemed to belong to this walking, perhaps in anticipation of her next move, or perhaps I already knew it, having walked it too. Yet I also remember attending to the division of the stage space into sections as the light sliced the air into wedges of darkness. Poised in-between the meaningless and the meaningful, the intrinsic ambiguity of the presentation effectively undermined my efforts to decode or translate it univocally. This is not to say that I did not try to bring preconceived notions of meaning to bear on this experience: it is merely to suggest that the elements emerging in the event of the performance did not make sense to me at first. Instead, they stood out as poetic manifestations that enthralled by being ambiguous and suggestively open to interpretation.

Seen this way, Beckett's theatre of affect participates in what Gilles Deleuze and Felix Guattari term 'traditions of sorcery' (2014: 287); i.e. it participates in a tradition of writing that trails a thin line between the meaningful and the meaningless to create a whole range of 'becomings and multiplicities' (2014: 293). Such writing ostensibly produces stage images that cannot be reduced to a specific meaning but 'have *an increasing or decreasing number of dimensions*' or potential meanings (2014). May's walking is therefore neither meaningful nor meaningless, nor is it first meaningless and then meaningful. Rather, it has the capacity to produce multiplicities of potential meanings predicating on the ongoing processes of becoming that constitute the movement. Consequently, as Brater points out, the 'footsteps of infinity on Beckett's narrow space complicate rather than elucidate the meaning of *Footfalls*' (1978: 38).

The emphasis on linguistic ambiguity in Beckett's drama thus reconfigures the conditions for interpretation. The theatre of affect seems designed to nudge spectators out of touch with familiar or habitual strategies of perception as the vitality of the dramatic presentation is founded on the redistribution of aesthetic attention from content to form, and from sense to sensation. In such presentations, 'meaning is no longer a property of the artist, nor does it reside in solely in the work of art; it emerges in the encounter between spectator and the artwork, or performance' (Einarsson 2017: 149). That is to say, the stage presentations that make up Beckett's theatre of affect (and *Footfalls* is here a case in point) are not symbolical in any conventional sense but emerge in the event of performance as invitations to experience, and it is the experience, not the presentation, that is loaded with potential.

In light of this, Beckett's emphasis on an 'inexpressive' art is not merely a means to create a 'new occasion' or 'a new term of relation' (Beckett 1983: 145), but a way to bring us closer to the 'truth' of a knowing that arises from experience. Admittedly, we usually come to a work of art expecting some kind of meaning and consequently try to piece the fragments together. Yet only when we are denied our habitual means of appropriating meaning, that is, only when we are prepared to give up trying to understand or control, may we begin to embrace that which we have no memory of 'having never seen it before' (Beckett 1983: 145). To be affected by Beckett's theatre, then, is to accept an invitation to be completely in the moment.

Accounting for affect is therefore not linking text to context – whether local, regional or global – in order to gauge its social or cultural impact; it is about tracing the potential effects of the forces that emerge in the event of performance. Seen this way, accounting for affect in *Footfalls* entails 'endeavouring to configure *a* body [not "the body" or "any body"] and its affects/affectedness, its on-going affectual composition of *a* world [not *the* world], the *this-ness* of a world and a body' (Gregg and Seigworth 2010: 3). The theatre of affect predicates on the structure of the dramatic work to allow for the possibility of *not* understanding the significance of the presentation meaningfully or univocally in language. Catering for ignorance, incomprehension and the perpetual alterations and adjustments of perception that follows in its wake, the theatre of affect thus undoes the relation to the world in order to allow for a more authentic encounter between spectator and work.

Notably, the notion of affect used here resonates with an understanding of affect as 'an inventory of shimmers', as suggested by Melissa Gregg and Gregory J. Seigworth in the introductory chapter to *The Affect Theory Reader* (2010). Affect, they explain, 'is in many ways synonymous with *force* or *forces of encounter*', even if the definition is a 'misnomer since affect need not be especially forceful' (Gregg and Seigworth 2010: 2). This description also leads them to Deleuze's inquiry into the workings of affect, which seeks to bridge the human/non-human divide (Gregg and Seigworth 2010: 6). According to Deleuze, however, Spinoza's philosophy could already be seen to straddle this divide (human/non-human), specifically through the realization that the 'environment is not just a reservoir of information whose circuits await mapping, but also a field of forces whose actions await experiencing' (Hurley 1988: ii).

Finding one's bearing in the intellectually and conceptually rich (and muddied) field of affect theory is admittedly difficult; not least since, conceived in terms of charged psychological states, affect is conventionally associated with emotions (see Tomkins 1962). Yet to address affect as an emotional response is ostensibly to reduce the term to a mere fraction of its explanatory potential. Over the past decades, affect theory has been increasingly broadened to comprise a wide range of 'orientations that undulate and sometimes overlap in their approaches' (Gregg and Seigworth 2010: 6). Given that accounting for affect as 'a field of forces' is a far cry from accounting for emotional responses (see Hurley 1988: ii), my discussion is less concerned with subjective responses to the dramatic presentations and more with the way Beckett's theatre orchestrates affect as potential (i.e. the Deleuzian brand of affect). Accounting for affect, then, is not only accounting for the potential effects of non-propositional forces in performance, it is also to account for the structure of the aesthetic presentation as the condition of possibility for experiencing without knowing. In fact, accounting for affect is realizing that 'understanding is not necessarily of the mind' (Metha 1989: 142), and the challenge is to respond to the 'shimmerings' of affect, without trying to conceptualize, emotionalize or reduce its effects.

If to create is to delineate a tension between the real world and the work of art, then Beckett's theatre of affect emerges at the junction between such resonating levels of worldedness. As David Lloyd explains, '[T]heatre for Beckett is the space in which what takes place is the happening of the moment as a thing in and of itself' (2018: 210). What is worlded, however, is not an aesthetic world, but an attitude allowing the momentary relief from understanding. Attending to the structural organization of unformed and untranslatable elements of performance (e.g. the sound of falling feet) is therefore to reconfigure the meaning of the artwork *as* experience. Yet it is only in the moment of giving in to the perpetual flow of Beckett's 'theatre of becoming, of deterritorialization, a decomposition moving towards re-composition, itself decomposing' (Gontarski 2015: 167), that we may become sufficiently alive to actually feel the power of such experiencing.

Such a position in no way excludes that 'disinterested' aesthetic experiences may not be culturally, socially or historically coded or that attending to such experiences may not increase our understanding of the artistic expression as an aesthetic and as a cultural phenomenon (whether in literature or in art more generally). Indeed, as Hayot points out, 'World creation happens consciously, but also in the ideological "unconscious" of the work, not as an expression of what the work does not know, but of what it knows most deeply, and thus says the least' (2012: 50). Viewed thus – and even though it is possible to relate Beckett's artistic presentations to (post-) modernist ideas, for example the crisis of the subject or the problem of representation, epitomized in his treatment of language – what Beckett's work seems to 'know most deeply and thus say the least' is not that linguistic meaning is unattainable, but rather that it is predictable. Consequently, Beckett takes precautions to secure the necessary conditions for his theatre of affect through staging situations that break down or resist conventional meaning-making.

The organization of aesthetic elements in performance is therefore an important aspect of worldedness in Beckett's work, and the meticulous stage directions, which record and document the aesthetic variables which comprise such worldedness are invaluable clues to understand the relation between the spectator and the work envisioned by Beckett.

Notably, Hayot's concept of 'amplitude' makes it possible to address the significance of adhering to Beckett's meticulous stage directions. According to Hayot, amplitude corresponds to 'the internal openness of the diegesis' (2012: 60). Large gaps in a narrative web emerge, for example, where speech does not serve to 'externalize thoughts' or where the characters' speech is directed to phenomena, situations or other characters, who are not part of the narrative besides being absences (see Hayot 2012: 55–6). Such a distribution of narrative elements will create worlds that are '"comparatively spacious"', as opposed to work in which the foreground and background are barely differentiated (Hayot 2012: 60). To illustrate this point, Hayot evokes Eric Auerbach's analysis of the Homeric narrative about Odysseus and the story of Abraham and Isaac. According to Hayot, 'Auerbach's great contribution is to conceptualize and name representational ground' (Hayot 2012: 55), and his analyses of these stories are presented as examples of two '"basic types" of literary representation', one in which '[e]verything is there for the reader' (i.e. the Homeric narrative) and one in which only 'certain parts [are] brought into relief others left obscure' (i.e. the Biblical narrative) (Hayot 2012: 55). Building on Auerbach's analysis, Hayot claims that a work which distributes narrative attention 'equally among all parts of the diegesis', as for example the Homeric story, 'produces […] a strong sense of foregroundedness, which is, in effect, the mark of *zero amplitude*' (Hayot 2012: 56). In contrast, works that distribute attention unequally among the various parts of the diegesis produce 'the sensation of mystery and wonder that permeates the twenty-second chapter of the book of Genesis' (Hayot 2012: 57). The latter is thus an example of a story in which, paradoxically, the background registers as conspicuously absent, which is to say it comes to the fore as a lack, enigma or gap. This is not to say that such a gap needs to be epistemological, as in Auerbach's example (see Hayot 2012: 59), nor is it a question of 'texts that are "all" foreground […] and ones that leave things largely unexpressed' (Hayot 2012: 57). Rather, given that all texts have both foreground and background, the question is to what extent do things left out register as absent in the diegesis (see Hayot 2012: 57). Ultimately, uneven distributions of attention between foreground and background produce high amplitude, whereas even distributions of background and foreground tend to produce low amplitude.[8]

Returning to *Footfalls*, then, it would appear that representational ground is here characterized by high amplitude. The uneven distribution between foreground and background renders sounds and shapes conspicuously foregrounded as enigmas to be experienced in the event of performance. To Gontarski's claim that productions that overemphasize the narratological aspects of Beckett's play do so at the expense of other aspects (2015: 11–15), we could therefore add the perspective of amplitude – not least since its effect seems to be a '[q]uestion of degree' between registering a '[t]otal object complete with missing parts' and a 'partial object' (Beckett 1983: 138).

However, the concept of amplitude may also help explain Beckett's objections to productions that failed to adhere to his meticulous stage directions. Take, for example, Gilas Bourdet's production of *Endgame* in 1988. Not only did Bourdet's staging displace 'the values contained and expressed by formal mastery such as Beckett's' (Scanlan 2000: 149), but in so doing, he disrupted the play's amplitude – thereby collapsing the production's capacity to present unformed and untranslatable elements as prompts for meaning-making processes. As the Swedish translator Göran O. Eriksson notes, Gildas Bourdet's production took 'extreme scenic liberties with' Beckett's *Endgame*, yet the main problem was not that the production seemed to go against Beckett's own creative vision but that it failed to take the degree of the work's openness into account. According to Eriksson, then, 'Gildas Bourdet was mistaken, but his mistake was not to violate a principle [the principle of authorial intention], it was to misunderstand the material' (1995: 189).

Clearly, the silence on temporal and spatial location is a key element of the openness in Beckett's theatre, and adding or alluding to explicit situations or meanings will therefore effectively close the gaps that contribute to produce high amplitude. Yet there is also an important difference between preserving the gaps (social, narrative, affective etc.) that emerge in Beckett's drama (as well as the degrees of communication between such layers of the presentation) and failing to notice their existence. Whereas the first stance entails sustaining the openness, which is to say the degree of incompleteness presented in the work, the other is running the risk of collapsing the intrinsic openness of such presentations, thereby reducing their power to affect – a circumstance that might render Beckett's authorial interventions in productions that failed to retain this openness more comprehensible. Given that experience is a function of form, the structure specified in the stage directions must be retained so as to allow for affect.

This idea seems corroborated by Jacques Derrida's response to Beckett's work. In an interview with Derek Attridge, Derrida relates his experience of teaching Beckett's prose and concludes that it would be impossible for him 'to extract a few "significant" lines from a Beckett text' (cited in Attridge

1992: 61). According to Derrida, experiencing the singularity of Beckett's work takes precedence over explaining it:

> [T]he composition, the rhetoric, the construction and the rhythm of his works, even the ones that seem the most 'decomposed', that's what 'remains' finally the most 'interesting, that's the work, that's the signature, this remainder which remains when the thematics is exhausted (and also exhausted, by others, for a long time now, in other modes)'.
>
> (cited in Attridge 1992: 61)[9]

The process of 'countersigning' (a phrase borrowed from Derrida) entails responding to the performance as a participatory event. Thinking about the world-constituting structures in Beckett's theatre of affect thus entails modifying the notion of interpretation.

This is not to say that we need to abandon our position as interpreters of individual works, yet we should be careful about the questions we ask. Indeed, as Gontarski observes, 'The apposite question may be less how Beckett was rendering our recognizable world than how he was creating new and unfamiliar worlds, decreating the worlds we thought we knew' (2015: 154). That is to say, the performance event invites spectators to reconfigure their situation in the world – a position that in no way excludes that works of art may also be contextualized culturally, socially or historically. However, the extent to which Beckett's theatre of affect resembles or represents the real world, or the place of such dramas within the world system of globalization, while interesting, cannot help us come to terms with the singularity of experience they offer. What is being worlded in Beckett's theatre is not the truth in relation to a particular context, but the possibility for authentic acts of judgement – this, finally, is also how Beckett's drama allows the spectator access to the ethical realm identified by Attridge (see 2004: 126–31).[10] In fact, Attridge stresses that '[t]o respond to the demand of the literary work as the demand of the other is to attend to it as a unique event whose happening is a call, a challenge, and obligation' (2004: 131). Beckett's theatre of affect predicates on such interdependence.

Looking at the distribution of unformed and untranslatable elements in *Footfalls* as world-constituting forces and trying to account for the way such forces emerge to affect spectators is thus to reconfigure the relation between world and artwork: a shift of perspective that may allow us to appreciate the wide applicability of Beckett's work. On a larger scale, accounting for affect allows us to reconfigure Beckett's place in the history of world literature, to notice how his work crosses the boundaries set by the conventional periodization of literature and to compare his prose with his drama.[11] We may also notice how Beckett's theatre of affect comprises an invitation to experience what is 'here' and 'now'. Watching a Beckett-play, audiences are invited to give up their privileged positions of autonomous meaning-makers in favour of recognizing an inclusive community of sentient, but essentially non-sovereign beings: an invitation to experience that also has ethical dimensions. Of course, as members of a global community (past, present or future), all human beings participate in various groups or contexts, but as Timothy Garton Ash asks, 'When you say "we", who do you mean?' (2005: 3). The answer to this rhetorical question underpins Beckett's theatre of affect.

Notes

1. As Enoch Brater suggests, Beckett's first play, *Waiting for Godot* (1953), owes its 'wide applicability' to its universalist tendencies and its vagueness about local reference and context (2003: 156). Notably, this essay does not deny the significance of his analysis; indeed, the title is inspired by this idea.
2. Nixon and Feldman's comprehensive anthology covers the reception of Beckett's work in the United States, Ireland, Poland, Japan, China, Spain, Italy, the Low Countries, the Nordic countries and in West and East Germany.
3. See, for example, Attridge (2011: 329–43; 2017: 10–23); Gontarski (2004: 194–208), the introduction to Gontarski (2014, 2015); Uhlmann (2005); Piette (2011: 281–95); Walsh (2011: 110–23).
4. Notably, Gontarski's methodological approach often pays more attention to the way in which Beckett deploys affect as a constituting factor in the lives of his characters than to the potential effects of such textual organization on its readers. His work is nonetheless highly applicable to the issue of how Beckett's drama affects audiences, not least as affect in the context of Beckett's theatre predicates on experience.
5. This is perhaps most noticeable in the dramatic works yet, as noted by Attridge, even Beckett's prose works could be seen to invite readers to pay attention to the elaborate organization of aesthetic features in the text over linguistic meanings (2017: 12).
6. Even if Hayot does not specifically discuss Beckett's work (he does mention it), his exploration of 'worldedness' in literary works seems highly relevant and useful also for the analysis of Beckett as world literature.
7. What emerges in a work of art is not only the work itself but also the tacit assumptions that could be seen to belong to the 'background beyond the aesthetic world proper' (Hayot 2012: 56). Ideological assumptions inevitably seep into works of art as part of the expectations on which the aesthetic work is founded and against which it takes its stance and as a result, 'world-creation happens both consciously [and] in the ideological "unconscious" of the work' (Hayot 2012: 49). A work of art, therefore, is 'an epistemological engine: a mechanism for the generation and exhibition of knowledge about itself as totality' (2012: 50).
8. Amplitude also emerges to be registered on the scale of social, affective, psychological or emotional aspects in a work, and '[a]mplitudinal norms [also] change over time' (Hayot 2012: 59).

9   This idea is also at the centre of Attridge's keynote at the conference 'Beyond Historicism: Resituating Samuel Beckett', 7–8 December 2012 at the University of New South Wales, Kensington, Sydney. Even if Attridge's discussion in the keynote centred on the prose work, specifically the three novels *Molloy*, *Malone Dies* and *The Unnameable*, this idea is equally relevant to Beckett's dramatic work, as evidenced by the effect of formal features.
10 Beyond the question of what counts or does not count as literature in a given time and place lies the question of what literature does, namely allowing us to participate in 'a particular kind of event', which Attridge calls 'performance' (even when referring to literary works) and which, he suggests, allows the reader access to the 'realm we call "the ethical"' (2004: 2).
11 Hayot convincingly outlines the potential benefits of attending to worldedness in literary works and my conclusion is inspired by his discussion.

Works cited

Ash Garton, T. (2004), *Free World*, London: Penguin Book, 2005.
Attridge, D., ed. (1992), *Jacques Derrida: Acts of Literature*, New York: Routledge.
Attridge, D. (2004), *The Singularity of Literature*, London and New York: Routledge.
Attridge, D. (2011), 'Once More with Feeling: Art, Affect and Performance', *Textual Practice*, 25 (2): 329–43.
Attridge, D. (2017), 'Taking Beckett at His Word: The Event of the Unnamable', *Journal of Beckett Studies*, 26 (1): 10–23.
Beckett, S. (1983), *Disjecta*, London: Calder.
Beckett, S., and S. E. Gontarski, eds. (1993), *The Theatrical Notebooks of Samuel Beckett*, general editor: James Knowlson, *Vol. VI, The Shorter Plays*, New York: Grove Press.
Brater, E. (1978), 'A Footnote to *Footfalls*: Footsteps of Infinity on Beckett's Narrow Space', *Comparative Drama*, 12 (1): 35–41.
Brater, E. (2003), 'The Globalization of Beckett's Godot', *Comparative Drama*, 37 (2): 145–58.
Deleuze, G., and F. Guattari, *A Thousand Plateaus*, translation and foreword by Brian Massumi, London: Bloomsbury, 2014.
Einarsson, P. C. (2017), *A Theatre of Affect: The Corporeal Turn in Samuel Beckett's Drama*, Stuttgart: *ibidem* Verlag.
Eriksson, G. O. (1995), 'Anvisningarna för spelet', in *Tala om Teater, Texter om teater och översättning i urval av Jane Friedman Eriksson, Leif Nylén och Katja Waldén*, 186–189. Stockholm: Nordstedts förlag.
Gontarski, S. E. (2004), 'Beckett and Performance', in L. Oppenheim (ed.), *Palgrave Advances in Samuel Beckett Studies*, 194-208, London: Palgrave.
Gontarski, S. E., ed. (2014), *The Edinburgh Companion to Samuel Beckett and the Arts*, Edinburgh: Edinburgh University Press.
Gontarski, S. E. (2015), *Creative Involution: Bergson, Beckett and Deleuze*, Edinburgh: Edinburgh University Press.

Gregg, M., and G. J. Seigworth (2010), 'An Inventory of Shimmers', in Melissa Gregg and Gregory J. Seigworth (ed.), *The Affect Theory Reader*, 1–25, Durham and London: Duke University Press.

Hayot, E. (2012), *On Literary Worlds*, Oxford and New York: Oxford Literary Press.

Hurley, R. (1988), 'Preface', in Robert Hurley (ed. and trans.), *Spinoza: Practical Philosophy*, i–ii, San Francisco: City Light Books.

Lloyd, D. (2018), *Beckett's Thing: Painting and Theatre*, Edinburgh: Edinburgh University Press.

Metha, Rohit (1989), *Krishnamurti and the Nameless Experience*, Delhi: Motilal Banarsidass.

Nixon M., and M. Feldman, eds. (2009), *The International Reception of Samuel Beckett*, London and New York: Continuum.

Piette Adam (2011), 'Beckett, Affect and the Face', *Textual Practice*, 25 (2): 281–95.

Scanlan, R. (2000), 'Performing Voices: Notes from Stagings of Beckett's Work', in Lois Oppenheim (ed.), *Directing Beckett*, 145–54, Ann Arbor: The University of Michigan Press.

Tomkins, Silvan S. (1962), *Affect Imagery Consciousness: Volume I, The Positive Affects*, London: Tavistock.

Uhlmann, A. (2005), 'Expression and Affect in Kleist, Beckett and Deleuze', in Laura Cull (ed.), *Deleuze and Performance*, 54-70, Edinburgh: Edinburgh University Press.

Walsh, Fintan (2011), 'From Enthusiasm to Encounter-Event: Bracha L. Ettinger, Samuel Beckett and the Theatre of Affect', *Parallax*, 17 (2), 110–23.

5

100% guaranteed Beckett: An intercultural reading of Beckett's *Waiting for Godot* as world literature

Mary O'Byrne and Wei Zheyu

This chapter gives an account of an attempt of interdisciplinary, collaborative, intercultural translation to engage with the text of *Waiting for Godot* as world literature. Ten sessions of performative research, carried out by a three-person research team of Drama and Beckett scholars, resulted in the delivery of a paper entitled '100% Guaranteed Beckett', including a performed reading of Lucky's speech in Act I of the play and a hand-held recording of the original French version of the speech read by the Chinese translator Yu Zhongxian at the Beckett and World Literature Conference in the University of Kent in May 2016. The aim of the research was to create and implement a model to read Samuel Beckett as world literature and to use it to examine the problematic of translation, the mode of circulation, cross-cultural performative reading and, at the same time, to grapple with the impossibility of language to confer meanings that remain stable across cultures or even within the same one. In this model the participants read, translated, performed, communicated and reflected all together in real time so that the text was interrogated in a way similar to how Beckett describes artistic experience in *Proust* as 'the free play of every faculty' (1999: 20). The project involved a coming together of participants of diverse cultural backgrounds, of varied skill sets, from different departments to explore the text outside of our established patterns of researching in order to examine Beckett's work from the perspective of interculturalism. This meant that the researchers had to leave to one side the conventional and cultural interpretations of the text and to this extent the research team sought to enact Beckett's commendation in *Proust* to '"[l]ive dangerously" that victorious hiccough in vacuo as the national anthem of the true ego exiled in habit' (Beckett 1999). We had to relinquish our habitual and conventional ways of interpreting the text and be open to the necessary dialogue about our experience of voicing the text out loud.

Our particular research methods necessitated repeated readings of Lucky's speech together live, using voice and body and reflecting on the theoretical issues raised. Three researchers participated in ten separate working sessions, and the work was accumulative. Our team consisted of Wei Zheyu, from the Department of Drama, School of Creative Arts, and Mary O'Byrne, School of English, both in Trinity College Dublin, joined by their colleague Li Yanshi, based in Foreign Language College, Taiyuan University of Technology, Taiyuan, Shanxi province, China. The ten two-hour meetings took place between 22 February and 27 April 2016. Li Yanshi participated from her home in Taiyuan, starting from 21 March 2016 in real time in an online video call. After reading the text we shared our experience, comparing, contrasting, identifying themes and issues related to working with it in the context of world literature. After each session a Learning Log was written up, then read and reflected upon, accompanied by further reading by the project members in preparation for the next working session. Video clips of various aspects of performance were examined; for example, Jean Martin's account of visiting a psychiatric hospital in order to visualize how Parkinson disease effected body movements during his preparation for playing Lucky in the 1953 Paris premiere and Wu Hsing-kuo, the Beijing opera actor and his Contemporary Legend Theatre's (CLT) 2005 crossover production of Samuel Beckett's *Waiting for Godot* in Taipei's Metropolitan Hall. The following printed editions and translations of *Waiting for Godot* were examined: the 1956 English version published by Faber and Faber in *Samuel Beckett: The Complete Dramatic Works*, the 1954 Grove edition of Beckett's translation from French to English, Shi Xianrong's 1983 translation from English to Chinese, Liao Yuru's 2008 translation from English to Chinese and Yu Zhongxian's 2006 translation from French to Chinese.

The participant role of the researcher was key, bringing her/his performative self to the process of intercultural exchange. As Beckett writes in his essay on *Proust*:

> The individual is the seat of a constant process of decantation, decantation from the vessel containing the fluid of future time, sluggish, pale and

monochrome, to the vessel containing the fluid of past time, agitated and multicoloured by the phenomena of its hours.

(1999: 20)

Our project commended each practitioner to 'perform' the decantation, that is, to embody the endless process of intercultural exchange, meaning-making and self-forming. Out of the decantation emerged a form or model of translation that enabled the intercultural exchange of meaning to remain open, active and not be dominated by a particular language or set of literary or performative conventions. The translation was ongoing and never completed. A Beckettian spirit guided the work; that is, the project was doomed to 'try again' and 'fail again' (1995: 101). Yet the project strove also to 'fail better', so as to express '[t]he expression that there is nothing to express, nothing with which to express, nothing from which to express, no power to express, no desire to express, together with the obligation to express' (1999: 103).

A crucial aspect of the process of embodied creative translation of Lucky's speech was an exploration of the musicality of multiple versions of *Waiting for Godot*. Musicality in this context meant the musical sensibility of the text, the modulations, rhythms, tones of the language and, particularly in a Chinese context, the potentiality of character creation in the language. After the first reading we experienced grappling with questions relating to how to voice the text in our own respective language – English and Chinese, including issues regarding grammar, style and intonation. For example, we found that the recurring three-syllable English word 'unfinished' was translated as *weiwanchengde* 未完成的 in Chinese, which had four syllables. The intonation of this Chinese word presents a different repetitive rhythm compared to the English word. The sense of *anxiousness* evoked in 'unfinished' changed to one of *pity* in '*weiwanchengde*'.

What is more, the use of tones in Chinese added to the complexity of voicing the translated text. Such kind of alteration of sounds changed its musicality. At this point, the connection between the signifier and the signified in the English language failed to guarantee a path for the exchange of ideas into another language. A video clip was examined of Lucky's speech from the 2005 adaptation of *En Attendant Godot*, performed by the CLT in the Metropolitan Hall, Taipei, directed by Wu Hsing-kuo. From a non-Chinese-speaking perspective, the focus of the listener was on the musicality of the voice of the actor, which was deep and strong, accompanied by stylized and precise movements and the sound effects of the bells on Lucky's feet. The sound of the bells was interpreted as an event of subjugation. The musicality of the bells was interpreted as animality such as bells on a pet animal. In the CLT's production the name Pengzu replaced Puncher, who was an ancient legendary Chinese man who lived for 800 years. Another Chinese perspective was how the theological and cultural aspects of the text could be read in the context of Buddhism. For example, the translation of the name Anan, a monk disciple of Buddha, replaced the name Wattman. The sounds of 'Quaquaquaqua' evoked French in a Western context but in a Chinese context evoked thoughts of steps, such as a lady in high heels, soldiers and the sound of ducks. Therefore, the research became an event where the sound of the language mattered as much as specific conceptual meanings. Be that as it may, the rearrangement of the musicality of the text was displaying disconcerting potentialities. The experience was disconcerting in the sense that the text came to be experienced as a site of unknowingness as well as of possibility. The word 'unknowingness' is not meant as failure in a negative sense but in the sense that Peter Malekin and Ralph Yarrow define: 'the mind becomes less, not more active, eventually leaving the subject-object relationship behind. It exchanges knowing about things in a theoretical and abstract way, for knowledge through uniting with the object of knowledge' (1997: 28).

Moving on to a discussion of the problematic of translation and Beckett's work, we encountered the necessity of dismantling the linguistic and cultural context of *Waiting for Godot*. We paid considerable attention to issues such as the accents, dialects, tones and modulations of sounds within English and Chinese. For instance, we found a resemblance between ancient Chinese literary texts and Lucky's speech, both of which had no punctuations. We started to wonder which type of English should be used in the reading. For instance, the place name 'Connemara' raised issues of whether to voice it in its Irish form as a post-colonial site of resistance or whether to voice what lexicographer Professor Terence Dolan terms Hiberno-English, a form of English whose grammar is based on the Irish language. The words 'Testew' and 'Cunard' suggested standard British English but lurking beneath their surface was a sense of a Beckettian basic-English-and-dirty-word humour, to borrow and adapt Ruby Cohn's description of Beckett's comedy in French (1959: 13).

In the second session of research, comparisons between two dramatic devices employed in performance were considered in the context of the musicality of the text. One was Jean Martin's adaptation of the effects on the voice, speech and body of Parkinson's disease to portray Lucky in the Paris premiere, and the other was *xiangsheng*相声, the traditional Chinese comedic art of crosstalk. We discussed two different cultural objectives: the Chinese interrogation of the human need to impress and the European concern with suffering, both being aspects of humanity's attempt to make sense of lived experience. What emerged as common to both cultures was a complicated response to what Stanton Garner describes in Beckett's work as 'a set of essentially phenomenological questions concerning subjectivity, embodiedness, and perception' (Garner 1994: 25). Both dramatic devices were a vehicle for expressing performative movements of possibility but also impossibility in language. For example, we examined the Beckettian creation 'quaquaqua' to explore how the connection between the signifier and the signified within the impossibility of exchanging ideas in language might be negotiated in translation. We discussed whether the negotiation held firm during the next reading session or there was a return to the point of departure or whether the process deducted certain ideas and movements of language that could not cross over into other languages and cultures.

Our work explored the necessity and impossibility of translation, by thoroughly analysing the transmutation of meaning, especially that of the proper names or nouns across different languages. The problematic of identity creation and the issues involved reflected back on our own subjectivity and foregrounded the responsibility we carried in translating Lucky's speech. Norman N. Holland describes the participative methodology adopted by our team:

> Identity re-creates itself... That is, all of us, as we read, use the literary work to symbolize and finally to replicate ourselves. We work out through the text our own characteristic patterns of desire and adaptation. We interact with the work, making it part of our own psychic economy and making ourselves part of the literary work – we interpret it.
>
> (Holland 1975: 124)

What we did in our project was to endeavour to embody the performance text, being not only conscious of our own process of self-replication but also to voice this experience out loud and open ourselves to hearing the responses from another cultural world view. In this way, we became aware of the intercultural and intracultural tensions found in Beckett's work.

The way Beckett's dramatic aesthetic deals with the proper nouns in *En Attendant Godot* that have specific French cultural references and become difficult to translate or even 'untranslatable' in his own English version showed us how language is fluid in the act of translating and in performance. For instance, 'Acacacacademy d'Anthropopopopométrie de Berne-en-Bresse' was translated into 'the Acacacacademy of Anthropopopopmetry of Essy-in-Possy', and 'Poinçon et Wattman' and 'Testu et Conard' were anglicized as 'Puncher and Wattman' and 'Testew and Cunard' (Beckett, 2006: 42). Harry Cockerham notes that a number of connotations of the French proper nouns have been lost in the English translation (see 1975: 148–9). However, new meanings and therefore new amusements were generated in the translation. Beckett cites the narrator in his monograph *Proust* with emphasis: 'The duty and the task of a writer (not an artist, a writer) are those of a translator.' Casting the writer as a translator, Beckett's argument appreciates the Latin preposition 'trans', seeking to bring these influences 'across' into his work not as mere imitations but to a more advanced point (Pilling 1993: 238). Our method of working with his text, likewise sought to go beyond imitation, to reinvigorate his usage of language and to grapple with the impossible-to-translate. Furthermore, we drew upon his aesthetics involving echo, re-soundings and resistance as expressions of the musicality of impossibility.

The focus upon the impossibility-to-translate led the team to consider going beyond the necessity of rational meaning-making and to consider other diverse possibilities of translating Lucky's speech while remaining true to the textuality of the text. Following in the wake of Beckett as translator, we found that the movement and direction of the work was one of distilling through the layers of possible meanings towards the 'idea', described by Beckett in *Proust* as 'the heart of the cauliflower or the ideal core of the onion' which represents 'a more appropriate tribute to the labours of poetical excavation than the crown of bay' (Beckett 1999: 29).

The reduction also sought to foreground the musicality and rhythms of every image detached from an object or category of substance and moreover to explore the role of comedy and humour in Beckett's aesthetics. For example, our initial loud readings of Lucky's speech involved attempting to place a logical structure on the stream of words, imaginatively applying commas to the text where none existed. We remarked how in later readings this approach was abandoned because breath control became more urgent. Beckett declared, '[B]reathing is habit', and in our experience Lucky's speech forced the speaker to stop randomly and breathe (Beckett 1999: 19). We found that this disrupted the surface of a coherent individuality. While this was disconcerting, Beckett identifies it in *Proust* as a kind of freedom and a source of creativity. We found that it was possible to read Lucky's speech as an angry feminist, when words such as 'cunt' were heard in Cunard and a hidden violence in the name Punchman. Furthermore, the intercultural, multilingual collaborative condition of our project facilitated putting to the test this Beckettian 'perilous zone' because of the lingual freedom it fostered. It reminded of Beckett's remark cited by Ruby Cohn in her article 'Samuel Beckett Self-Translator': '"The kind of work I do is one in which I'm not master of my material"' (Cohn 1961: 613). This lack of mastery was reflected in the way Lucky's speech repeats and reverts back to the starting point, to echo, or to resound.

At this point it is important to acknowledge that our lack of mastery of the text involved a certain force of resistance, interpreted as the violence of translation. To Lawrence Venuti, violence 'resides in the very purpose and activity of translation' (2008: 14). He writes:

> The reconstitution of the foreign text in accordance with values, beliefs, and representations that preexist it in the translating language and culture, always configured in hierarchies of dominance and marginality, always determining the production, circulation, and reception of texts. [...] [A] translator is forced not only to eliminate aspects of the signifying

chain that constitutes the foreign text, starting with its graphematic and acoustic features, but also to dismantle and disarrange that chain in accordance with the structural differences between languages, so that both the foreign text and its relations to other texts in the foreign culture never remain intact after the translation process.

(Venuti 2008)

Siding with Milan Kundera, Venuti criticizes domestication strategies[1] that integrate a foreign text violently into overriding values and concepts at home, destroying the very foreignness that caused the translation to be called for. Beckett's translation involved domestication but he successfully stroke the balance between domestication and foreignness, which retained the sense of the text. And our research demonstrated how domestication and foreignness coexist and may be experienced in translation.

First of all, domestication is inevitable (especially for translations for theatre because the spectator does not have as much time to digest the 'foreignness' as a reader of a text does), and the process of domestication needs the sense of foreignness to begin with. In the meantime, a certain degree of foreignness will somehow be preserved whenever domestication happens. For instance, even though in Beckett's translation of Lucky's speech Petermann was anglicized as Peterman, the English element of the latter (when the colonial history of Ireland is considered) echoes the German element of '-mann' in the French text, which both implicate a sense of foreignness. Likewise, the sense of foreignness also existed in the Chinese translations, which we engaged with in our project; for example, Pengzu彭祖 and Anan 阿難, the legendary or religious figures in China have a similar musicality to 'Puncher and Wattman' but different connotations. According to Feng Wei, CLT's emphasis in their interpretation of the text is the connection between Zen Buddhism and absurdist existentialism (Feng 2017: 24–5). Therefore CLT's translation of the 'untranslatable' aims to link the proper nouns in English to Chinese names with Buddhist or related traditional Chinese cultural references. In this way a new vocabulary arises, which is special for the performance itself in the specific sociocultural context, and it renews both traditional Chinese theatre and the understanding of Beckett's work as part of a world literary canon.

A particular Chinese strategy of translation was to look for the dramatic/comic tension in his Chinese reading to provoke amazement/laughter in the audience. This was done realizing how vaudeville, clowns and slapstick played a similar significant role in European comedy. Furthermore, the translator Yu Zhongxian offered the team a recording of his reading of the French text with a more 'standard pronunciation'. In an Irish context, Emilie Morin's argument that Beckett's avant-garde practices are bound up to the problem of his Irishness (Morin 2009: 69) led to an exploration of Irish accents at certain points in the text, precarious though the process was.

The knowledge of Beckett's decision to write in a second language in order for 'a greater simplicity and objectivity' and, furthermore, to 'concentrate on a more direct expression of the search for "being" and on an exploration of ignorance, impotence and indigence' enabled Yu's insistence on the 'proper pronunciation' of his French reading (Knowlson 1997: 357).

In the meantime, by exposing the participants' contrasting ways of interpreting the text, the violence of identity labelling in the project was acknowledged. As our project title satirized, while the consensus of the team was that translation should always strive to convey the essential idea of the original text, 100 per cent authority of the understanding and authenticity of the interpretation could never be guaranteed. After playing the game of exchanging hats, Didi and Gogo still can neither think nor settle on a singular identity. In an analogous way, our project could not guarantee the originality of the language emanating in our cultural exchange in the translation of the text. Instead, what we provided was our inter-subjective responses to the text. Such responses were always under the threat of being 'renamed' with either overgeneralized or over-specific labels. Because of our identities (nationality, ethnicity, culture etc.), a great number of images that by no means were relevant to us were also conjured up by these imposed identities. By addressing the 'impossibility' of 100 per cent authenticity, we, on the contrary, approached Damrosch's idea of world literature as 'what is gained in translation' (Damrosch 2003: 6). Examining how variable the experience of reading Beckett can be, the project reflected on world literature's nature, as Damrosch puts it:

> The variability of a work of world literature is one of its constitutive features – one of its greatest strengths when the work is well presented and read well, and its greatest vulnerability when it is mishandled or misappropriated by its newfound foreign friends.
>
> (Damrosch 2003: 5)

In order to open up possibilities and to address the ambiguities of the translation/performance process we examined what the effect was on Lucky's speech when we substituted a number of proper nouns in the text. For example, names such as Puncher and Wattmann, Testew and Cunard, Miranda and Bishop Berkeley were changed to randomly selected names (Cheng Nuohan 程诺涵, Cheng Xue 程雪, Shen Haibo 申海博, Shen Haiche 申海澈 etc.). We used proper names of characters in classical fictions (Lin Daiyu 林黛玉 in *The Dream of Red Chambers*) and contemporary celebrities (such as Guo Degang 郭德纲, a renowned *xiangsheng* performer). The randomness of the names was conditional: it was limited by the specific cultural and socio-historical context of the team as translator/practitioner. Interestingly, the names of *Cheng* and *Shen* were found on a few bulletin board systems (BBS), posts where the users were invited to give suggestions for names for new babies.

The naming (especially of the babies) and meaning-creating process in the 'backstory' became symbolic in the project for the translator/practitioner,[2] as the project aimed to bridge the gap between languages and cultures and in this way to give birth to a hybrid that, while composed of incongruous elements, spoke to different cultures. Moreover, to us the translation was not solidified but on the contrary still fluid. In new readings it would be encouraged that new random names be chosen, along a similar procedure of reading and listening to each participant and to reflect on one another's response.

The translation of the performance text in our project focused more on the *affect* of the audience than on the precision of the literary meaning. Affect is the subjective experience in response to the text. Derrida's reading of Walter Benjamin's essay 'The Task of a Translator' proposes the argument: 'Translation does not have as essential mission any *communication*' (2001: 180), especially for a poetic or sacred text. In such a long and fast monologue as Lucky's it seemed impossible to us for the audience to grasp all the puns and references at once (or at a single performance). What was more important in the performance than the literal meaning of the text performed was how the musicality and rhythms of the speech brought thoughts and ideas to mind. Peter Hall remarks of directing the UK premiere of *Waiting for Godot* in Arts Theatre in London in 1955: 'I soon felt secure in Beckett's rhythms. This was real dramatic poetry, not applied but organic' (2003: n.p.). Beckett famously says, 'Drama is following music. I never write a word without first saying it out loud' (Olk 2011: 391). We tried to convey the musicality through the project, to respect the poetic text of Beckett and explore the essence of translation beyond *communication*. The resemblance between Lisa Dwan's performance of *Not I* (2014) and traditional Chinese *xiangsheng* skills of *guankou* 贯口 struck the team as an inspiration of how an intercultural interpretation of Beckett was possible. By fast-paced utterance of the text we experimented with the ways to evoke audience responses through musicality. Beckett in *Godot* writes about the 'audience response' of Pozzo, Vladimir and Estragon:

1 Vladimir and Estragon all attention, Pozzo dejected and disgusted.
2 Vladimir and Estragon begin to protest, Pozzo's sufferings increase.
3 Vladimir and Estragon attentive again, Pozzo more and more agitated and groaning.
4 Vladimir and Estragon protest violently. Pozzo jumps up, pulls on the rope. General outcry.

(Beckett 1954: 28)

While this series of reactions is not what may be usually expected from a theatre audience, it foretells the kind of response remembered by Peter Hall who directed the UK premiere of the play in 1955. He writes of the cheers and counter-cheers of the audience and how 'bafflement and derision were everywhere' in the response of the critics (Hall 2003: n.p.). The passage of the play above was worth close scrutiny when we conducted our own performed reading of the text. If the musicality or rhythms of Lucky's speech were interpreted as a Derridean hyperbole: 'from whose heights thought is announced to itself, *frightens* itself, *reassures* itself against being annihilated or wrecked in madness or in death', it was possible to experience it as an event of transcendence, an action of inauguration (Hall 2003). It allowed access or passage from one language to another, to translation.

However, translation and writing were found to be always partial. Derrida suggests that the 'attempt-to-say-the-demonic-hyperbole' is always followed by a transition to an economy that overcomes its height with a violence that brings it back down to earth, so to speak (Derrida 2001: 75). Lucky's speech was experienced as a condition for silence. The reactions of the other characters to his 'thinking' aimed to establish a regulated relationship between reason, madness and death. They dramatized the complex possibility-impossibility of communication. Our reading of Pozzo's reactions was of dejection, disgust, agitated groaning and finally attack. He failed, with increasing intensity, to listen and to hear thinking itself. Vladimir and Estragon paid more attention and gave greater ear to Lucky's speech but ultimately failed to sustain listening. The collective idea emerging in this passage of play was the wilful interplay between the phenomena of writing, listening and reading. In this sense the target of our performed translation of the text sought to voluntarily remain in the area of possibility *as* impossibility. Hall cites Kenneth Tynan's response of how the play forced him to 're-examine the rules which had hitherto governed the drama; and having done so, to pronounce them not elastic enough' (Hall 2003: n.p.). The elastic form of Beckett's dramatic text enabled it to be accessed in different languages. Hall concludes that Waiting for Godot 'remains a poetic masterpiece transcending all barriers and all nationalities' and while this may be the case, our project indicated that such a crossing-over must bear witness to the strangeness or foreignness of the text (Hall 2003).

We also found that the humour in Beckett's writing worked as an important device to accommodate strangeness, foreignness and even suffering. The argument was that Beckett deconstructed agony. Even death – the ultimate fear of the human – was disrupted by Estragon dropping his pants later on in the text. Such 'cosmological comedy', which as Ruby Cohn argues is one 'that resides not in any given society but in the cosmos as it appears to human sense', led us to compare it with dual *xiangsheng* comedies (Cohn 1959: 14). *Xiangsheng* involved the supporting actor *penggen* 捧哏 constantly commenting on the performance of the lead actor *dougen* 逗哏, to create a hilarious scene. In our project, the translation was inspecting its own flaws or incompleteness reflecting the humour of the characters' responses to Lucky's speech.

Equally, in our project we spent a lot of time reflecting on our own readings and commenting on each other's. We acknowledged the practitioner/translator's presence so that our role in the circulation of Beckett – a mockingly '100% Guaranteed Beckett' – across cultures was examined. This aspect of the project was brought to the attention of the attendees at the University of Kent conference in 2016 with Li's rendition of CLT's text heard on a Walkman held by Wei who walked around the room. In this way, we hoped to cross the boundaries of time, space and culture and connect Beckett with the spectators coming from different backgrounds. Yu's voice from the cassette recorder sounded so remote and at the same time frequently interrupted that it resembled the past. The fact that Beckett's original text was coming to us from the mouth of the translator also reminded us how his works may travel, be re-invigorated as world literature and return.

In conclusion, our project engaged in the critical cosmopolitanism that Ric Knowles proposes, that is, to locate the 'analysis within specific national and global contexts' and to provide 'scrutiny of complex negotiations across different stakes and scripts' (Knowles 2010: 58). What travels between languages and how Beckett's works may travel globally offer inexhaustible opportunities for research and interpretation. The different voices (of O'Byrne, Wei, Li and translator Yu) as well as the texts (of Beckett and the three collaborators) created a diverse cultural space where other dimensions overlapped. This multiplicity of dimensions included temporality, technology and media, together with embodied hospitality of lips, tongues, what the protagonist of *Not I* describes as 'all those contortions without which... no speech possible' (Beckett 2006: 379). The voices conveyed a great deal of sociocultural codes, and we put the voices together so that a new process of decoding and recoding began.

Notes

1 To Venuti, the domestication translation strategy is to minimize 'foreignness', or the strangeness of the foreign text by 'invisibly inscrib[ing] foreign texts with [target language] values and provide readers with the [...] experience of recognizing their own culture in a cultural other' (1999: 15). But for him the term has negative connotations.
2 It is also important to note that in the Chinese language people have much more freedom in choosing names.

Works cited

Beckett, S. (1954), *Waiting for Godot: A Tragicomedy in Two Acts*, New York: Grove Press.

Beckett, S. (1995), *Nohow On: Company, Ill Seen Ill Said, Worstward Ho: Three Novels*, London: John Calder.
Beckett, S. (1999), *Proust and Three Dialogues with Georges Duthuit*, London: Calder & Boyers.
Beckett, S. (2006), *Complete Dramatic Works*, London: Faber and Faber.
Cockerham, H. (1975), 'Bilingual Playwright', in K. Worth (ed.), *Beckett the Shape Changer*, 139-60, London: Routledge.
Cohn, R. (1961), 'Samuel Beckett Self-Translator' *PMLA*, 76 (5): 613–21.
Damrosch, D. (2003), *What Is World Literature*, Princeton and Oxford: Princeton University Press.
Derrida, J. (2001), *Writing and Difference*, trans. Alan Bass, Abingdon, OX: Routledge Classics.
Feng W. (2017), 'Xi yu Dengdai Guotuo: jingju dui "huangdanju" de gaibian [*Chairs* and *Waiting for Godot*: Jingju's Adaptation of "Theatre of the Absurd"]', *Xiju yishu* [*Dramatic Arts*], 196 (2): 22–31.
Garner, S. (1994), *Bodied Spaces: Phenomenology and Performance in Contemporary Drama*, New York: Cornell University Press.
Hall, P. (2003), 'Godotmania', in *The Guardian*, 4 January, Arts, Stage Theatre.
Holland, N. (1975), 'Unity Identity Text Self', in Jane P. Thomkins (ed.), *Reader-Response Criticism*, 118–33, Baltimore: Johns Hopkins University Press, 1980.
Knowles, R. (2010), *Theatre & Intercutluralism*, London and New York: Palgrave Macmillan.
Knowlson, J. (1997), *Damned to Fame: The Life of Samuel Beckett*, London: Bloomsbury.
Malekin P. and R. Yarrow (1997), *Consciousness, Literature and Theatre: Theory and Beyond*, London: Palgrave Macmillan.
Morin, E. (2009), *Samuel Beckett and the Problem of Irishness*, London: Palgrave Macmillan.
Olk, C. (2011), '"A MATTER OF FUNDAMENTAL SOUNDS" – The Music of Beckett's "Endgame"', *Poetica*, 43 (3): 391–410.
Pilling, J. (1993), 'Beckett's Proust', in S. E. Gontarski (ed.), *The Beckett Studies Reader*, 9–28, Gainesville: University Publishers of Florida.
Venuti, L. (1999), *The Scandals of Translation: Towards an Ethics of Difference*, London and New York: Routledge.
Venuti, L. (2008), *The Translator's Invisibility: A History of Translation*, Abingdon and New York: Routledge.

PART II

Adaptation

6

Modernism, medium and memory

Mischa Twitchin

Beckett's ambivalence (not to say distress) concerning his reception into the canon of World Literature[1] is perhaps symbolized by his non-appearance at the award of his Nobel Prize (being represented instead by his French publisher, Jerôme Lindon (Craig et al. 2016: 160)). According to the Nobel citation, 'born near Dublin... as a renowned writer [Beckett] entered the world almost half a century later in Paris' (Gierow 1969). If, as Beckett famously observed, '[b]irth was the death of him' (1986: 425), what might be the consequence of having 'entered the world' after leaving behind his literal place of birth? What – or, indeed, where – is this Pantheon of Literature if it is conceived of as a world removed from the 'godforsaken hole' to which Mouth, for example, is introduced in *Not I* (1972) (Beckett 1986: 376)? Given that the works of many Nobel laureates are now all but forgotten, it is not in virtue of belonging to the canon of World Literature that Beckett is still read today, but, rather, because of what is particular in his writing, to the sense of what he called 'a world of [its] own'. Indeed, Beckett observes of the modern period that it is no longer possible to be a 'universal' artist (such as Leonardo was): when 'the tie between the self and things no longer exists... one must create a world of one's own in order to satisfy one's need to know, to understand, one's need for order' (McMillan and Fehsenfeld 1988: 231).

Claims about – and for – a 'world' literature (in lower case) put Beckett's example in its own perspective; not least, concerning 'the politics of untranslatability' (Apter 2013), as a question of experience to be read in, or between, Irish-English and French. To draw on just one of the philosophical 'heterocosms' cited by Emily Apter (2013: 190), Jean-Luc Nancy, for instance, offers reflection on an 'untranslatable' term in French, *mondialisation*, distinguishing between '"creation" (up to this point limited to theological mystery)' and '"world-forming" [*mondialisation*] (up to this point limited to economic and technological matters, generally called "globalisation")' (Nancy 2007: 29). In this context, then, distinct from the creation of 'the' world by God, Beckett's sense of creating art worlds 'of one's own' also contrasts with the colonial-capitalist era of 'globalisation', conceived not in terms of the imagination but of exploitation.

The sense of what 'world-forming' is 'limited to' – especially in its self-constituting distinction from 'creation' – echoes Adorno's analyses of linguistic modes of commodification, where the transformation of social relations into relations between things extends into their conditions of expression, now celebrated by champions of the so-called experience economy. Adorno's reading of Beckett is profoundly informed by this sense of 'pseudo-logical connections, and galvanized words appearing as commodity signs – as the desolate echo of the advertising world – [being] "refunctioned" (*umfunktionert*) into the language of a poetic work that negates language' (Adorno 2010: 162–3). How Beckett's 'refunctioning' of language in terms of 'lessness' might fit the World Literature – or World Theatre – agenda will be explored here through two examples of his work on screen.

To follow Adorno's negative appreciation of modernism 'as the obsolescence of the modern' (Adorno 2010: 171) means refusing the ornamentalism of the postmodern when engaging with what remains of art in the twentieth century. With its potential resistance to the irrepressible tide of the conventional (not least, in works of art), Beckett's principle of 'lessness' (or, in Adorno's term, 'subtraction' [Adorno 2010: 178]) advances an impossibility that is the very test of the possible, a failure that is the test of the effort required for it. In Adorno's anti-Cartesianism, what remains of and for the modern artist, rather than the ego of indubitable doubt, is 'the dust thou art' (Adorno 2010: 170, 173) – beautifully evoked in the lines of Clov's leave-taking in *Endgame*: 'I am so bowed I only see my feet, if I open my eyes, and between my legs a little trail of black dust. I say to myself that the earth is extinguished, though I never saw it lit' (Beckett 1986: 132). The balance between the tragic and the comic in Beckett is epitomized by Clov's following reflection: 'When I fall I'll weep for happiness' (Beckett 1986).

As there is no risk of not stating the obvious here, the argument of this essay is far from concluded. Rather than the national languages into which we are born (even as these admit of bilingualism or, indeed, of multilingualism), this chapter will consider the residua of untranslatability in terms of medium. Taking as an example Beckett's last play, *What Where* (1983), the essay will explore a comparison between Beckett's own translation of the play for television (Beckett 1985) and the version made for the prize-winning *Beckett on Film* project (Beckett 2001b).[2] What conception of 'world' is evoked – or supposed – in the very title of *What Where*? How does the question of World Literature – or, indeed, of World Theatre – give us to think about this short text, and, vice versa, how might a reading of (or with) Beckett's play give us to think about such worldly concepts (or institutions) as Literature or Theatre, even as they turn to dust in the very claims of their conceptual consistency?

Although the Dublin film project aimed to give Beckett's work a global reception, it promoted itself with the stamp of a 'made in Ireland' authority. Indeed, according to a promotional article based on an interview with one of the project's producers, Michael Colgan (then director of the Gate Theatre in Dublin), 'a sense of place is provided by well-known Irish actors' (Riding 2000).[3] Paraphrasing Colgan, the article proposed that the 'Beckett Film project... attempt[ed] to reclaim him as an English-language writer, and an Irish one at that'. With this 'sense of place' – of, precisely, 'what where' – conceived of in terms of the actors' nationality, the Dublin version fails to engage with the particular world of Beckett's writing – a failure not in Beckett's artistic sense (as the best that could be hoped for), but in the mundane sense of ignoring literal specificities in favour of metaphors that are themselves 'commodity signs'.

*

Caught briefly on camera, Beckett can be heard telling Stanley Gontarski that *What Where*, although 'written for the theatre', was 'much more a television play than a theatre piece', and in a letter, he comments, 'Thinking of proposing *What Where* to *Süddeutscher Rundfunk* [the South German broadcaster]. For once a stage play that invites TV – as I feel it now' (Craig et al. 2016: 624). How does writing 'for' performance in one medium or another come into question, then, through its translation between these mediums – rather than being read as simply the analogy for an 'original' intention, one which would not be specific to either medium? Beckett's own account of his play – as himself a director (Gontarski 1999) – need not involve us in an interpretative teleology, retrospectively supposing a sense of the work's inception. Indeed, the play (like all of Beckett's 'dramaticules', with their poetics of dust) offers a parable of the impossibility of such a sovereign conception of 'what where' – even for its author. Despite 'being given the works', no one finally answers the play's own questions, giving rise to its own much-quoted suggestion 'make sense who may' (Beckett 1986: 476).

This makes the Dublin film version's title (with its ostentatious possessive apostrophe), 'Samuel Beckett's *What Where*', all the more odd – especially given that its claims to textual 'fidelity' are demonstrably false in their own terms (as one might have expected the Beckett estate to have noted). However, it is those terms themselves that are fallacious, in supposing that the pragmatic and the conceptual be separated, even if this is the prevailing expectation of staging – one which Beckett, precisely, set out to resist. As Steven Connor notes (in discussing Enoch Brater's remarks on the earlier example of *Quad* (1981)):

> In one sense the performance... is its own text, and has, if anything, a higher status than the actual written form, which in some ways it modifies and supersedes. But if this written form comes before *and after* the performance, then both text and performance repeat and perhaps displace each other, the text being one 'original' for the production, just as the production is another 'original' for the text.
>
> (Connor 1988: 166)

That reading in one medium becomes rewriting in another – quite literally with Beckett's changes to the play in light of his directorial experiences – complicates any assumption about its translation, but this does not mean that any interpretation is equivalent to any other. The issue remains as to the work's resistance to an interpretation that would merely assimilate it to the conventions of the medium into which it is being translated, requiring perhaps a change in the understanding of that medium – indeed, a failure, even, in its supposed literacy. *What Where*'s proposal to 'make sense who may' does not forestall its translatability but, precisely, holds it open. In this way, assumptions concerning what is primary (text) and secondary (performance) – as between the what and the where of a drama – are challenged by the aesthetic truth of the 'world' of the work.

Exemplifying an aesthetic 'not [of] abstraction but subtraction' (Adorno 2010: 178), or, in Beckett's own words, of 'getting rid of every superfluity' (Gontarski 1987: n.p.), Beckett's own work for television contrasts with the aggrandizement of the Dublin translation. Indeed, comparison between the two films allows us to address issues that go beyond the particular example to consider how Beckett's play resonates, in a deeper critical context, with Rosalind Krauss's sense of a modernism in which 'the medium is the memory' (Krauss 2011: 127), as key to its resistance to kitsch – or, in Beckett's own terms, to the 'parody' of his work.

*

Although it is the singular term 'medium' that is invoked here (as indicating questions of aesthetics, distinct from the ubiquitous 'media' of cultural studies), performance on both stage and screen occurs through a hybrid of audio-vision. Despite the fact that we habitually refer to *watching* television, and going to *see* a play or a film, these performances are as much heard as seen, and it is the relation between these senses that constitutes the *theatre* of Beckett's late plays. Like the performance of music (in Beckett's preferred analogy), this is a theatre in which questions of space and time, sound and sight, constitute the 'drama', rather than the conventions of character and setting with which 'stagings' are typically conceived. As Beckett wrote to Alan Schneider, for example, about his stage characters (in this case Mouth in *Not I*): 'All I know is in the text. [The character] is purely a stage entity, part of a stage image and purveyor of a stage text. The rest is Ibsen' (cited in Harmon 1998: 283).

In the Dublin film, it is as if the play was to be read as a transferable set of dialogues, rather than, precisely, an attempt to address the very medium of its performance as Beckett proposed. This is the basic mistake of conceiving such translations in terms of a primary text and a secondary performance – as if the stage directions were not equally part of the drama. When Beckett says that a 'production that dismisses my directions is a complete parody of the play as conceived by me' (cited in Kalb 1991: 79), he addresses this misconception of a translation between mediums – a misconception engendered by reading Beckett as if he was (in his own example) Ibsen. Following Beckett's comparison of his theatre making with chess (see McMillan and Fehsenfeld 1988: 231), the pieces and the rules allow for the freedom of play. It is not the individual moves that constitute the game (or a Beckett performance) but the rules (see Twitchin 2019).

Given that *What Where* is contemporary with what Krauss called a 'post-medium condition' in the arts, why specify medium as a key for making sense of its possible 'world'? Why is resistance to the postmodern claim that medium no longer makes sense important for translatability in Beckett's case, not least in the enduring fascination of an otherwise anachronistic artistic modernism? Crucially, the questions of the work (between the what and the where that is said in the play) resist the conflation of the medium with a supposed audience. Without publicly funded facilities (such as Beckett had access to in Stuttgart for his own version), advertising – and with it, 'accessibility' – comes to define the medium in terms of a target audience. The attempt to identify the latter – as if to write for a medium was the same as to write for a specific audience – is one of the more depressing consequences of the commercial imperative. When a work is conceived of in terms of product and ratings, the medium itself becomes a commodity, rather than being an artistic concern.

In the critical, modernist sense of the world of imagination – referring to specifically aesthetic conditions for an understanding of medium (or, perhaps, its 'world'), addressed in the material or technical conditions of and for its concept – Beckett's own translation of *What Where*, indeed, 'make[s] sense'. As Krauss, one of the few critics who still invokes questions of medium specificity, observes, '[I]n order to sustain artistic practice, a medium must be a supporting structure, generative of a set of conventions, some of which, in assuming the medium itself as their subject, will be wholly "specific" to it, thus producing an experience of their own necessity' (Krauss 1999a: 26). Although this criterion of 'necessity' may seem not only anachronistic but also, in the eyes of many, conservative (or even reactionary), it lies at the heart of what makes Beckett's work still contemporary and challenging in affirming a 'world of [its] own'. After all, not everything that may be thought of after modernism is necessarily postmodern, especially as the latter is characterized by an omnivorous mixing of genres which Beckett despaired of.

*

Questions of medium (and of its corollary, aesthetic 'autonomy') can be related to an essay by Beckett on the poet Denis Devlin where he writes, with a merciless historical irony, that '[a]rt has always been this – pure interrogation, rhetorical question less the rhetoric – whatever else it may have been obliged by the "social reality" to appear, but never more freely so than now, when social reality (*pace* ex-comrade Radek) has severed the connection' (2001: 91). This reference to the World Literature debates of the 1930s, with their diverging claims for 'bourgeois cosmopolitanism' and 'socialist internationalism', is worth recalling. Before he too fell victim to Stalin's show trials, Radek's suggestion that Joyce's *Ulysses* (1922), for instance, offered the reader 'a heap of dung, crawling with worms, photographed by a cinema apparatus through a microscope' (1977 [1935]: 153) is among his more pithy insights addressing a cultural politics of 'social reality' as 'severed' from art. Suffice it to note that Beckett's own cinematic point of reference, Sergei Eisenstein – with whom he had even aspired to study – was by this time himself under personal threat from the commissars of 'socialist realism', the totalitarian translation of 'social reality' into modern aesthetics.

While the appearance of 'social reality' is regularly invoked by critics with respect to the drama of *What Where* (together with *Catastrophe* (1982) and *Rough for Radio 2* (1961)), the keyword in Beckett's reflection on Devlin – as for any modernist aesthetics – is 'less,' as it points to a reality that is specific to art, as *pure* interrogation, as that which is itself in question through its medium (addressing the 'world' as its 'literature'). Indeed, if there is one word that characterizes Beckett's sense of the rhetoric of aesthetic interrogation in and for the theatre, it is, precisely, 'less' – or perhaps, more expansively, 'lessness'. This is not, then, a question of more *or* less, but rather of that modernist mantra that less *is* more. Beckett refers precisely to 'the principle that less is more' (which is usually credited to Mies van der Rohe) in the writing of *That Time* (1975), anticipating objections that its proposed relation between image and word (in any possible translation) would be thought insufficiently 'theatrical'. And of his own translation of

What Where, Beckett referred – with respect to the work in Stuttgart – to a 'process of elimination' (Gontarski 1999: 431).

*

Evoking it as a 'field of memory' (Gontarski 1999: 415 , 450), Beckett makes the question of his characters' appearance in *What Where* specific to the play's concept of embodied experience, examined rather than simply located in its medium-specific sense of time and space. By contrast, the opening of the Dublin film forestalls the conceptual-pragmatic questions concerning the what-where of a performance by providing a location unrelated to the medium (or game) of the play's sense. This turns the play text into a narrative text, such as one might indeed associate with Ibsen. In a revealing interview, Alan Moloney (one of the producers of the Dublin film project) declares that '[i]n the making of a film, you need to do certain things. You need to contextualize things, and create an environment that – in its purest form – Beckett's writing doesn't require' (cited in Herren 2007: 192).

This shift (using again Jean-Luc Nancy's distinction) from 'world creating' (in 'its own necessity' [Krauss]) to 'world forming' (or 'contextualisation' [Moloney]) – where a potential acting 'environment' is applied *to* the text rather than derived *from* it – is further elaborated by the director of the Dublin screen version, Damien O'Donnell, who remarks of the playing space in 'the original play' that 'there is no set' (2001). Insisting that he 'wasn't allowed to change the text, or the staging', O'Donnell acknowledges the question of medium only by a negation that is allowed no meaning for itself (see O'Donnell 2001). That there is no set is regarded as a lack to be made up for, rather than as the very clue to the play's conception of 'staging' its own world. Paradoxically, the possibilities of time and space (as of the medium of performance) are not the least of *What Where* is concerned with – making sense with (and of) its play between light and dark, voice and vision, memory and image – even in the possibility of imagining the 'abuse of power' (or, '*pace* ex-comrade Radek', its 'social reality'), for which O'Donnell sees his added library setting 'as a metaphor' (Sierz 2013: 144).

This anti-modernist (indeed, anti-Beckettian) aesthetic remains focused on an associative message or content, where the translation of (and between) 'worlds' is conceived in terms of an expectation of 'acting' which Beckett's work specifically eschews. As Beckett wrote to Deirdre Bair: 'Not for me these Grotowskis and Methods... the best possible play is one in which there are no actors, only the text. I'm trying to write one' (cited in McMillan and Fehsenfeld 1988: 16). Indeed, in contrast to its self-image, the 'universal' translation machine of 'acting' marks the Anglophone theatre as distinctly parochial in relation to European, never mind world, theatres. For the *What Where* production in Stuttgart, Beckett initially proposed 'mimes', wanting 'no "interpretation"': 'In a word a discipline and self-consciousness hardly to be expected of "seasoned" actors and indeed too much – or too little – to be asked of them' (Craig et al. 2016: 631–2). What is gained, in this context, by the Dublin insistence on Irish actors is hard to fathom. Exposing the contradictions of the Dublin claims to textual fidelity, these differences in translating the what and the where of the play are pertinently expressed by Eckhart Voigts-Virchow, when he observes that '[t]he real alternative that Beckett's minimalist, abstract TV vision has to offer contemporary media culture is its definition of space as a void and an absence – the denial of vision and spectacle' (2001: 121).

This is particularly apparent in the way that O'Donnell's film locates the play's Voice, not with the action of fading in and out, but by intercutting the actors coming and going with shots of the presiding megaphone. Paradoxically again, the megaphone – which was eliminated in Beckett's small screen production and in the subsequent Paris stage performance (directed by Pierre Chabert, under Beckett's supervision) – becomes an index of the 'filmed theatre' that the Dublin project supposedly set out to avoid (as Beckett and Marin Karmitz successfully did in their collaboration on a film version of *Play* (1963)). A curiously antique anomaly in an otherwise futuristic, automated environment, the visual presence of the megaphone anchors that of the characters in the eye of the camera rather than that of the screen. Here the failure to question the medium – 'we wanted to create a cinematic feel, rather than just filmed plays', as Moloney put it (cited in Sierz 2013: 141) – returns on an epic scale, assimilating translatability to the generic conventions of that 'cinematic feel'. Any possibility of dramatic 'lessness' is precluded by additions made in the name of the play's supposedly missing 'contextualization'. It is as if O'Donnell's understanding of the film language with which to adapt *What Where*'s 'field of memory' was learnt from James Cameron rather than Beckett himself (or still less, in Beckett's case perhaps, from Wilhelm Röntgen). The Dublin film version reduces the aesthetics of memory to a field of oblivion (or kitsch), pursuing a sense of 'cinematisation' that – like 'globalisation' in Nancy's account – 'has already translated everything in a global idiom' in contrast to 'preserv[ing] something untranslatable' (Nancy 2007: 28).

*

Beckett's ambiguity, in the play of identity and repetition (both material and memorial), as to whether the voices speak *as*, or *about*, the 'I' who hears them (and who might, then, imagine himself to be no longer alone) is lost in the Dublin version by eliding voice and vision, memory and speech, the mental and material image, through the 'contextualized' appearance of the actors. In place of the expected synchronicity of word – or rather voice – and image, the 'action' of *What Where* involves the Voice recalling a body which may or may not be its own, oscillating between memory and imagination (as between face and screen). The beauty of Beckett's own translation is that the emanation of both voices and faces could be a phantasy of the medium, as if the screen were dreaming to and of itself. By contrast, O'Donnell's resort to the convention of shot/counter-shot to visually narrate the interrogation between different voices abstracts the play from its own world of medium reflexivity, that is, from its specific question of memory. Identifying *what* and *where* with the expectations of narrative cinema editing – in which dialogue is presumed to be inter, rather than intra, subjective (let alone, as it were, intra-medial) – Beckett's play is subsumed by cinematic conventions. What Moloney called the 'literacy... associated with making a film' (cited in Sierz 2013: 143), which was disparaged by Beckett as the expectations of 'industrial film' (Fehsenfeld and Overbeck 2009: 312), is emblematized from the very beginning of the Dublin version with a standard opening top shot. With this typical cinematic scene setting, the *question* of space – as that of locating memory in the world of the play (at least, in the translation between one medium (stage) and another (screen)) – is answered before it can even be posed.

The Voice is no longer the promise of an image that may or may not be seen, but the index of a narrative visibility that is not in question artistically. The ambition of the Dublin film project, to offer a 'World TV' version of Beckett's work, offers a reaffirmation – on screen – of everything that Beckett's writing for theatre sought to resist. As Martin Puchner has observed:

> The sequential arrangement of gestures and speech – stage direction and direct speech – is not just an accidental feature of one text but a structuring principle of many of Beckett's plays... Beckett's technique of interruption... [is] thus directed against what since Aristotle had become the purpose of drama: the representation of action. It is a strategy that uses the dramatic text against the theatre and stage directions against the integrity of actors.
>
> (Puchner 2011: 168, 169)

This concerns the aesthetic politics of what is – or is not – at stake in the example of medium translatability, when the paradox of the play's resistance to its own potential performance (in its writing for that medium) is simply ignored with a claim to make the work globally accessible or comprehensible in that very medium (paradoxically, here even in Beckett's name).

What O'Donnell describes as the 'restrictions' of the text (2001) – upon the language of film, as a medium of and for the play's translation for the screen – are precisely the potentials of and for its resistance to (or 'untranslatability' in) the medium of its performance that make it *this* play, *What Where*, and not simply a generic, filmable drama with and for actors. In terms of a modernist critical judgement, this is what makes Beckett's translation art and the Dublin version kitsch, where – between these two examples of imaginable worlds – there passes a dividing line of aesthetic politics which demands that one takes a position. As Rosalind Krauss writes:

> If [certain examples] are not instinctively felt to be meretricious, arbitrary, and thus the simulacrum of art rather than the real thing, this is because kitsch has become the polluted atmosphere of the very culture we breathe. Their identity as kitsch derives from their feckless indifference to the idea of a medium, so long ago condemned by Greenberg's admonishment in *Avant-Garde and Kitsch*. Kitsch he defines as the corruption of taste by the substitution of simulated effects for that recursive testing of the work of art against the logic of its specific conditions, a testing he named 'self-criticism'.
>
> (2011: 68–9)

This is not to advocate an artistic show trial, orchestrated by a political committee (such as in Radek's case), but to experiment with the critical demands of thinking with and through a medium. As previously noted, this work of translating involves what Beckett (reflecting on *What Where* specifically) called a 'process of elimination' – but only in the sense of 'pure interrogation', in which the possibility of autonomy in aesthetics remains a promise for that in politics.

*

With respect to what Krauss identifies as 'both projective and mnemonic' as 'concerns the idea of a medium' (1999b: 296), the example of *What Where* evokes an aesthetic resistance to the sort of translation produced by the corporate recycling of media that represses the *work* of both modernist cultural memory and its historical politics. It is precisely in this context that Thierry de Duve's acknowledgement of Greenberg (generally dismissed as 'outmoded', as if the concept of history that permits such a judgement were not itself in question) is significant: 'While everyone else was crying from the rooftops that the avant-garde was an anti-tradition, Greenberg saw it as the sole authentic defence of the tradition before the erosive force of kitsch' (de Duve 2010: 8).

Perhaps the most famous counterpart of this in Beckett is his insistence on the hope of 'failure'. Film, which was once emblematic of the culture industry (before the rise of digital media), pioneered the use of audience previews for making a 'final cut', ostensibly to protect the producer's investment from the director's vision (eloquently satirized in Godard's *Le Mépris*). The model of what has already been made (and successfully sold) now feeds the cannibalism of cinema in the endless pursuit of 'remakes'.

The Dublin version of *What Where* is itself an instance of what Friedrich Kittler called 'McLuhan's law' – 'according to which the content of a medium is always another medium' (1990: 115) – precisely in its failure of not offering 'filmed theatre'; that is, in simply reproducing the conventions of stage acting on screen. The production (and promotion) of kitsch – in the negation of medium memory – always pretends to be both de-aestheticized and depoliticized.

In conclusion, given that the power of Beckett's writing is so much bound up with its testimony to the fractured possibilities of cultural memory within modernism, it is perhaps worth quoting another of Krauss's appeals to the critical value of the concept of medium, as its own world. This again poses both the problem and the possibility of conceiving the example of *What Where* in the context of World Literature or World Theatre:

> The aphorism… *the medium is the memory*… specifically opposes Marshall McLuhan's aphorism 'the medium is the message.' McLuhan exalts in the *non*-specificity of the medium, its 'message' always referring to another, earlier medium… 'The medium is the memory' insists, instead, on the power of the medium to hold the efforts of the forebears of a specific genre in reserve for the present. Forgetting this reserve is the antagonist of memory… The paradigm of the medium could thus be mapped as *memory versus forgetting*.
>
> (Krauss 2011: 127–8)

Echoing Voice's call in *What Where* to 'make sense who may', the question here would be how the play dislocates its supposed translatability in the field of 'World Media'. How, after all, do such media engage with the relation between the senses and technology, meaning and medium, when it is a question of Beckett's *art*? To give the last word to Beckett himself, how might such translation make sense of a world in which it may be said, 'In dark and silence to close as if to light the eyes and hear a sound' (2003: 24)?

Notes

1. I have opted to capitalize the term 'World Literature' to distinguish – as Emily Apter suggests – between a 'disciplinary construct' and any reference, in lower case, 'which may be considered as a descriptive catch-all for the sum of all forms of literary expression in all the world's languages' (Apter 2013: 2).
2. I have also made a performance-film experiment with Beckett's text but will not discuss it here (Twitchin 2013).
3. In the case of *What Where*, specifically, these were Gary Lewis and Sean McGinley.

Works cited

Adorno, T. (2010), 'Notes on Beckett', trans. D. Van Hulle and S. Weller, *Journal of Beckett Studies*, 19 (2): 157–78.
Apter, E. (2013), *Against World Literature: On the Poetics of Untranslatability*, London: Verso.
Beckett, S. (1985), *What Where*, dir. Samuel Beckett, SDR. Available online: http://www.ubu.com/film/beckett_what.html (accessed 11 July 2019).
Beckett, S. (1986), *The Complete Dramatic Works*, London: Faber and Faber.
Beckett, S. (2001a), *Disjecta*, London: Calder.
Beckett, S. (2001b), *What Where*, dir. Damien O'Donnell, RTE and Channel 4. Available online: https://web.archive.org/web/20120510055447/ and http://www.beckettonfilm.com/plays/whatwhere/synopsis.html (accessed 11 July 2019).
Beckett, S. (2003), *Company*, London: Calder.
Connor, S. (1988), *Samuel Beckett: Repetition, Theory and Text*, Oxford: Basil Blackwell.
Craig, G., et al., eds. (2016), *The Letters of Samuel Beckett*, Vol. 4 (1966–89), Cambridge: Cambridge University Press.
De Duve, T. (2010), *Clement Greenberg: Between the Lines*, trans. B. Holmes, Chicago: University of Chicago Press.
Fehsenfeld, M., and L. Overbeck, eds. (2009), *The Letters of Samuel Beckett*, Vol. 1 (1929–40), Cambridge: Cambridge University Press.
Gierow, K. (1969), *Nobel Award Ceremony Speech*. Available online: https://www.nobelprize.org/prizes/literature/1969/ceremony-speech/ (accessed 7 June 2019).
Gontarski, S. (1987), 'Beckett Speaks'. Footage of Beckett in 1987, taken from 'Waiting for Beckett: A Portrait of Samuel Beckett', Global Village Production, 1994. Available online: https://www.youtube.com/watch?v=1ohAssRQsjM (accessed 19 September 2019).
Gontarski, S., ed. (1999), *The Theatrical Notebooks of Samuel Beckett, IV, The Shorter Plays*, London: Faber and Faber.
Harmon, M., ed. (1998), *No Author Better Served: The Correspondence between Samuel Beckett and Alan Schneider*, Cambridge: Harvard University Press.
Herren, G. (2007), *Samuel Beckett's Plays on Film and Television*, London: Palgrave Macmillan.
Kalb, J. (1991), *Beckett in Performance*, Cambridge: Cambridge University Press.
Kittler, F. (1990), *Discourse Networks 1800/1900*, trans. M. Metteer and C. Cullens, Stanford: Stanford University Press.
Krauss, R. (1999a), *'A Voyage on the North Sea': Art in the Age of the Post-Medium Condition*, London: Thames & Hudson.
Krauss, R. (1999b), 'Reinventing the Medium', *Critical Inquiry*, 25 (2) (Winter): 289–305.
Krauss, R. (2011), *Under Blue Cup*, Cambridge: MIT Press.
McMillan, D., and M. Fehsenfeld (1988), *Beckett in the Theatre*, London: Calder.
Nancy, J.-L. (2007), *The Creation of the World or Globalisation*, trans. François Raffoul and David Pettigrew, New York: SUNY.

O'Donnell, D. (2001), *Interview*. Available online: https://web.archive.org/web/20120205062930/ and http://www.beckettonfilm.com/plays/whatwhere/odonnell.html (accessed 11 June 2019).

Puchner, M. (2011), *Stage Fright*, Baltimore: Johns Hopkins University Press.

Radek, K. ([1935] 1977), 'Contemporary World Literature and the Tasks of Proletarian Art', in H. G. Scott (ed.), *Soviet Writers' Congress, 1934: The Debate on Socialist Realism and Modernism*, 73–163, London: Lawrence and Wishart.

Riding, A. (2000), 'Finding New Audiences for Alienation', interview with Michael Colgan, *New York Times*, 11 June. Available online: https://web.archive.org/web/20120523023208/ and http://www.beckettonfilm.com/colgan_interview.html (accessed 11 June 2019).

Sierz, A. (2013), '"A Relevant and Cinematic Environment": Filming Beckett's Plays', in M. Buning, et al. (eds.), *Samuel Beckett Today*, Vol. 13, 137–49, Amsterdam: Rodopi.

Twitchin, M. (2013), *Field of Memory 1*. Available online: https://vimeo.com/60040714 (accessed 11 June 2019).

Twitchin, M. (2019), 'What Chance Failure?' in T. Fisher and E. Katsouraki (eds.), *Beyond Failure*, 37–54, London: Routledge.

Voigts-Virchow, E. (2001), 'Face Values: Beckett Inc., the Camera Plays and Cultural Liminality', *Journal of Beckett Studies*, 10: 119–36.

7

Knock, knock, who's there? The circulation of *Macbeth*, *Ulysses* and the myth of Echo and Narcissus in *Ohio Impromptu*

Laurens De Vos

Part of the reason why Beckett has become a canonical figure in world literature lies in his reliance on various texts from different cultures, languages and periods. The dissemination of an author's texts to large parts of the world and the longevity of this status is enhanced by the academic world that makes sure a writer's work is studied in depth. In addition, as gatekeepers, academics contribute to the survival of certain texts by passing them on to future student generations through lectures and reading lists. Hence, how strongly literary texts are embedded in the academic world at least partly determines how long they circulate in world literature. Texts that make a lot of use of intertextuality are often given more attention by academics, and this holds true for Beckett too. His rewriting of myths that seem to touch upon a universal sensibility has definitely contributed to the circulation of Beckett on a global scale.

From his earliest writings, the Narcissus and Echo myth has been of special interest to the Irish playwright. His first, long unpublished novel *Dream of Fair to Middling Women* features Belacqua, who is to return shortly in *Echo's Bones*, a short story that should have complemented *More Pricks Than Kicks* (1934), but which wasn't published until 2014 with the expanding academic interest in Beckett studies. In light of Beckett's preoccupation with self-alienation and the search for autonomy the recurring motif of Narcissus and Echo comes as no surprise. What fascinates Beckett is the impossibility of a complete self-realization (the merger with one's image) and the awareness that the process of self-development can only be reached through the mediating instrument of language. This language, moreover, functions as a foreign body while at the same time being the primordial constructor of one's identity and being. Thus, language not only builds, but paradoxically also dispossesses one of one's true self. Echo can only express herself through the words that she is given from outside, by the Other. Narcissus, on the other hand, rejects this observation and refuses any self-realization that has an external source; his self-image does not allow for any Other to complement it, forgetting, however, that it is exactly what it says it is: an image, the visual counterpart of the aural echo, cast back to build up that very image of one's identity. In this sense, I is always an Other. It is this existential split that finds its artistic translation in the ghosting of doubles, alter egos, pseudo-couples and repetitions that haunt all of Beckett's work.

Man's tragedy, says Beckett, is not that he is either Narcissus or Echo, but – seemingly impossible – both at the same time. Accordingly, Daniel Katz sees in this 'echoing narcissism' a self-defying alterity:

> Beckett's narcissistic structure is in fact unthinkable without the returns and retrievals, which both enable and disable the apparently static structure of specular self-contemplation. It is in this context that Beckett's investigations of the linguistic temporality of Descartes' cogito need to be examined. This sort of 'echoing narcissism' defies any easy opposition between visual/aural, image/language, body/mind, or imaginary/symbolic. [...] [Beckett's] rereading of the Narcissus and Echo myth, can be seen as attempts to put into play a structure of alterity that a metaphysics of reflection might tend to deny. For if Narcissus seems to reside in an imaginary, totalitarian view and viewing of 'self', Echo only has meaning through her repetition, her haunting, and her stony embodiment of what she is not.
>
> (Katz 1996: 66)

The ambiguity that arises from this position results in the figure of the ghost that invades Beckett's entire works. Belacqua himself, of course, is no exception. After having died in *More Pricks Than Kicks* he is resurrected in *Echo's Bones*, the testimony being that despite his seeming corporeality he casts no shadow. Many other characters have met the same fate. In what follows I will analyse this ghosting not so much within this work but in Beckett's oeuvre. In particular, I will question the way in which Belacqua offers a gateway in order to better understand and interpret the roles of

Reader and Listener in the late dramaticule *Ohio Impromptu* (1981). In addition, I will point out how this playlet not only is indebted to a few canonical texts from world literature, but also can itself be seen to reflect on the very ideas of authorship and world literature.

Ohio Impromptu stages two elderly men, similar in appearance. Reader reads out a story from a book while Listener listens, every now and then interrupting Reader by knocking on the table, whereafter Reader resumes reading with a repetition of the last sentence. The story is about a man who has suffered a great loss and is comforted by another man visiting him at night and who reads from a worn volume till dawn, after which he disappears. We are left in the dark as to what he reads, but we may gradually assume that the story *told* merges with the story *staged*. Thus, the story merges with the act of telling the story, which unfolds as it is being narrated.

Throughout this playlet these knocks on the table dictate the rhythm of the speech and narrative. Abstract though it may be, the story in itself is fairly cohesive, but due to these knocks the text becomes fragmented and triple-layered. How are we to interpret these knocks that seem to be overlooked or ignored too easily in critical literature, which instead focuses primarily on the monologic narrative? What does this editing process consist of? Why does Beckett stage a character that cuts a story into several fragments? Of course, it bears reminiscences to other plays in which editing is a major motif, such as *Krapp's Last Tape*, but can we distinguish more profound parallels with other works based on the motif of the Narcissus and Echo myth?

The short play bears an uncanny, ghostlike stamp. Not only do both men act like Doppelgängers, but their appearance – long black coat, long white hair – also gives the scene a spooky impression. In addition, the indeterminate setting, both of the theatrical environment and of the fictional location (though with references to the Isle of Swans in Paris), as well as the lack of context and background of the story told, contributes to the eerie and spectral atmosphere. However, this internal ghosting, whereby the fictional and the theatrical haunt each other, is compounded by a form of external ghosting. This can be understood in the sense that Marvin Carlson attributed to the term 'haunting', as a theatrical translation of what literary and cultural studies might call intertextuality. Nevertheless, I prefer to interpret the concept of ghosting in Derrida's terms. In *Specters of Marx* Derrida criticizes modern human propensity to exorcize the ghosts from the past and live with the illusion of ontological presence without the traces of what was and what is yet to come. Absence is a necessary prerequisite of meaning. Presence can never stand on its own but is always moulded by the spectral, by what is not present. While the dead return, those who are not yet living cast their shadow too, and thus all interfere with the living. Derrida calls this living with ghosts *hauntology*. It is in this sense that we should understand *hauntology* in Beckett's work as well, i.e. as a perpetual challenge of ontology, the halting of the dialectical movement that underlies the terms and brings them to a standstill in an end position. Spectres occupy a twilight zone between being and non-being, between absence and presence, between the organic and the inorganic. But what is equally important is the revisiting of the past that informs Derrida's interpretation of *hauntology*, particularly with regard to *Ohio Impromptu*, a play that is so drenched in melancholy in its evocation of a lost past. The *hauntology* at work in this dramaticule goes way beyond the spectral phenomena that mark the impossibility of any presence whatsoever.

Beckett's work in general summons up a lot of ghosts, very often explicitly but even more so implicitly. Who are these two men in *Ohio Impromptu*, reading and listening? And who is the dear face with the dear name that determines what both men in the narrative do? The first two seem to be mirroring each other; both '[a]s alike in appearance as possible', with each a '[l]ong black coat' and '[l]ong white hair' (Beckett 2006: 473), they seem fragments of the same person, sharing a narrative in which the protagonists are once 'so long alone together' (474), then '[w]ith never a word exchanged they grew to be as one' (475). Several fictional layers entwine – first, the theatrical staging of Reader and Listener; second, the tale told onstage by Reader about a man who in his loneliness is visited by another man; and third, the story told by this last man to his companion he has come to comfort. On all these levels, separation and unison, appearance and disappearance alternate. The flowing of the river in the story is a metaphorical reflection of their personal predicament, particularly since the protagonist in the narrative stops to look into the water. From both sides of the islet both arms of the river eventually join each other and flow united on.

As mentioned earlier, *Ohio Impromptu*, like most of Beckett's writings, takes place in a fairly indefinite setting. However, the playwright does give us some very concrete topical references. Besides the Isle of Swans that the main character in the story can see from his window he could be seen pacing the islet with his 'old world Latin Quarter hat' (474). Both elements can be read as clear nods to his friend, mentor and compatriot James Joyce. Back in his early youth, Beckett used to take walks with Joyce on the Île aux Cygnes, mostly in silence, as the young Beckett was too much in awe to speak a great deal with the great master (Knowlson 1996: 101). In his early twenties, as an aspiring young writer, Joyce also used to wear a Latin Quarter hat in order to look like a bohemian artist and 'dress the character', an autobiographical element that he also attributed to Stephen Dedalus in *Ulysses*.

> My Latin quarter hat. God, we simply must dress the character. I want puce gloves. You were a student, weren't you? Of what in the other devil's name?
>
> (Joyce 2000: 51)

However, after drawing attention to this extravagant headwear, Joyce also makes a clear reference to *Macbeth*. In an almost hallucinatory scene, the setting of the castle in *Macbeth* turns into a nightmarish underworld after King Duncan has been brutally murdered. Both Macbeth and Lady Macbeth start to hear a knocking sound, the origin of which is not traceable – 'Whence is that knocking?' (807). Later in the play, the same noise anticipates the arrival of Macbeth at the witches (826) and in her madness Lady Macbeth again hears a 'knocking at the gate' (837) so that the knocks dictate the rhythm of the play. The first appearance of the knocks after the murder extends into the next scene, where the kings' porters nightmarishly have transformed into the gatekeepers of hell. In this scene the sound of knocking announces a sinner waiting at the gates of hell to be let in.

> Knock, knock. Who's there, in th'other devil's name? Faith, here's an equivocator that could swear in both the scales against either scale, who committed treason enough for God's sake, yet could not equivocate to heaven. O, come in, equivocator.
>
> (808)

It is probably no coincidence that *Macbeth* too, just like *Ohio Impromptu*, is a ghost play, set in a twilight zone, where concepts and values constantly turn into their opposites: 'Fair is foul, and foul is fair' (793), bearded women resemble men and Mucduff is not 'of woman born' (826). On a political-religious level these ambiguities reflect the lewdness propagated by the Jesuit Henry Garnet at the time, whose *A Treatise of Equivocation* advised Catholics how they could avoid telling the truth in court without lying. Yet of course they also add to the unstable, spectral atmosphere that permeates the whole play.

In adopting Joyce's twofold allusion to the hat and *Macbeth*, Beckett's device in *Ohio Impromptu* to have Listener knock to stop the narrative and in some way oblige Reader to repeat the last sentence is a conscious intervention in order to evoke the deathly, ghostly atmosphere of Shakespeare's play. Moreover, the name of this piece of land, the Isle of Swans, with its reference to a dance of death, also evokes the river Styx. The narrative, then, would take place in some underworld, the islet with its river being a site of death. However, '[t]he dead die hard, they are trespassers on the beyond' (Beckett 2014: 3), as Beckett states in the opening sentence of *Echo's Bones*. With a perpetual oscillation between leaving and coming, between being and dissolving, the underworld rather resembles limbo. It seems that Reader, Listener and their alter egos within the stories are inhabitants of Purgatorio, a state of sitting on the fence, neither here nor there.

But, as already mentioned, not only do these knocks in *Ohio Impromptu* bring to (semi-)life *Macbeth*'s ghosts, they also disrupt the narrative. In a much-quoted fragment from *Dream of Fair to Middling Women* Beckett writes, 'The experience of my reader shall be between the phrases, in the silence, communicated by the intervals, not the terms, of the statement, between the flowers that cannot coexist' (1992: 137). If we take Beckett's word, it is from these knocks – the intervals and silences of the play – that true meaning emerges. Here of course we notice Lacan's belief that one can only find oneself in the gaps of language, where discourse halts or breaks down, where the logics of the narrative and the flow of the coherent story yield to the inconsistencies that – fragmentary though they may be by necessity – reveal a meaning that keeps on insisting, thus resulting in a diarrhoea, an outburst of fragments. Six times (exactly as many times as the knock within resounds in scene II.3 in *Macbeth*) through his knocks Listener forces Reader to stop and recapitulate the previous sentence, as if the sound of death halts the flow of the narrative of life. And this is precisely what happens indeed. The narrative in Beckett is a flow itself that comes to a halt, takes turns, then moves on. As death and life play hide-and-seek in Beckett's work, narration and the blockage of narration equally alternate, resulting in fragmented, kaleidoscopic pieces of literature.

Listener in *Ohio Impromptu* takes on a very similar role to little Ernst, Freud's grandson, who showed him how children cope with the alienation process from their mother. Throwing away a spool then pulling it back, accompanied by yelling respectively 'fort' and 'da', the boy teaches himself to be in control of a situation that is in reality beyond his command. In *Beyond the Pleasure Principle* (1920) Freud relates how this simple game is a way of dealing with an initial trauma – the separation from his mother – through the process of symbolization. Thus, it forces the little child to give up on his incestuous desires towards his mother and redirect his desire to external objects.[1] Listener's knocks are analogous to Ernst's spool that is alternatively thrown away and then pulled back. They are the punctuation in the stream of language that other characters in Beckett such as Mouth in *Not I* (1972) lack and that puts Listener in a controlling position.

Beckett's aforementioned phrase 'The experience of my reader shall be between the phrases, in the silence' can hardly be overestimated. Silence marks the spectre of death haunting what is still alive. In her essay on Antonin Artaud Susan Sontag argued that his attempt to put an end to all dualisms was bound to lead either to madness, suicide or silence (see 1988: liii). Obviously, Beckett's characters are no more capable of reaching silence than of killing themselves, as Estragon acknowledges, but being 'incapable of keeping silent' may protect them from hearing '[a]ll the dead voices' (2006: 54). Silence seems a privilege that is not within reach of Beckett's protagonists. Krapp, for one, does experience some moments of absolute silence. These take place at instances of perfect balance. In Beckett's circular world the epicentre or the exact middle is the only space of rest, peace and silence – the space where the organic body eventually turns into inorganic stone. The desire to occupy this middle can be associated, then, with Freud's death drive – it is a very persistent longing that Hamm in *Endgame* formulates most poignantly, demanding Clov push him 'right in the center' (2006: 109). Several texts mention the neologism womb-tomb, which can be interpreted as the stage in which all opposites are erased, a stage that amounts to a pre-Oedipal, symbiotic state of existence. It bears the promise of the erasure of the lack of the subject, resulting from the sin of having been born. Therefore, the epiphany that Krapp experiences takes place during that 'memorable equinox' (2006: 223), the moment when day and night are exactly equally long. Only then and there can life indeed turn to stone, to the inorganic stage of the unborn where nothing stirs and all is silent: 'Never knew such silence. The earth might be uninhabited' (2006: 229). This moment is the equivalent to the end of *Ohio Impromptu*: 'they sat on as though turned to stone' (476).

Following Beckett's adage that form should follow content, the ghostly figments of a character require fragmentary textual structures. If anything, plot lines should be decomposed, and unity and linear form be avoided in order to escape from 'the "chloroformed world" of Balzac's novels, where, he claimed, characters are turned into "clockwork cabbages", on whom the novelist can "rely on their staying put wherever needed or staying going at whatever speed in whatever direction he chooses"' (Knowlson 1996: 146). *Echo's Bones*, the apocryphal narrative that did not make it into *More Pricks Than Kicks* because it gave publisher Charles Prentice – in his own words – the jim-jams (Beckett 2014: xi), definitely conforms to this principle. The narrative opens with Belacqua who is resurrected after having been dead for what might at least have been forty days. The character of Belacqua, of course, is taken from the waiting figure in Dante's *Purgatorio*, and considering the neither-nor position that defines this place, it is not in the least surprising that we find the resurrected Belacqua sitting on a fence. If not for the neither-nor associations with the expression it evokes, this seeming detail is emphasized a little bit later by the third-person narrator in his description of how Belacqua was brought back to life.

> To begin then at the beginning, he felt himself nodding in the grey shoals of angels, his co-departed, that thronged the womb-tomb, distinctly he felt himself lapsing from a beatitude of sloth that was infinitely smoother than oil and softer than pumpkins, he found himself fighting in vain against the hideous torpor and the grit and glare of his lids on the eyeballs so long lapped in gloom, and the next thing was he was horsed as it were for major discipline on the fence as see above, the bells pealing in all the steeples, his pockets crammed with cigars.
>
> (2014: 4–5)

Quite some elements link this fragment to *Ohio Impromptu*. In the mystification that surrounds him like an aura, the man who pays nightly visits in the story read by Reader could easily be considered an angelic figure.

> One night as he sat trembling head in hands from head to foot a man appeared to him and said, I have been sent by – and here he named the dear name – to comfort you. Then drawing a worn volume from the pocket of his long black coat he sat and read till dawn. Then disappeared without a word.
>
> [...]
>
> Till the night came at last when having closed the book and dawn at hand he did not disappear but sat on without a word.
> [*Pause.*]
> Finally he said, I have had word from – and here he named the dear name – that I shall not come again. I saw the dear face and heard the unspoken words, No need to go to him again, even were it in your power.
> (475)

Besides the silent and nightly setting of the scene that provides this visitor with angelic features, there is this enigmatic phrase – 'and here he named the dear name' – that must give us pause. Who else but God is so transcendent that even mentioning his name comes close to blasphemy? Particularly in the Jewish tradition mentioning the name of God in vain – and this is almost every use outside prayers and reading from the Torah – is strictly prohibited. This reading seems to be supported by the suggestion that the messenger, like an angel, operates under the command of an almighty – 'even were it in your power' (475).

Another similarity between *Echo's Bones* and *Ohio Impromptu* can be found in the interference of the third-person narrator who disrupts the story with references to the physicality of the book and the paper on which the narrative is written. In the first text the narrator breaks up the rhythm of the story by explicitly pointing out the repetition of Belacqua sitting on the fence ('as see above'), and a comparable disruption interrupts the flow of the story in the dramaticule: 'Now with redoubled force the fearful symptoms described at length page forty paragraph four' (475).

Belacqua, of course, in his name also refers to the myth of Narcissus, that split mythological character that tries to unite with himself and has to pay for it with his own life, and it appears that figments of the myth have made their way in *Ohio Impromptu* too. Given the fact that the character halts at the top of the islet to look into the conflowing arms of the river, could we not conclude, then, that he – and by extension Reader and Listener – is another apparition, another resurrection of Belacqua?

> Day after day he could be seen slowly pacing the islet. Hour after hour. In his long black coat no matter what the weather and old world Latin Quarter hat. At the tip he would always pause to dwell on the receding

stream. How in joyous eddies its two arms conflowed and flowed united on. Then turn and his slow steps retrace.

(474)

And is not the repetition of Reader's phrases after Listener's knocks in itself a repetition of the echo by the mythological figure that gave her name to the title of Beckett's narrative written in 1933? And when Reader and Listener end up very much like both men in the narrative, i.e. 'as though turned to stone', we should not forget that this is exactly the fate of Echo's bones, which is not only why *Ohio Impromptu* ends with this stony image, the third and last part of Beckett's early story *Echo's Bones* also has Belacqua sitting at his own headstone, and as the coffin is opened up what they find there is, indeed, a 'handful of stones' (51).

I do not think it is exaggerated to consider *Ohio Impromptu* as Beckett's return to Ovid's myth and recognize in Listener another figment of Echo: mute throughout the play, with only the capacity for repetition. And as with Echo, his only freedom lies in his choice when to knock and hence which phrases will be repeated. Listener's knocks trigger an echo of Reader's last words. Reader in his turn seems to be a Narcissus figure, who does not find his alter ego in the water's reflection but in the fictional character of the story he is narrating and with whom he increasingly builds up a parallel, mirroring world.

So what is left once Echo's bones are petrified is her disembodied voice, but Beckett's close is paradoxical. The very last sentence indeed is repeated: 'Nothing is left to tell. [...] Nothing is left to tell' (476). However, the content seems to contradict the repetition that seems willing or inclined to continue. And yet the book is closed, leaving Listener and Reader silent, unblinking, expressionless, inorganic. In returning to his earliest writings dating from almost half a century earlier, with *Ohio Impromptu* Beckett not only closes the book but also the circle meanwhile silencing Echo too.

In conclusion, metafictionality plays on several levels. Beckett uses canonical texts of world literature, such as *Ulysses* and *Macbeth*, that echo throughout *Ohio Impromptu*, as a means to integrate his own text in it and thus participate in this whirling stream of global literature. In this way his own texts may become a side river that joins the stream of world literature: 'in joyous eddies its two arms conflowed and flowed united on' (474). His playlet dramatizes this circulation of narratives both thematically – through the resonation of the Echo and Narcissus myth – and dramatically – by means of the knocks but also through the narrative that Reader reads out to Listener mirroring the theatrical situation of Reader and Listener themselves. As Listener and Reader are each other's alter egos, so are the act of narration and the narrative, and so does the dramaticule *Ohio Impromptu* echo *Echo's Bones* as an alter ego. If the poetics, as Ann Lecercle has argued, of *Echo's Bones* is 'a poetics of suture', aiming at 'suturing the original gap' (cited in Hunkeler 1997: 197), this underlies the fragmentary structure of

Ohio Impromptu too. Thus, it serves as an echo of Beckett's first writings, going back as early as *Dream of Fair to Middling Women* and *More Pricks Than Kicks*. With a time span of fifty years, the circle of a career is equally closed. But additionally, mirroring the hide-and-seek game of narrative and the act of narration, at the end of his life, in *Ohio Impromptu* Beckett makes up the balance and seems to assess his own position as a writer in relation to world literature. Can we not see the river as a metaphor for the literary canon to which Beckett, as a tributary, contributes his oeuvre? Dwelling on the stream of his own work that joins the main river, he realizes that he has been able to add his part to those works that travel the world.

Note

1. Little Ernst's play with a spool brings to mind Krapp's fetish with his audio spools, and indeed, the underlying dynamics are exactly the same. This play too is strongly about separation and finding ways to – literally – come to terms with this kind of alienation. Also see my book *Cruelty and Desire in the Modern Theater*: 'Although Krapp was engaged in several relationships if we are to believe his autobiography, he makes sure never to really commit himself and break up with the girl before his narcissism is threatened too much. Rapprochement and departure alternate in a never-ending fort/da story' (De Vos 2011: 196).

Works cited

Beckett, S. (1992), *Dream of Fair to Middling Women*, Dublin: Black Cat Press.
Beckett, S. (2006), *The Grove Centenary Edition (vol. III): Dramatic Works*, New York: Grove Press.
Beckett, S. (2014), *Echo's Bones*, London: Faber and Faber.
De Vos, L. (2011), *Cruelty and Desire in the Modern Theater. Antonin Artaud, Sarah Kane, and Samuel Beckett*, Madison: Fairleigh Dickinson University Press.
Hunkeler, T. (1997), *Echos de l'Ego dans l'oeuvre de Samuel Beckett*, Paris: L'Harmattan.
Joyce, J. (2000), *Ulysses*, London: Penguin Classics.
Katz, D. (1996), '"Alone in the Accusative": Beckett's Narcissistic Echoes', in Sjef Houppermans (ed.), *Beckett & La Psychanalyse & Psychoanalysis*, 57–71, Amsterdam: Rodopi.
Knowlson, J. (1996), *Damned to Fame. The Life of Samuel Beckett*, London: Bloomsbury.
Shakespeare, W. (1997), '*Macbeth*', in Stephen Greenblatt (ed.), *The Norton Shakespeare*, 783–846, New York: W. W. Norton.
Sontag, S. (1988), 'Artaud', in Antonin Artaud (ed.), *Selected Writings*, xvii–lix, Berkeley and LA: University of California Press.

8

Echoes, rags and bones: A few Brazilian Becketts on the way

Fábio de Souza Andrade

When considering Beckett's reception in Brazil, one must sound at least a bit like Caliban (see Morse 1981: n.p.). The necessary perspective is of one being completely seduced by, yet at the same time rather suspicious and resentful of the compelling power of a master's voice, even if not one's own master's voice. How to avoid being converted into an echo chamber of such a prestigious, precise and alluring architecture of ruins? Is it at all possible not to be completely swallowed by his work, to read Beckett's plays and prose from an interested, active, unusual point of view, but still preserve the spirit of his poetics, so strictly connected to the flesh of his revolutionary form? Studying the Brazilian reception of Beckett's work provides an invaluable occasion for considering how world literature builds on the basis of a permanent political and aesthetic debate, a rather complex, active and not at all innocent process. Even though translation and untranslatability, editorial history and academic critical readings are also crucial aspects of this reception, nowhere are these conflictive aspects more visible than in practical matters concerned in staging and adaptation.

Some violence is intrinsic to any process of conceptual appropriation; reverence is constantly mixed with occasional fury. To misquote Titus Andronicus, a creative reading does not have to – and should not, by the way – 'grind your bones to dust/and with your blood and it [...] make a paste', a vital elixir that keeps no trace of its starting point. Beckett's backbone is far more resistant than that, *et pour cause*. Like the resurrected

Belacqua, in the recently published *Echo's Bones*, attending a concept play we must anxiously wait, breath suspended, to find out in the end if the current grave-diggers did not destroy the object of their quest in the hurry of revealing it. That certainly stands valid for Brazilian readings of Beckettian drama in our days.

This chapter provides an overview of the twenty-first-century reception of Beckett in Brazil, giving an account of three very recent local productions of his work: Isabel Teixeira's *Fim de jogo* (*Endgame*), Isabel Cavalcanti's *Moi lui* (based on *Molloy*) and Fernando and Adriano Guimarães's *Ocupação Sozinhos Juntos* (*Together Alone Occupation*). All of them are fully accomplished examples of the challenges involved in staging Beckett in a peripheral cultural context, each of them dealing with distinct and complementary aspects of his canon – early plays, late plays and the transposition of prose fiction to the stage.

Though many other contemporary Brazilian productions could be mentioned as well, none were exemplary as these mentioned above, having in mind Beckett's fundamental ambiguities. All three of them, each in its own way, pay a successful tribute to his profile as an artist, radically exploring an aesthetic of fragments, resistant to allegorical readings, firmly grounded on the tense instability of *aporia*, oscillating, on the page or on the stage, between the chaos of modern experience and the transfiguring power of fancy, presence and absence, physicality and imagery.[1]

Fim de jogo (*Endgame*), Isabel Teixeira, Renato Borghi and Élcio Nogueira, 2016

Almost sixty years after the world première (and the Brazilian one too, as a matter of fact), Isabel Teixeira directed *Fim de jogo* (*Endgame*) in strict adherence to the original text, avoiding the trap of pinning down the characters to particular historical circumstances, such as life after the nuclear holocaust or under military dictatorship. Like previous Brazilian productions, it has managed to escape legal battles and public controversy, as JoAnne Akalaitis's American *Endgame* (1984), for instance, had not. Even in a globalized world, Brazilian stages are still quite remote and Brazilian directors enjoy an occasional indulgence, far away from the vigilant eyes of the Literary Estate of Samuel Beckett.

And yet this production is rather on the experimental side. The young director, Isabel Teixeira, and the also young stage partner of Renato Borghi, Élcio Nogueira, were both responsible for a very prolific Beckettian workshop in 1999. Meant for actors, playwrights, sound and light designers, it resulted in a series of Beckett-inspired performances, as well as visual installations and musical compositions. Teixeira directed a staging of *Eleutheria* (2013) gathering the actors that were graduating that year at the Laboratory Theatre of Escola de Arte Dramática (EAD), the drama school at the University of São Paulo.

It is worth mentioning that at the same school Alfredo Mesquita (about whom Beckett wrote to Jerome Lindon, asking for his permission concerning the performance rights) produced the first Brazilian *Esperando Godot* (*Waiting for Godot*) in 1955. Actual productions of *Eleutheria* are rare and Teixeira corresponded to the explicit avant-gardist mood of the play in her production in many aspects. Having to deal with a plethora of characters in a rather modest theatre, without proper wings or backstage space, she even multiplied these characters into several actors playing the same role; the rotating platform on which the action was meant to take place, comprising both Victor's bedroom and the Krapps' living room – the latter occupying a growing part of the setting in each new act of the play – was replaced by a lit rectangular area at the centre of the stage, surrounded by niches in the dark. The costumes were colourful and very sharply angled, of modernist inspiration.

The famed Brazilian actor Renato Borghi, who played Hamm, has taken part in most of the key moments of recent Brazilian theatrical history, from the incorporation of twentieth-century politically engaged North American realism to the very origins of a modern local dramaturgy, an attempt to deal directly with Brazilian issues and, simultaneously, to assimilate the international language of the avant-garde. He has trodden the whole path from a Brechtian epic acting school to the rising role of physicality in performance, at the expense of the centrality of the text. He was personally involved in the founding of one of the most daring and long-lasting Brazilian avant-gardist companies, Teatro Oficina. Besides that, he took part in productions of another politically engaged sixties group, Arena, associated with Augusto Boal, during the first steps of what would turn out to be Teatro do Oprimido. He has discussed and digested from Stanislavski to Grotowski and has won several of the most prestigious awards in Brazil.

The confluence of Borghi and Teixeira around *Endgame* brought together, on the one hand, a whole life devoted to acting, directing and producing, with a yearning to sum it all up and, on the other, that of two young artists in search of new perspectives. The meta-theatrical material of the play was at the core of the project from the very beginning, as well as the *parti pris* that they were not going for a conventional production. What they most had in mind was to concentrate on the radical interrogation of the contemporary possibilities and limits of drama. They were not working on the same project for the first time though, for Élcio Nogueira and Renato Borghi have run their own company for more than ten years, having directed and produced Brecht, Chekhov and Genet, among others.

Endgame is a play about characters trapped in the stage so that spatial issues, such as scenic architecture and the symbolic or allegorical interpretations raised by the setting, are crucial to its dramatic effect. Aware of this, and willing to stress the theatricality and the reflexivity that sustain the text, Teixeira began by entertaining the possibility of producing it in a solemn house, such as the São Paulo Municipal Theatre, built after the Parisian Opéra Garnier. She envisaged the action as limited to the stage elevator. The audience would be reduced to a few spectators each night accommodated in temporary seat rows improvisated back stage, opposite to the splendid, unoccupied velvet seats. Though inventive, this plan proved to be extravagant and costly enough not to be carried through.

Nonetheless, obsessed by the thought of relocating not the action in *Endgame* but the spatial circumstances involving the performance, the acting itself, she came across her solution looking through the wrong side of the eyeglasses, just like Clov. Instead of a sumptuous hall, they decided to invade another alien space: Borghi's own ground floor apartment's living room, conveniently emptied for the occasion. As in Kantor's experiences, their *Endgame* was now conceived as chamber, or rather pocket, theatre introduced in a strange, if not frankly hostile, domestic environment. Closeness and intimacy reinforced the play's tendency to be apprehended first by the nerves and only secondarily by the intellect.

Teixeira decided to recuperate solutions that Beckett had considered and eventually discarded during the process of writing the play. Exploring proto-versions and archival typescripts such as '*avant fin de partie*' and '*early endgame*', kept in Reading, Dublin and Austin, she decided to go back in time and restore a moment in the creative process when the actors on stage were only two, the pair of protagonists, Hamm, the blind tyrant confined to a chair, Clov, his factotum unable to sit, and both multiplying their voices to incorporate Nagg and Nell. The falsetto and transvestism once cogitated by Beckett found their way back into the play, as formal procedures that re-enact its reflexive essence.

Another layer of meaning came from the fact that Renato Borghi and Élcio Nogueira actually live together as a couple and the former had just overcome a long physical ordeal, which resulted in temporary paralysis due to excruciating pains in the spine. During Borghi's recovery period, Nogueira performed as his nurse for a certain time, and both suddenly realized that they were already living *Endgame*'s routine, tied to the house and involuntarily repeating circular dialogues. Jan Kott and Marjorie Perloff have written about the sort of memories Beckett's plays can activate in those who live the routine of being ill, restricted to a bed or a chair, in hospital, for instance, and have shown the great importance insignificant objects may acquire in these situations.

Beckett's plays farcically recapitulate modern dramatic history, parading, as Adorno points out, its failed techniques and senile conventions and producing a second-degree realism made of fragmented expressions, meaningless words and reasoning leftovers. These make a profound impression on us, creating a language so flagrantly familiar and at the same time so very foreign. The same applies to the portrayal of forced confinement in an enclosed space, the delirious verbal fancy trying to counterbalance the lack of variety, the multiplied imaginary voices trying to fill the void of life 'together alone', as Beckett names this experience in *Ohio Impromptu* (1981). In this production, a realistic resonance of that kind certainly is part of the game, as Borghi recalls having performed as a young actor several times in private residences for the delight of wealthy people, but this is far from being a key for interpretation.

Taking seriously the confinement so dear to Beckett, particularly in his late drama, and having chosen to perform the play 'together alone' in the living room of the apartment they would continue to live in during the season, dealing with the complicated logistics was nothing compared to the consequences of having only a pair of actors on stage. Suppressing the actual physical presence of Nagg and Nell is by far the most profound and consequential intervention. They still are in the play but now, symbolized by portraits, turned into things, or rather puppets, now dependent on Clov to be activated. Though the text has not been cut and their lines are all delivered, their bodily presence, sometimes veiled, sometimes explicit, is no longer there. The grotesque elements such as their severed limbs, the sand, the alluded corporal holes, the hunger, tend to become more abstract. On the down side, though they are still the repositories of the infernal pregnancy of yesterday in the present day, accompanying the remembrance of the Lake Como narrative by a waltz – and discreet use of music is part of this show – simplifies their role in provoking pathetic nostalgia.

The transformation of the stage into a domestic space also brings surprising interpretative consequences to the production. Arriving at the apartment is part of the strangeness of the experience. After queuing at a cultural centre five minutes' walking distance from Borghi's house, the spectators are given tickets and a map. The role of welcoming the audience at the front door is taken by a prompter, an addition to Beckett's text, a new character that also operates light and sound during the play. Located behind the audience, he also repeats, once or twice, allegedly forgotten lines. The right window is the room's own window, facing the car entrance of the building, and the left one is represented by a lit opening in a wardrobe on the opposite side. There is a real kitchen, close to the left window, visible through an occasionally open door, where Clov still finds his shelter, and a real toilet, from where he speaks, out of scene, to Hamm. Two drawers, respectively at the right and left extremities of a large sideboard (a family piece of furniture) placed behind Hamm's chair, provide wombs/tombs for Nagg and Nell, who are represented by pictures of Borghi's actual parents.

Left to the audience, off centre, close to the prompt, a false mantelpiece decorated with several of the prizes collected by Borghi throughout his career (with busts of Molière and Shakespeare among them), displays an artificial blue light, the play's equivalent of Lake Como, where Nagg and Nell fly to, conducted by Clov's hands, when approaching their final silence. Playing Clov and Nagg, Nogueira uses the busts as puppets, helping him to tell the tailor's anecdote. When representing the tailor, he has Molière in hand and talks in French accent. When representing the Englishman, he holds Shakespeare's statuette.

Besides altering the dialectical interplay between immobility and movement, so vital in the play, the new stage configuration simultaneously changes the dynamic of the eye, for now there is action taking place close to the mantelpiece. Hamm's prerogative at the centre is no longer unique. At the same time, the intimacy of a minimum and less peopled setting, excluding the actors that play Nagg and Nell, so close to the audience, goes further in exploring the visual meanings that the symmetric and asymmetric postures adopted by the actors on stage suggest. A visual translation of this occurs in the final *agon*, when Clov, even if unable to sit, does so and faces Hamm directly, indicating perhaps a new correlation between them. In this production, actors are always on the edge of physical contact, recuperating the persistent menace of violence and tenderness already important in the final text, but much more so in the proto-versions of the play. As for the potential strangeness of the props, which might be naturalized in the context of the domestic realm, it is reinforced by the providing of a stick, taped as a splint to Clov's damaged leg, which later, when violently torn away from him, will alternately pass for a gaff, eyeglasses or a paddle.

The stress put on the meta-theatrical aspects of the play is reflected in the protagonists' acting, which is not naturalistic but suggests an implicit ironic subtext, a silent comment on their gestures, attitudes and words. Revealed or not, the uncertain aspect of the characters' memories, desires and intentions, a mix of presence and absence, invention and remembrance, assumes in this production a very concrete and material scenic translation and extreme physicality rules.

One might say that the fictional and dramatic voice of the late Beckettian style, dramatically consummated in the complex enunciative devices of *Nohow on* (1989) or plays like *Ohio Impromptu*, retroacts and influences the interpretative decisions of this production. This seems to be a good way of avoiding the risk of an officialized version of Beckett, by exploring the possible internal resonances of the different phases of his oeuvre *ex post* and renewing his own artistic procedures and experiences by providing new contexts to them.

Before moving on to another Brazilian production of Beckett's work, I should point that arrangements are being made to repeat this version of *Endgame*, this time replicating the whole apartment for a short period in a cultural centre; the strange and the familiar are duplicated a second time. Overall, this would be perfectly coherent with the fundamental premise of the play – there's no other place allowed to the actor but the stage – and the rigorous attention to spacing, movement and position Beckett employed when writing it.[2]

Moi lui, Isabel Cavalcanti and Ana Kfouri, Sesc Pompeia, 2014

Isabel Cavalcanti, an actress and director from Rio de Janeiro, first approached Beckett as a scholar when writing a PhD thesis on the scattered I in his dramatic and narrative works, particularly in *Not I*, later published as a book (cf. Cavalcanti 2006). Her practical experience with his plays is also very significant and diverse, having directed Sérgio Brito, a recently deceased great Brazilian actor, in *Krapp's Last Tape* (1969) and *Act without Words I* (1957). His distinguished quality, his physical fragility on stage due to old age, and her informed intuition, following Beckett's indications very closely, resulted in a remarkable staging.

But it is precisely when she took risks in an already explored, though not nearly exhausted territory – the transposition to the stage of works originally conceived for other media – that Isabel Cavalcanti revealed herself as someone prepared to face the challenges Beckettian poetics poses. From Jack McGowran's *Beginning to End* (1968) to the recent production of the radio plays on the stage by the Pan Pan Theatre, this is a minefield which pays the lucky hits highly. Cavalcanti concentrated on the post-war works, namely on *Molloy* (1951), and directed Ana Kfouri performing solo extracts of the novel's first part, double billing with director Antonio Guedes's adaptation of 'First Love' (1941).

Both adaptations meant to materialize the voice's instability – permanently contradicting itself, suspending the truth of every single statement – and critically examine the way it plies into many. How to dramatically convey the characteristic self-analytical, self-despising, self-mocking process of the Beckettian prose of the period? From the title, a wordplay on the impossibility of saying I and a comment on the inevitable broken nature of modern subjectivity, her decision was to be as discreet and minimalist as possible, just underscoring the potential divisions of the voice already inscribed in the text. The choice of the fragments was faithful to the nature of the book and its peculiar form of plot, resistant to any attempt of paraphrase. Cavalcanti was successful in recreating on the stage the paradoxical nature of a voice in constant structural doubt and managed to avoid any trace of a conceptual framework which might have given birth to a misleading dramatic arc, non-existent in the novel.

Even though one will recognize episodes such as Molloy's sucking stones, his tumbling into social assistance, his sado-comic attempts at communicating with his mother, there is no imposition of a teleological progression upon them in the play. Dressed as a Beckettian clochard, set in a devastated land, she is alone on the stage, but for a few props (a lamp, projecting shades shaped like bicycle wheels, a suitcase, a wheelchair). Notwithstanding it is a woman playing Molloy, her very short haircut, as well as the sharpness of her features and diction conceal this circumstance. Playing to a small audience of about fifty people each night, Ana Kfouri utters the monologues as if they were a dialogue: dissenting from herself, alternating moods, darting here and there a suspicious and defying look, giving full release to her gangrenous, entropic voice, but not lacking humour (see Figure 1).

The moments when the play parts from this less-is-more aesthetics are only a few, but significant. In the opening section, Molloy is spoken of in the third person, suggesting he might be a character in the mind of an author unable to say I himself. The same happens in the final section, when a mist of glycerine invades the stage and a rope ladder falls from the top, similar to the bottle of water in *Act without Words I*, somehow suggesting a common ground to Beckett's several assaults on conventional language, both narrative and dramatic.

FIGURE 1 *Ana Kfouri directed by Isabel Cavalcanti in* Moi lui, *2014. Dalton Valério.*

Primeiro amor (*First Love*), presented as a double bill with *Moi lui*, chooses a similar minimalist approach, observing the first steps of Beckett's first-person voice in the post-war period, its self-cancelling and scattering effects. The setting is arranged around a stone bench, central to the story, on which the protagonist remains seated throughout the whole play, alternatively staring at the audience seated in three improvisated rows very close to the action. On the ground, projections evoke some of the central elements of her tale such as the autumn leaves in turmoil, later converted into a whirlwind of projected words, mixed together by the hesitant memory and language of the protagonist, his self-reflexive verbal bursts denouncing his own fictionalized nature and complete mistrust in the efficiency of his report.

The search for a scenic equivalent for this uncertain and tentative voice, moved by a compulsion to fail, contrasts flagrantly with another Brazilian transposition of Beckett's fictional prose to the stage which took place practically at the same time. A company called Club Noir, with its focus on the investigation of the voice both as theoretical object and dramatic instrument, staged *Tríptico Beckett* in 2014, inspired by the so-called late trilogy.

In a black box, a particular favourite of the company's productions, and in the dark, three actresses – Paula Spinelli, Nathália Timberg and Juliana Galdino – speak alternately, fixed at precise spots during the whole play: Paula, left stage; Timberg, centre stage; and Juliana on the right. Their costumes mark them as women at different stages of their lives. Paula is dressed as a high school student; Timberg, the only sitting character, wears a black robe that contrasts with her long white hair, immediately recognizable as one of Beckett's late plays' female protagonists; and Galdino, wearing a jogging suit and running shoes, suggests a middle-aged woman. Each one performs extracts from a different volume: Spinelli recites some of *Company*'s second-person narrated memories, Timberg, passages from *Ill Seen, Ill Said*, and Juliana, parts of *Worstward Ho*.

In contrast to *Moi lui*, here the result completely ignores the beauty of the complex linguistic achievements of the narrator of Beckett's final prose. There's no trace left of the aesthetic and epistemological consequences involved in his writing. By suggesting that the same female voice runs throughout the three novels, reading them as sequential, the play creates a universe of its own, not only parallel, but rather plain, paying no heed to the anguishing pronominal war (to use Gontarski's phrasing) being fought in them. If drama is already there, taking place in language, there is no need to provide extra doses by forging a plot. Finally, the only meaningful stage prop is a huge skeleton, hanging close to the back wall behind the seated actress. It is almost impossible to figure out how one could be more literal, annihilating the huge evocative power of the expression/image 'frescoes of the skull'. The contrast between these two simultaneous productions demonstrates how much reinventing Beckett depends on being conscious of his own formal consciousness, extremely demanding and precise in the origin.

Fernando and Adriano Guimarães's *Ocupação Sozinhos Juntos*, SESC Belenzinho, SP, 2015

Not only has Beckett frequently meditated on the imaginative process from the point of view of a fine connoisseur of visual arts – in his essays, notebooks and correspondences – but often inspired the imagination of composers, choreographers, video artists and painters as well, from Morton Feldman to Maguy Marin and Bruce Nauman. In Brazil nowadays, one of the most interesting and active aspects of the contemporary reception of his works relates to this feature. Adriano and Fernando Guimarães, known as *Irmãos Guimarães* (Guimarães Brothers), originally visual artists, migrated to performance and theatre and have been exploring sculpture and video art to promote exhibitions based on Beckett ever since. They also direct his plays, training and specializing actors in Beckettian procedures (both teach in Brasilia). They have also performed worldwide: in Avignon, L.A., Paris and London.

Their most recent Beckettian season, *Ocupação Sozinhos Juntos* (*Together Alone Occupation*), four weeks of intense and varied activities in a cultural centre in São Paulo in May 2015, started with *Act without Words I* and *II*, then *Footfalls* and *Ohio Impromptu*, and the television plays *Quad I* and *Quad II*. The Guimarães Brothers organized a series of debates, productions of the plays and of plays inspired by them, as well as performances inspired by Beckett's prose. In one of them, for nine hours in a row, an actor occupying a glass room reads *The Unnammable* (1953) without interruption until exhaustion. Under constant observation and submitted to a diminishing light, he physically experiments a growing uneasiness, analogue to the one experimented by the novel's elusive I. In another one, the spectators sitting in total darkness on randomly disposed chairs listen to a blend of memories and fiction narrated by an actress who rambles between them, always hesitating between third and first person.[3]

As a whole, *Ocupação Sozinhos Juntos* offered a repertoire of Beckettian procedures and concerns – the exploration of series and repetition, care for the fragment and the presentational and representational aspects of the image – translated and recreated with diverse degrees of freedom by artists that have been digesting it for a long time. In alternate nights, two double-bill programmes, entitled *Fôlego* (Breath I) and *Sopro* (Breath II), brought together *Footfalls* and *Act without Words I* on the one hand, and *Act without Words II* and *Ohio Impromptu* on the other. The spirit oscillated between a staging modelled after Beckett's own productions of his plays, tied to the instructions he inscribed in the texts, and frank recreations *d'après* Beckett. *Footfalls* and *Ohio Impromptu* were conceived in the former mode, both *Acts* in the latter.

The most impressive of all these productions is certainly *Act without Words I*. The Sisyphean dynamics of the play, the learning of resistance by desistance, was completely reinvented from the first intuition of an image: a huge industrial fan propellers like the ones employed by the airplane and car industry. Having *Breath* (1969) in mind, converting the stage itself into a gigantic breathing body, an ephemeral and entropic machine whose brief span a blink condenses and symbolizes, the Guimarães Brothers replaced the mythological background of the Beckettian mime for a modern domestic context, without neutralizing its strangeness. An extremely fragile old lady painfully crosses a long and narrow stage from left to right leaning on a stick. Half way, she passes a cupboard storing cups, kettles, towels; at the right end, a table, presumable place of her tea, waits, close to the fan, gradually gathering speed; at the left end, a music stand supports a ream of white paper.

The fan takes on the role of the unpredictable and sadistic machinery that in the original *Act without Words I* prevents the protagonist from fulfilling his plans and drinking his water. During her many attempts to set the table and prepare her tea, the intensity of the wind and the deafening noise increase exponentially, resulting in an invincible vortex. Against all odds, however, the old lady goes on trying, fragile, but resilient. Elements such as her long dancing foulard, the flying pieces of paper and the water coming out of the kettle that never reaches the cup visually materialize the wind's cruelty. The final image of great impact, just before the curtain closes, is of her drinking the tea under the implacable noise of the fan (see Figure 2).

This image subverts, in a way, what is implied by the final refusal of the thirsty dying man of *Act without Words I*, giving up the deceptive offers and finally finding out the power of resisting through denial. In the Guimarães reading of the play, ultimately and against all odds, the lady manages to have her tea, in contrast to the man who gives up on the carafe of water. This subversion shows how deeply the Guimarães have penetrated *in terra samueli*s, as collectors that developed a sharp internal memory of Beckett's dramatic universe, allowing themselves daring recombination of fragments, exploring the tattered syntax in their own fashion.

The same stands valid for *Quadrado* (*Square*), a new recreation for the stage of the televisual plays, *Quad I* and *II*, set in a big black box. Abandoning the small screen frame, they have also left behind the single perspective which the camera forces on the spectators, who are now distributed on chairs that are placed along three walls surrounding the stage proper: a central square delimited by light. The naked actors wait for the audience to come in, under dim light, and take seats next to them, already sitting here

FIGURE 2 *Yara de Cunto directed by Guimarães Brothers in* Sopro *(d'après* Act without Words I), Ocupação Sozinhos Juntos, *2015. Ismael Monticelli.*

FIGURE 3 Quadrado (d'après Quad), Ocupação Sozinhos Juntos, *directed by Guimarães Brothers, 2015. Ismael Monticelli.*

and there. Then the lights go off to the point of a complete blackout, only to come back very timidly and gradually, illuminating once more the central area, rather guessed than seen until then, in which the actors reappear, barely recognizable, combined in a huge collective body made of interwoven limbs. It takes some time before one can conclude that they are moving across the stage. Their minimal and slow movements, almost imperceptible under the feeble light, also intensify gradually (see Figure 3).

When the reflectors provide plenty of light, the collective body dissolves and the actors, four men and three women, rejoin the audience, to fetch boxes full of clothes, which they empty on the three sides of the square, leaving them on the floor. The square is visible once more and the following action brings some chaos and chance into *Quad*'s original structure, as they come in and out of it, alone, in twos or threes, and walk within its limits, avoiding collisions. At the same time, they pick up and dress some of the abandoned clothes, no manifest method to be found: either just a skirt or a blouse and a coat, or only underwear, all of different colours and regardless of gender. In this come and go, when out of the arena, they sit again next to the audience, occasionally naked or half naked.

Two different moments follow: back on the stage, the actors first engage in dressing the clothes one piece over the other and, subsequently, begin to share the same piece of clothing simultaneously, one getting into the other's garments, building up sculptural pairs and trios, assuming multiple configurations, materializing androgynous and mutant bodies, the human origami, as Stanley Gontarski calls it, typical of late Beckettian prose. Finally, glasses and bottles are added to the game, complicating the choreography through their attempts of serving one another.

In his televisual works Beckett dismissed the supposed documentary realism this medium is associated with, exploring different non-synchronous rhythms of voice-over and images, recurring to big close-ups and unusual framings and deconstructing conventions of televisual language. *Quadrado* is a performance that translates this interrogative drive into another medium, incorporating the suspension between the representative and presentative, an ambiguity typical of his late work. Is it a body, many bodies, what you nearly see? Are we talking about men and women or a new creature, multi-limbed, a sort of human crab?

The superb light and setting design suggest this oscillation between form and formlessness, systolic and diastolic tempo that embrace Beckett's final images, simultaneously evanescent and full of energy, finding a performative, plastic-choreographic equivalent to it. They bring to one's mind the eventual androgyny of the closed space narratives' characters, the moving population in the cylinder from *The Lost Ones* (1970), the power games in the mimes.

It is hard to tell from these three examples if we could possibly extract a single common tendency in the Brazilian reception of Beckett's work, a Brazilian way of combining his unique language to local traditions and debate. To extract unpredictable consequences of Western modernist drives has always been a way of affirming Brazilian identity and the melting pot has been a current (and accurate) metaphor to describe the process. Resistant to complete dissolution in a new synthesis, his paradoxes and aporias made of remains persist as irreconcilable foreign bodies in each new artistic resonance, hard as bones. In a way, the following lines from Yeats's later years finely sum up the reception of Beckett in Brazil:

> Those masterful images because complete
> Grew in pure mind but out of what began?
> A mound of refuse or the sweepings of a street,
> Old kettles, old bottles, and a broken can,
> Old iron, old bones, old rags, that raving slut
> Who keeps the till. Now that my ladder's gone
> I must lie down where all the ladders start
> In the foul rag and bone shop of the heart.
>
> (Yeats 1989: 347–8)

Notes

1 For a historical approach of Beckett's Brazilian reception, see Correa (2007) as well as Andrade (2014).
2 Indeed, a second production of Teixeira's *Fim de jogo* (*Endgame*) was staged in Rio's *Cassino da Urca*, in August 2016. Abandoned since 1946, when gambling was declared illegal in Brazil, the place was in ruins. After the end of the play's season, a complete renovation of the ancient building began.
3 On the Guimarães Brothers and the art of performance, see Gatti (2015).

Works cited

Andrade, F. de S. (2014), 'Facing Other Windows: Beckett in Brazil', in S. E. Gontarski (ed.), *The Edinburgh Companion to Samuel Beckett and the Arts*, 445–3, Edinburgh: Edinburgh University Press.
Cavalcanti, I. (2006), *Eu que não estou aí onde estou: o teatro de Samuel Beckett*, 7 Letras, Rio de Janeiro.
Correa, R. (2005), 'A recepção crítica de Esperando Godot no teatro brasileiro', *Revista Gestos (Irvine/California)*, 40: 113–12.
Correa, R. (2007), 'Finding Godot: Samuel Beckett, Fifty Years in the Brazilian Theatre', *Journal of Beckett Studies*, 15: 124–44.
Eleutheria (2013), [Play], Dir. Isabel Teixeira, Brazil: Teatro Laboratório Eca/Sala Alfredo Mesquita, São Paulo. Cast: Ana Paula Lopes Vieira, André de Almeida Santos, Arthur Hiroyki Abe et ali.

Fim de Jogo [*Endgame*] (2016), [Play], Dir. Isabel Teixeira, Brazil: Itaú Cultural, São Paulo. Cast: Renato Borghi, Élcio Nogueira Seixas.

Gatti (2015), 'Ocupação Sozinhos Juntos: Samuel Beckett segundo o Coletivo Irmãos Guimarães', *Questão de Crítica*, VII (65): 1–27.

Moi Lui: Projeto Beckett [*Molloy*] (2014), [Play], Dir. and adapting. Isabel Cavalcanti, Brazil, Sesc Pompeia, São Paulo. Cast: Ana Kfouri.

Morse, R. (1981), *O Espelho de Próspero: Cultura e Ideias na América*, Trans. Paulo Neves, São Paulo: Companhia das Letras, 1988 [*Prospero's Mirror: a Study in New World Dialectic*, Unknown Binding].

Ocupação Sozinhos Juntos [*Together Alone Occupation*] (2015), [Plays], Dir. Adriano e Fernando Guimarães, Brazil: Sesc Belenzinho, São Paulo. 1. Quadrado [*Quad I + II*] Cast: Edson Bezerra, Lavinia Bizotto, Leandro Menezes, Lina Frazão, Rafael Alves, Valéria Rocha; 2. Sopro (Passos + Atos sem Palavras I) [*Footfalls, Act Without Words I*] Cast: Liliane Rovaris e Yara de Cunto; 3. Fôlego (Ato sem palavras II + Improviso de Ohio) [*Act Without Words II, Ohio Impromptu*] Cast: Emanuel Aragão e Mateus Ferrari; 4. Performances (Nada se move + 59 minutos e 59 segundos + 99 a 1) [based on *Company, The Unnamable*] Cast: Yara de Cunto, Denise Stutz or Miwa Yamagizawa; Liliane Rovaris; Emanuel Aragão.

Oh Os Belos Dias [*Happy Days*] (2014), [Play], Dir. Rubens Rusche, Brazil: Sesc Santana, São Paulo. Cast: Sandra Dani, Luis Paulo Vasconcellos.

Tríptico Samuel Beckett [*Company, Ill Seen, Ill Said, Worstward Ho*] (2014), [Play], Dir. and adapting: Roberto Alvim, Brazil: Centro Cultural Banco do Brasil, São Paulo. Cast: Natália Timberg, Juliana Gualdino, Paula.

Yeats, W. B. (1989), *The Collected Poems of W. B. Yeats*, ed. Richard J. Finneran, New York: Palgrave Macmillan.

9

Samuel Beckett's *Fin de partie* in Hungary: A brief reception history

Anita Rákóczy

The first Hungarian *Waiting for Godot* (1953) (Thália Theatre, Budapest, 2 November 1965) opened up the way for studio theatre culture and absurd drama in Hungary. The number of *Godot* premieres has increased since 1989: according to the Productions Database of the Hungarian Theatre Museum and Institute, by 2015 there had been altogether twenty-two *Waiting for Godot* premieres. Hungarian-language productions of *Endgame* (1957) are significantly fewer in number, although *A játszma vége* or *Végjáték* (two translations for the titles *Fin de partie* and *Endgame*[1]) remains the second most frequently produced Beckett drama. It was directed for the first time by István Paál on 29 September 1979, at the Chamber Theatre of Szigligeti Színház, Szolnok. By 2016, it had been professionally staged altogether nine times. This chapter explores the first Hungarian-language TV and stage productions of *Endgame* (Gábor Zsámbéki in 1974; István Paál in 1979), through reviews, an available TV recording and newly conducted interviews, and it offers a brief insight into the preparations of its latest production: the Hungarian composer György Kurtág's *Fin de partie* opera (2018).

Special thanks to Bernard Adams for proofreading and to Márta Kurtág, György Kurtág and Gábor Zsámbéki for the interviews. All quotations are in the author's translation unless otherwise indicated.

Gábor Zsámbéki: *A játszma vége* (TV recording, 1974)

The Hungarian stage premiere was preceded by a nearly forgotten 1974 TV recording of *A játszma vége* (*Endgame*), directed under studio conditions by the young, upcoming theatre artist, Gábor Zsámbéki.[2] Currently one of the most acknowledged stage directors in Hungary, Zsámbéki, who graduated from the University of Theatre and Film Arts in 1968, was at the time at the beginning of his career.[3] The Database of the Hungarian Theatre Museum and Institute does not include it in Zsámbéki's directorial oeuvre, perhaps because this production of *Fin de partie* has no attachment to a particular theatre. It was produced as part nine of '... *And All the Men and Women Merely Players*', a ten-programme TV series on the history of theatre. The playwright, poet, dramaturge and university professor Miklós Gyárfás[4] was the writer, editor and host of the programme: he selected the plays and their directors. Part one of the series, '*Man enters stage*', began with scenes from Ancient Greek tragedies (Aeschylus's *Persians* and Sophocles's *Antigone*) (see Körmendi 1973: 28), while part nine, the 14 May 1974 broadcast of Samuel Beckett's *Fin de partie* was given the title *Man Exits Stage*.

The programme started with a brief introduction to the play by Gyárfás, whose thin figure appeared leaning against a large-sized metallic ashbin. Zsámbéki joined him shortly after at the other side of the bin, and they discussed the directorial challenges of approaching *Fin de partie* before the actual broadcast of the play began. In an interview conducted on 28 March 2018, Zsámbéki recalls Gyárfás's suggestion that they should emerge from two bins and conduct their introductory conversation from there: 'I didn't like the idea. And I admit that I didn't accept it, that is why we are not sitting in the bins. Also, I doubt that I would welcome this suggestion today. I think that it is Beckett's job to mean and disclose, and not those that are working on him' (Zsámbéki 2018). Zsámbéki remembers Gyárfás fondly up to this day. When asked about his choice to direct *Fin de partie* for television in 1974, he replied:

> I owe this to Miklós Gyárfás. He was my dramaturgy-professor at the university. [...] Gyárfás's personality is very memorable to me. He wasn't a good playwright, but he was an excellent teacher. As dramaturge, he introduced us to works that no one else showed us that time. I remember that he brought us and also translated to us plays by Ionesco that in those years weren't available in Hungarian at all. [...] I believe that he was a strongly favoured, popular literary figure of the 1950s, meaning that he wrote terribly bad 'production plays' too,[5] so he constantly seemed to

feel some kind of self-accusation and remorse. However, this made him even more likeable.

(Zsámbéki 2018)

From his 1957 review of contemporary French comedy, it is apparent that Gyárfás showed a great interest in Beckett's work from early days, even if the first Hungarian production of *Waiting for Godot* only took place as late as November 1965. A lengthy and heated literary debate in the *Nagyvilág* journal preceded the premiere: scholars, critics and historians of literature argued over the suspicious Westerner Samuel Beckett's play and oeuvre. It had to be decided whether *Godot* is a 'literary bluff', a 'rather weak and repulsive literary bungle' with failed dramaturgy and philosophy or a drama worth introducing to the Hungarian audience (Hegedűs 1965: 1715–19, cited in Rákóczy 2017a: 288). As Károly Kazimir, *Godot*'s co-director, explained to the audience and Socialist party officials, standing on the stage, delivering his apology for *Godot* on the opening night before the play began, we in 1965 considered the absurd, anti-dramatic theatre 'highly problematic' (Rákóczy 2017a: 289). Gyárfás realized Beckett's potential as a playwright in 1957 and found a key to make his work digestible to both Hungarian spectators and authorities: 'Samuel Beckett's recently produced comedy, *Fin de partie*, depicts how the last four surviving people on earth torture each other to death. The staging of Studio des Champs-Elysées has caused a great stir. It is only natural – humanity is living in such an age that nervous journalists and calm scientists equally talk about that certain final catastrophe' (Gyárfás 1957: 4).

In the conversation prior to *Fin de partie*, Gyárfás wonders whether a play can be dramatic at all without action or any kind of progress. Gábor Zsámbéki argues that *Fin de partie* is highly dramatic, although Beckett provides very limited possibility for the actors and director to create anything spectacular in the staging.

Its four characters are in a post-apocalyptic state. We don't exactly know what kind the catastrophe is, we principally think of a nuclear catastrophe. And, in a closed space, they are waiting for the end to come, for total annihilation. This situation is very dramatic. And the response to be given to this, whether to hasten the decay or to resist is the most exciting question for us now.

(Zsámbéki 974)

At this point in the discussion, a brief, scarcely discernible smile appears on both faces, and a quick exchange of glances acknowledging the mutual awareness of double-talk.

In terms of the set, Zsámbéki's direction follows Beckett's instructions: a grey, bare interior, tattered walls of some indefinable material, two small windows, two ashbins touching each other. One alteration is that Zsámbéki introduces the meta-theatrical device of opera glasses instead of Clov's telescope, which adds an extra pun to the scene in which he examines the audience from the top of the ladder. László Inke's Hamm is lost in the enormous armchair in the centre of the stage, with a rather large head compared to his arms and body. These proportions are repeated in Hamm's dog: a hairy, black stuffed toy animal with a colossal head. Istvá Iglódi's Clov in this production is a young and extremely mobile, flexible character with rapid movements, without much physical discomfort. His mood changes repeatedly, often without good cause: from a simple-minded, half-witted, helpless and enervated fool, he turns to an aggressive rebel and back in no time and without consequence. Zsámbéki chose Iglódi for the role of Clov because they had been fellow students at university, and Zsámbéki considered him a brilliant actor and a great talent. Inke's robust figure as Hamm reflects the director's decision to emphasize the tension between the two characters and their situations.

Looking back at his 1974 production in 2018, Zsámbéki reveals that he had considered the relationship between Hamm and Clov of great importance and that it could also be detected in the casting:

> A master-slave relationship that we can essentially find in the case of Pozzo and Lucky as well. And of course this was expressed physically too between the vigorous Hamm and the rather thin and tiny Iglódi.
>
> (Zsámbéki 2018)

Although Clov's rapid mood changes are not always justified, the characters of Nagg (Sándor Kőmíves) and Nell (Margit Andaházy) are undoubtedly merits of the production. Zsámbéki treats them with such sensitivity that the rhythm of the entire play changes whenever they appear from or disappear into their bins. Nell's recollection of Lake Como and its clean, white water is a slow close-up, which returns when she recalls her memories again. Simple, not over-lyricized, it is perhaps the subtlest moment of Zsámbéki's direction.

Writer and theatre critic András Pályi raises the question whether Beckett's *Fin de partie*, 'which is about the final and complete collapse of the world, the total senselessness and hopelessness of life, absolutizing the fall of capitalism, [...] is really the kind of work that Hungarian television should produce?' (1974: 6). This dilemma must have given the programme-makers a lot of thought; as opposed to all other parts of this series that were broadcast during prime time on weekday evenings, Beckett's play was shown at a considerably later hour. As Zsámbéki recalls, artists and directors encountered these inept and infantile variations of censorship often, if a particular production was not banned, some kind of restriction was introduced. For example, at times a play was allowed to be performed locally, but it could not leave town or go on tour; at others some parts of the text had to be cut, or the show had to start later than the usual 7.00 pm starting time (Zsámbéki 2018). It was also a routine censorship technique to reduce the allowed number of the audience by either assigning the production to a studio or narrowing down the auditorium to a smaller size. In his review, Pályi argues that Zsámbéki's sensitive approach to *Fin de partie* succeeded in bringing the drama closer to the Hungarian audience, thus giving a new standard and meaning to the public demand for entertainment. It is definitely one of the greatest merits of the production that Zsámbéki, in the beginning of his career as a director, courageously introduced Beckett's *Fin de partie* to the Hungarian public.

Although Pályi declares that 'no violence has been exercised on the play' under Zsámbéki's direction (1974: 6), the TV recording reveals that several textual modifications, mainly retrenchments, had been made to *Fin de partie*. Not only were the mention of Mother Pegg and its resonances absent, but the heart of the drama was fully cut from the production: Hamm's complete storytelling scene, the prayer and Nagg's fatherly curse. Omitting these key scenes was a dramaturgical flaw for Hamm and Clov's relationship loses its dynamics and several layers of interpretation as a consequence even if Pályi states that it was because Zsámbéki decided to focus 'on the dramatic power relation between the two main characters' (1974: 6). Unfortunately, Zsámbéki does not recall whether it was his own cut or whether Gyárfás had given him an already retrenched copy, which had been subject to his dramaturgical simplifications. The cuts are precisely and systematically exercised so that all references to Hamm's story, hints to any kind of past wrongdoings, are deleted, as are almost all mentions of the painkiller. The story scene, being a time-demanding monologue, is removed in its entirety. Such brutal omission can only occur due to censorship, which Zsámbéki (2018) denies with the remark 'one remembers every restriction', or to fit the tight airtime of the series. The latter is not unlikely, as parts of the programme varied in length between fifty and eighty-five minutes, including a general series animation and a ten-minute opening discussion before each broadcast.

Zsámbéki argues in 1974 that Beckett's plays contain circus elements too, and his characters are clowns to some extent in their dialogues and movements. In his opinion, it is of great importance that the directions of Beckett's plays reveal this flavour of clownery and not only the gloom, as 'laughter connects the audience with the one they laugh at' (Zsámbéki and Gyárfás 1974). However, Gyárfás adds:

> Actually, the clown's situation is also completely hopeless and comfortless. Since the clown whose head is constantly being hit by another clown is in an equally desperate condition. The child laughs at this. The adult

spectator is filled with distress, and the more he knows about life the more anxious he is because of the blows and the clown's hopeless state.

(Zsámbéki and Gyárfás 1974)

István Paál: *A játszma vége* (Chamber Theatre of Szigligeti Theatre, Szolnok, 1979)

The stage premiere of *A játszma vége*, directed by István Paál, took place on 29 September 1979, over twelve years after the French-language premiere of *Fin de partie* in the Royal Court Theatre. Interestingly, the first Beckett-stagings in Hungary have often signalled the opening of new, experimental theatre spaces. Just as the first *Waiting for Godot* was the opening show of Thália Studio, and thus the first studio theatre production in the country, the studio space called the 'chamber theatre' of Szigligeti Theatre in Szolnok was launched by Paál's *A játszma vége*. The studio production is relatively well documented by photographs and theatre reviews, which indicate that Paál's revolutionary direction was a groundbreaking theatrical achievement of the time. As László Bérczes[6] argues, '[R]isk taking is not a strong point of our theatres. By their go-slow policy they provide long periods of grace for new theatre phenomena, authors or plays. It is indeed this time that István Paál intends to shorten with his directions' (1979: 7).

Instead of a detailed description of the staging, the reviews pay a great deal of attention to Beckett's ambiguous reception in Hungary. In 1966, László Kéry closed the polemic of the *Nagyvilág* debate with a 'symptomatic' question mark in his essay *The Drama of Motionlessness* (Szekrényesy 1979: 25). The *Epilogue to the Godot-Debate* announced, '[T]his [*Waiting for Godot*] is not the only work in the bourgeois literature of the last half-century that raises the hard question: how can a work of art be relevant and in certain aspects valuable if its ideology is highly problematic or downright unacceptable?' (László 1966, cited in Szekrényesy 1979: 26). By the time of the 1979 premiere, Beckett's 'Hungarian trial' was over; critics and audiences had come to the understanding that 'Beckett does not need our contribution to his glory but perhaps the other way round' (Szekrényesy 1979: 25). The reviews indicate that the first staging of *Fin de partie* in Hungary might have signalled some kind of a watershed in our approach to Beckett and the pleasure we take from his dramatic works.

In the absence of a video recording, little is known about the actual production; its rhythm, atmosphere and subtleties can only be partially reconstructed if at all. The reviews focus mainly on Beckett's world view and its defence, balanced out with the 'obligatory' gesture of emphasizing the Hungarian 'ideological and political superiority and power' over the

Western, decadent welfare states (Bérczes 1979: 7). However, there are a number of recurring observations in the critical writing about Paál's direction that provide us with an impression of this peculiar theatre event.

Most reviewers agree that 'the production sticks firmly to the author's stage directions' (Szekrényesy 26) and that 'Paál follows Beckett's instructions to the letter without becoming calculated and pedantic' (Koltai 1979: 7). It is also apparent that the cast did a brilliant job in providing the spectator with a thrilling theatrical experience. László Huszár's Hamm built up his character from two main components: the self-confidence of omniscience and the despair of defencelessness. Hamm, as Bérczes recalls, 'lifts the gaff like a victorious commander, he holds it out with dignity as a monarch would hold a sceptre, then he attempts to push himself farther in a mad rage, like a child trying to run away from darkness' (1979: 7). István Jeney's Clov was also a complex case study and made special use of his eyes when forming all shades of his character: at times his eyes reflected the irony of wisdom, while in other moments he seemed innocent, almost naive, a simple-minded fool or a deranged lunatic. Through pointless, mechanical obedience, his main drive was to escape the question: 'What is happening, what is coming' (Bérczes 1979)?

Indeed, this question leads to another common feature of the reviews, namely the discussion of post–Second World War traumas – nuclear warfare, the cold war and the armaments race – that critics instantly linked to the play. As Júlia Szekrényesy puts it, '[W]e have been living in an almost sexual intimacy with the forces that threaten our existence' (1979: 25). Although the average Hungarian spectator of the 1970s could naturally relate these frightening events with *Fin de partie*, as we saw in Gyárfás's 1957 review, these topics also became a common and accepted means of making Beckett acceptable, not only to the audience but primarily to the Hungarian political authorities. It was a graspable and universal message that, in spite of our unquestionable political superiority, Hungarians could not feel 'entirely safe, because a possible conflict would not only result in the destruction of certain people, but of the whole of mankind' (Bérczes 1979: 7).

Two more points are crucial with regard to the reception of Paál's *A játszma vége*: the humour of the production and its finale. Several reviews address its problematic humour, noting that neither the audience nor the critics themselves reacted to the jokes and humour in the play in a light-hearted way. As Bérczes declares, 'Paál does not kill the frightening humour in the play, but he takes away the liberating joy of joking around and making the audience accomplices. Our fear is not eased but increased by laughter' (Bérczes 1979: 7). István Váncsa admits that although the performance is full of humour, 'it lacks all relieving effects; it is not jolly but overwhelming' (1979: 15107). Due to this special effect of Beckett's comedy, Hungarian audiences traditionally rarely laugh during a Beckett production. After the first production of *Waiting for Godot* (1965) up until 1989, a Beckett premiere was more about rebellion against the regime through the language of art, a silent and solemn event rather than fun and laughter.

In Paál's production, after Hamm covers his face with his bloodstained handkerchief, he remains motionless, sitting in his chair, with Clov near him wearing his hat, an umbrella on his arm, standing still. Dead silence. Only Hamm's breathing was audible in that small studio space. As Váncsa records:

> [S]ilence grows longer and longer, then the audience slowly sneaks out of the room. [...] There is no applause, absolutely no expression of approval breaks out. What is more, as I observed, the spectators sidling out of the auditorium did not begin to discuss in between themselves what they had seen. [...] [A]s far as the audience's (relative) perplexity is concerned, this again goes without saying; I must admit that if then and there in the foyer I had had to say something, even a single valid sentence about the production, I would have not been able to utter more than a 'Well ...'. And I am not even ashamed about it.
>
> (1979: 15107)

It is every director's dream to stage a play after which no applause follows. However, as this reflex of approval is deeply rooted in Hungarian theatre culture, it requires a combination of factors to discourage the audience from clapping their hands, and even the most elaborate advanced directorial planning might fail on the spot. After István Paál's production of *A játszma vége*, there was no applause, no curtain call. The tension between the two main characters had perhaps contributed to this result, as had also the intimacy of the space, as people 'breathed together in physical proximity' with the actors. Paál's direction deliberately made it difficult for the spectator to distance oneself from the production. In the first place, the audience had to reach the studio up the stairs with footprints on them, go through a door, then be led along a narrow, dark corridor, passing a coat-rack with a hat, an umbrella and a travel bag almost falling over a dog-like clump of fur before reaching the stage through another door and stepping into the play itself. And, as Bérczes recalls, 'there's no way back' (1979: 7).

Preparations for György Kurtág's *Fin de partie* opera (Teatro alla Scala, Milano, 2018)

Following the Hungarian-language staging of *Fin de partie* that opened at the National Theatre, Târgu-Mureș, under the direction of Gábor Tompa on 13 May 2016, the latest production of the play has been György Kurtág's *Fin de partie* opera. Although the opera is composed in the original French language, it has a strong Hungarian relevance, given that Kurtág is Hungarian and a great part of the creation process took place in Budapest. Initially commissioned by the Salzburg Opera Festival, he began the great project in 2010. In May 2016, the opera was still in an advanced work-in-progress phase, with the premiere expected to be in November 2018 in Teatro alla Scala. Similar to Beckett's working method, writing and rewriting, composition, decomposition and re-composition are fundamental characteristics of Kurtág's creative process. Showing great interest in the genesis of *Fin de partie*, with the permission and help of the Beckett International Foundation and the Estate of Samuel Beckett, Kurtág studied the *Fin de partie* manuscripts that are located in the Samuel Beckett Collection of the University of Reading. These became invaluable sources of inspiration for him; their direct and indirect effects on the opera, as well as Kurtág's several discarded variations and reworkings of *Fin de partie*, are likely to provide a subject of research for generations of musicologists to come.

In his opera, Kurtág focuses on the character of Nell. The first production of the play he ever saw was in Paris in the autumn of 1957:[7] together with Robert Klein, he attended Roger Blin's *Fin de partie* (Varga 2009: 93). As he recalls:

> I comprehended very little when I was there in the auditorium. I understood the play later when I bought it, and started reading it together with *Godot* in a serious way, several times. So I strongly remember Hamm's Veronica-veil, with the blood-stains and all. It was a very dirty handkerchief.
>
> (Kurtág 2016)

So strong was the impression left in Kurtág's memory by the red colour that appeared on both the cloth and on the actors' faces in Blin's direction that he decided to use the colour in his opera even though at a later stage Beckett consistently eliminated red from his *Fin de partie* productions. However, what Kurtág remembers most is the character of Nell, 'that is why she has become a major character in the opera' (Kurtág 2016).

Kurtág explains that the piece opens 'in total darkness. Then, perhaps in front of the curtain (if there is one) or in the dark (if there is no curtain) only Nell's head is visible. There is a spotlight on Nell's head – the rest is in darkness. Then gradually, "*on all that strand//at end of day*" (Beckett 2012: 205), the spotlight slowly blacks out again' (Kurtág 2014). Beckett's *Roundelay* is heard while the light accentuates Nell's head; there is a prelude and a music following the prologue, at the end of which, suddenly, from four different directions in space, a police whistle blows loudly. As Kurtág points out:

It is a significant element. It is beautiful, how Beckett, through these elements, approaches the subject; the drum [in some preliminary manuscript versions of *Fin de partie*] is so much less aggressive. This ear-splitting whistle takes place, and then, abruptly, blinding light; the whistling lasts for a long time, then, gradually, the Beckett-prescribed grey light sets in. This semi-darkness remains throughout the opera. This is my first addition.

(2014)

Kurtág further discloses that his opera would consist of four major sections. The first part spans from the mime to Clov and Hamm's first monologues. The second unit Kurtág calls the 'ashbin-scene', with Nagg and Nell in the centre, culminating in the latter's death. The third section is the 'novel', Hamm's magnum opus, which practically lasts until the end. The last scene constitutes of Hamm and Clov's final monologues (Kurtág 2016). In May 2016, Kurtág had just completed the Finale, but he felt dissatisfied with the result, for he intended to find the pivotal points, shorten, simplify – and start all over again.

Notes

1 This essay uses both titles *Fin de partie* and *Endgame* since the versions of the play carry significant differences. It was the French original that was translated into Hungarian, so in some cases it is adequate to stick to the original French title, especially in the case of Kurtág's opera, as it is in French and is entitled *Fin de partie*.
2 Gábor Zsámbéki, founder member of the Union of the Theatres of Europe, born in 1943, is an internationally acknowledged Hungarian stage director; he has been a leading director, artistic and managing director of Csiky Gergely Theatre (Kaposvár), National Theatre (Budapest) and Katona József Theatre (Budapest).
3 For a more detailed account of Gábor Zsámbéki's Samuel Beckett-related directorial oeuvre, see Rákóczy (2017b: 150–57).
4 Miklós Gyárfás (1915–92) was a popular playwright of the socialist regime; in his best years, he had as many as three to- four-stage premieres in a theatre season. His works were less frequently produced from the mid-80s. Although most of his plays are now forgotten, he is remembered and respected by students and artists as a dramaturg and professor.
5 Production plays in Hungary were schematic pieces fully imbued with the Communist ideology. They emerged from the late 1940s and flourished in the 1950s. Ideology was the main governing force behind dramatic action and character formation. An example of a production play would be Miklós Gyárfás's *Hatszáz új lakás* (*Six Hundred New Flats*) (1951).

6   László Bérczes, born in 1951, is a Hungarian literary historian, theatre critic, dramaturg and stage director. He has worked extensively at Bárka Theatre, Budapest and Csiky Gergely Theatre, Kaposvár.
7   György Kurtág spent a year in Paris from June 1957 to June 1958. His wife, Márta Kurtág accompanied him for a month and then returned to Hungary for their son, Gyuri. Despite an agreement that guaranteed her permission to return to Paris, the authorities did not allow her to leave Hungary again.

Works cited

Beckett, S. (2012), *The Collected Poems: A Critical Edition*, London: Faber and Faber.
Bérczes, L. (1979), 'A jászma vége', *Szolnok Megyei Néplap*, 14 October: 7.
Gyárfás, M. (1957), 'Egy szemtelen múzsa üdvözlése. Egy kis tájékoztató a mai francia komédiáról', *Népakarat*, 3: 4.
Hegedűs, G. (1965), 'Vita Beckett *Godot*-járól. *Godot*-t újraolvasva', *Nagyvilág*, November: 1715–1719.
Koltai, T. (1979), 'A játszma vége. Beckett-bemutató Szolnokon', *Népszabadság*, 27 October: 7.
Körmendi, J. (1973), 'A drámatörténet nagy színpada. Tíz plusz egy rendező', *Film Színház Muzsika*, 8 December: 28.
Kurtág, Gy. (2014), Interview conducted and recorded by Anita Rákóczy in St-André-de-Cubzac on 21 July.
Kurtág, Gy. (2016), Interview conducted by Anita Rákóczy, recorded by Judit Kurtág, Budapest, BMC, 22 May.
László, K. (1966), 'A mozdulatlanság drámája. Utószó a Godot-vitához [The Drama of Motionlessness. Epilogue to the Godot-debate]', in *Nagyvilág*, 1966 (2): 261–4.
Pályi, A. (1974), 'A honi néző igényeiről', *Magyar Hírlap*, 21 May, 7 (138): 6.
Rákóczy, A. (2017), 'Earth That Shakes, Earth That Covers: A Review of *Waiting for Godot* and *Happy Days*, Katona József Theatre, Budapest', *Journal of Beckett Studies*, 26 (1): 150–7.
Rákóczy, A. (2017), 'The *Godot*s That Arrived in Hungary. The First Budapest Productions before and after 1989', *Samuel Beckett Today / Aujourd'hui*, 29: 288.
Szekrényesy, J. (1979), 'Zárkombinációk? A játszma vége Szolnokon', *Színház* XII: 25.
Váncsa, I. (1979), 'A kép kimerevedik. Szolnok: A játszma vége', *Film, színház, muzsika*, 6 October: 15107.
Varga, B. A. (2009), *György Kurtág. Drei Gespräche mit Bálint András Varga und Ligeti-Hommagen*, Budapest: Holnap Kiadó.
Zsámbéki, G. (2018), Interview Conducted and Recorded by Anita Rákóczy, Budapest, 22 March.
Zsámbéki G., and M. Gyárfás (1974), Opening discussion preceding the broadcast of *Fin de partie*, in *... And All the Men and Women Merely Players*, TV series, 14 May.

10

Tracing Beckett in the avant-garde theatre of mainland China

Liu Aiying

'Avant-garde theatre' is a complicated term in mainland China. First, there is the problem of naming. In the decades after Beckett was made available in print, following the vein of Western avant-garde art, Chinese theatre demonstrated a great variety and multiple designations: Exploration Theatre and New Fashion Theatre in the 1980s, Experimental Theatre and Avant-garde Theatre in the 1990s, and Independent Theatre in the twenty-first century.[1] The term 'small theatre' is also used to cover the period from the 1980s to the present. Moreover, there is a lack of consensus about which theatrical work actually marked the birth of China's avant-garde. According to some critics, China's avant-garde theatre began with the Beijing People's Art Theatre production of *Absolute Signal* (1982),[2] with Gao Xingjian as playwright and Lin Zhaohua as director (see Zhang 2009: 36), while others argue that it began with Gao Xingjian's *Bus Stop* (1983), a one-act parody of *Waiting for Godot* (see Liu 2013: 142).

Despite the complexity of defining China's avant-garde theatre, various researches have shown that Chinese critical responses to the Theatre of

---

In the text as well as in the endnotes section, Chinese names are provided by following the Chinese convention of putting the last name before the first name. In the 'Works cited' section, the last name is followed by a comma.

the Absurd often feature Beckett as the leading absurdist playwright and *Waiting for Godot* as the most discussed and staged play (Lie and Ingham 2009: 129). In what ways has Beckett influenced the avant-garde theatre of mainland China? To what extent have the Chinese avant-garde artists adapted Beckett? So far as these question are concerned, S. E. Gontarski provides us with a cue in his preface to the twenty-two-volume Chinese translations of *The Complete Works of Samuel Beckett*: Beckett's work will continue to 'interact, germinate, and cross pollinate with the long and rich tradition of Chinese literature and performance' (2016: 21–2). Studying the major Beckettian performances of the past decades in mainland China proves Gontarski's perception of the dynamic interaction between Beckett and Chinese culture.

China's first Beckettian performance, *Bus Stop* (1983), directed by the Nobel Prize winner Gao Xingjian, was an attempt to adapt Beckett's *Waiting for Godot* in order to reflect the social reality of China, then at a stage of drastic social transformation. From 1977 to the high-culture fever of the 1980s, Chinese dramatists engaged themselves with two urgent tasks: reviving realist drama and adopting contemporary Western aesthetics. As Lin and Zhang point out, the sudden boom of publications, translations and criticisms of the Theatre of the Absurd 'almost invariably placed Beckett at the centre of this literary school' (2011: 416). Beckett secured his central position in China's literary scene mainly due to the fact that '[t]he subversive power in his works coincidentally resonated with the yearning of the intellectuals in China to throw off whatever shackles in their time' (Cao 2006). Thus in their endeavour to explore how to liberate themselves from the rigid dramatic conventions of the 1980s, China's avant-garde dramatists including Gao found Beckett's *Waiting for Godot* particularly relevant to China's post-cultural-revolution situation. According to critics such as Yang Rongli (1988), Luo Tian (Cao 2006) and M. Berne (2011), the striking likeness of the theme of waiting is an obvious connection between Beckett's *Waiting for Godot* and Gao's *Bus Stop*. Luo even identifies Beckett as a direct source of inspiration for Gao: '*Bus Stop*, which represents the avant-garde theatre in mainland China, was inspired by *Waiting for Godot*. This is a fact that no one can really deny' (Cao 2006).

Bus Stop, like Beckett's *Godot* (and as the title suggests), tells a story of an endless waiting at a bus stop in the suburbs where various characters wait to go to the city centre. Like Godot, who is both sure to come and certain to postpone his presence, the buses both give people hope and disappoint them for no reason. While Gao's characters quarrel over the importance of order for waiting in line, the buses come and go but do not stop. Like Vladimir and Estragon, Gao's characters have waited for a very long time and have seen the shifts of night and rain and snow – almost ten years according to Crabb (see 2006). One day, however, they suddenly come to realize that the bus stop is no longer in use. Nevertheless, the day-to-day waiting has evolved into a habit, routine or ritual so that Gao's characters go on waiting. Only one silent man is different: he leaves the bus stop and chooses to walk to the city centre. While the sense of disappointment and suffering accompanying a much-prolonged process of waiting does suggest the *Godot* motif, Gao's silent man is obviously different from Beckett's two tramps as well as from Gao's other characters who choose to wait aimlessly and endlessly at the bus stop. Gao's silent man has the will, strength and determination to change his repetitive and monotonous life, which is paralysing and perpetually hopeless. This particular detail transforms Gao's waiting into an optimistic one. This adaptation may seem strange, but it was a necessary alteration given that post-cultural-revolution society cherished emancipation, enterprise and hope.

Yet to adapt Beckett to properly accommodate this new social reality was a tricky issue. In an interview with his friend and poet Ma Shoupeng, Gao acknowledged Beckett as a source of influence on his work, although he denied this at a later date. No publications can ascertain the reason for this denial; yet perhaps the overwhelmingly negative responses to Gao's *Bus Stop* might serve as an explanation. The play was performed only six times to a limited audience in the rehearsal hall of Beijing People's Art Theatre. It was criticized for negating the socialist literary and artistic tradition (Shi 2013: 42), as well as for borrowing its aesthetics from Beckett's *Waiting for Godot* (Zhao).[3] As Zhao Yiheng expounds, although 'nearly everyone' in the 1980s was absorbing theories of contemporary Western art through translated works, they were also hesitant to acknowledge such apprenticeship while there were still people insisting on 'the socialist realism borrowed from the Soviet Union' (Zhao n.d.). Gao had to be strategic about how he engaged with Western absurdist drama and how his productions should be interpreted 'in the current political or aesthetical framework' (Shi 2013: 41).

Acculturation was a main concern in China's first full-length performance of *Waiting for Godot* (1986) premiered in Shanghai Changjiang Theatre with Chen Jialin of the Shanghai Theatre Academy as director. What is especially experimental about Chen's production is his effort to make Beckett's *Godot* develop certain Chinese artistic and cultural qualities. China has a long history of *Xiqu* art, the art of traditional opera, in which the Peking Opera is the most famous in the West. As Irving Lo points out, Chen's production shows 'affinity to the tradition of the Peking Opera' (1989: 237). Unlike Gao's *Bus Stop*, Chen's production of *Godot* is a demonstration of his cultural consciousness as well as of his innovative mind. As Chen Jialin explains in a 1987 review of his own production, he found it particularly exciting to employ *Xiqu* and achieve the traditional aesthetic goal of poetic conception. Keeping in mind the absurdist dimension of *Godot*, Lin decided to enrich the performance by means of the *Xiqu* style in which highly stylized gestures are used to create an effect similar to that of freehand brushwork in traditional Chinese painting. Since some of the students specialized in *Xiqu*, Chen made two particular requirements for their performance. According to Chen's first requirement, the students had to make proper use of their *Xiqu* training but not display the *Xiqu* conventions conspicuously in their performance. Chen's second requirement was that the actors employed a dancer's posture characteristic of Peking Opera. Thus, the students were asked to integrate *Xiqu* performance techniques in their performance of *Godot*, but without making rigid use of their *Xiqu* performance skills (Chen 1987: 70). With this *Godot*, Chen hoped to advance the Chinese 'understanding of the West and, at the same time, provide a new direction for our [Chinese] theatrical enterprise' (cited in Lie and Ingham 2009: 135). By 'new direction', Chen indeed had in his mind the acculturation of Beckett's *Godot*:

> Considering the fact that this was the first time for us to perform a dramatic work of the Theatre of the Absurd on the stage in our country, we of course had the obligation to introduce to the audience this particular school of drama. Therefore, we not only had to be faithful to the original work but also had to take into consideration the Chinese audience: we performed the play for them and should accordingly display some qualities characteristic of the performances in China.
>
> (Chen 1987: 71)

Chen's innovation, however, was not appreciated by those critics who cared about Beckett's strictness regarding the performance of his work. Walter Asmus, for instance, considered the employment of music and dance in the performance an almost blatant defiance of Beckett's authority.[4] Nevertheless, since the 1960s, Chinese literary and artistic circles have been inclined to a popularly known basic principle about how to deal with cultural legacies at large: 'Make the past serve the present and foreign things serve China.' It was thus not a big surprise when China's avant-garde dramatists adapted Beckett's work to reflect current social conditions or drama aesthetics in an era of tremendous changes.

Meng Jinghui's production of *Godot* (1991) also reflected this new social reality and aesthetics. Then a graduate student at Central Academy of Drama, this Beijing-based avant-garde stage director premiered his own *Waiting for Godot* in the small auditorium of the university. In this performance, a black piano and a white bicycle appear on the stage. Meng also has Beckett's emblematic tree hang upside down from the ceiling fan (see Liang 2006: 96–9). However, unlike the tree in Beckett's *Godot*, which has 'four or five leaves' (Beckett 1990: 53), the tree in Meng's production is apparently leafless and lifeless. Meng changes the characters, too. Beckett's two tramps are now two jobless young men, the messenger boy is replaced by twin sisters in nurse uniforms who speak and act uniformly, and a slim figure named 'That Man' who is supposed to be

Godot appears on the scene when the play is close to the end. Meng modifies Beckett's plot, too. For the first few moments the dry tree turns round and round to the accompaniment of Chinese folk music played on the bamboo flute. As Act Two opens, Vladimir, having performed his daily ritual with the boots, looks at the tree, and with his left hand touching the tip of a slender offshoot and his right hand holding an umbrella, begins to turn around feverishly under the tree, chanting a popular nursery rhyme. The nursery rhyme has various versions in different regions of China, but it generally tells the story of a family of ten children named Pockmark One to Pockmark Ten. After Pockmark One gets sick, the other Pockmarks begin to deal with this mishap in a way that is both admirable and amusing. In their division of labour, Pockmarks Two, Three and Four become the medic team and try to save Pockmark One's life with traditional Chinese medicine; Pockmarks Five and Six become carpenters and make a coffin for him; while Pockmarks Seven and Eight make funeral arrangements, dig a grave and bury Pockmark One. The nursery rhyme clearly recalls Vladimir's song about a hungry dog in Beckett's text. However, Meng also uses it to foreshadow the imminence of violence and death.

Towards the end of the play, Meng's Vladimir is angered by the postponements of Godot's arrival and takes out his anger by smashing two windows on the extreme right and extreme left of the stage. Shortly afterwards, That Man arrives and is strangled by the two men in a sudden fury. Nevertheless, Vladimir and Estragon talk about having to come back the next day to wait for Godot. Meng's production, therefore, conveys a sense of disillusionment reflecting, as Lie and Ingham argue, 'a pervasive dystopian mentality' (2009: 135). While Meng's changes are 'in the vein of Beckett', he also achieves an aesthetic of his own style: 'not superfluous, not spectacular; but cruel, poetic, humorous; demonstrative of violence – including the violence of language and the violence in the true sense of the word' (cited in Cao 2006). So far as the sociopolitical context is concerned, the rebellious and subversive tone of these adaptations constitutes a gesture of challenge against authority and mainstream artistic criteria.

Meng Jinghui continued to experiment with Beckett's work in the search for his own aesthetics. In his aborted work *Waiting for Godot* (2003), which was not staged owing to the SARS epidemic rampant in China, Meng deliberately replaced Beckett's bleak scene with that of one hundred actors performing fashionable postmodernist techniques, such as pastiche and carnivalesque. Furthermore, Meng turned to *Godot* again in his small-theatre comedy *Two Dogs' Views on Life* (2007). Premiered in Beijing's National Pioneer Theatre (originally Beijing Pioneer Theatre before 2005), one of the theatres affiliated to the National Theater Company of China, *Two Dogs' Views on Life* features two dogs named Laifu (meaning literally 'Lucky') and Wangcai (meaning literally 'Wealthy') who come from the country to a big city to pursue happiness. Laifu and Wangcai are two of a kind brothers suffering from the bitterness of life.

In the play, the two dogs refer to each other as 'younger brother' and 'older brother'. Interestingly, in Chinese an evident allusion to Beckett's 'younger brother' is pronounced as *didi*, while 'elder brother', *gege*. Laifu and Wangcai have shared memories of their life in the country and sing a popular children's song about the ducklings raised by the production team, which is a basic unit of cooperative production adopted in China's socialist agricultural economy from 1958–84. Meng's two dogs are seemingly naive, but they both hope for a better life. In the city, they experience a series of difficulties and failures in adapting to the new circumstances but encourage each other to face up to the challenges of life even when they have to consider returning to the country.

Two Dogs' Views on Life was an instant success and remains a box office hit in Meng Jinhui's repertoire. According to Meng himself, the play is another version of Beckett's *Waiting for Godot* (Liu 2013: 143). What Meng acknowledges is the affinity between the two works, with the latter being Meng's source of influence and inspiration. Yet in his exploration of a personal aesthetics, Meng not only draws from Beckett's *Godot*, but he also makes *Two Dogs' Views on Life* a brilliant pastiche of various discourses (social, political and academic), different styles of music and songs (from rock and roll to children's rhymes), different artistic genres (theatre and *Xiangsheng* – traditional comic dialogue) and diverse mass media productions (popularly received TV serials and films).

Compared with their Western counterparts, China's avant-garde dramatists seem to be less concerned with loyalty to Beckett's work than with finding original ways of localizing this work in the context of contemporary Chinese culture. Shi remarks: 'It was not clear if the Chinese artists knew about Beckett's objection against women playing *Waiting for Godot*' (2013: 89), but regardless, since the end of the 1990s China's avant-garde dramatists have demonstrated a great audacity, ardour and creativity by having women play Beckett's *Godot* in their productions. In one *Godot* performance (1998) premiered in the Beijing People's Art Theatre with Ren Ming as director, two women, Lu Fang and Wang Qianhua, act as Vladimir and Estragon respectively. Founded in 1952, this theatre is often recognized as one of strategic importance in terms of socialist values and conceptions of literature and art. In the same way that Beckett's *Waiting for Godot* became a representative work of Western absurdist drama, Ren's production was a groundbreaking event. Ren boldly adopts the perspective of the contemporary Chinese youth and adapts *Godot* to represent the new social phenomena that were changing the life style of many Chinese people. Ren's *Godot* takes place in a bar, symbolizing the newly emerging social life in the big cities of China in the 1990s. Of course, Vladimir and Estragon also change from male tramps in rags into slim and fair female bar customers. Pozzo visits the bar too; and Lucky, unfortunately, changes into a plastic model with a mutilated body. Ren's Vladimir and Estragon appear to be carefree, yet from time to time they complain about the boredom of life. They represent a new class of rebellious young women who are proud to show their femininity and take delight in feeling appreciated. Along with these changes, Ren also modifies *Godot*'s main motifs. In Beckett's work, the two tramps feel the boredom of life, yet they find it hard to free themselves from their habits and routines. In Ren's adaption, however, Vladimir and Estragon hate their drab life and simply want a change.

Critics such as Jiao Er regard Ren's adaptation a fiasco (1998: 12). To Jiao, the change of the setting from a country road to a metropolitan bar in contemporary China is already a faulty interpretation of Beckett (12), and Ren's modification of the plot leaves a deep dent on the original text:

> Estragon's trousers should fall about his knees [*sic*]. As soon as I entered the theatre, raised my head and saw the billboard, I was immediately aware that the most brilliant detail before the curtain would be spoiled. You can't ask a fashionably dressed beauty as Estragon to have her trousers suddenly fall like that! The problem lies in having a woman play Estragon!
>
> (1998: 13)

Ren may have misinterpreted certain details in Beckett's work, especially those leading to a metaphysical contemplation of human existence. However, like his contemporary avant-garde dramatists in mainland China, Ren is concerned with making the foreign serve a Chinese reality, and his adaptations do just that. His play captures the drastic social transformation China was undergoing, using the female body as a way to explore contemporary feminist issues.

Unlike Ren's *Godot*, Lin Zhaohua's *The Three Sisters Waiting for Godot* (1998), which premiered at the Capital Theatre, enjoyed a mixed reception. Some critics complimented him for his 'polyphonic structure blending Anton Chekhov's tradition with Beckett's subversion' (Cao 2006). As Lin argues, waiting is an eternal and universal theme, and thus 'it's waiting that brings the Russian sisters to meet the Parisian hobos in Beijing' (Qu 2008: 44). By juxtaposing Moscow (where the Russian sisters long to be) and Godot (whom Beckett's tramps are waiting for), Lin conveys 'his personal understanding of "waiting – hope"' (Qu 2007: 68). What matters most to Lin, however, is the act of waiting itself, not what the characters in the two works actually wait for:

> Noticeably, both Chekhov and Beckett find a tool, or excuse, to narrate waiting and express 'What we do' while waiting. In *The Three Sisters*, the excuse is Moscow, and in *Waiting for Godot*, Godot. Moscow is a real existence, the leading characters long for being there, but they end up in failure. From *The Three Sisters* we can perceive the spiritual emptiness

of the Russian intellectuals. There is elusiveness in Godot's existence, but the leading characters are ignorant about this and just wait for him to come. From *Waiting for Godot* we can sense the perplexity of the spiritual world of the modern man. Altogether, this is the real situation of our life.

(Qu 2008: 44)

Lin's play also calls into question a feminist issue. In his production, Lin keeps only the major characters of both plays. Actresses Chen Jin, Gong Lijun and Lin Cong act respectively as Chekhov's sisters Olga, Marsha and Irina. Actors Pu Cunxin and Chen Jianbin play roles in both works: with Pu acting as Vershinin and Vladimir and Chen acting as Tuzenbach and Estragon. Similar to the positioning of Mouth in *Not I*, another actor is situated on a framework above the stage and left of the audience. He performs several roles: doctor and Kulygin in *The Three Sisters*, the messenger boy and narrator in *Godot*, and a number of other minor roles. Capable of crossing borders, performing multiple roles and complicating the dramatic situation, Lin's male characters are obviously more dynamic than his female ones. Lin's stage design also consolidates the conception of male activity in contrast to female passivity. The sisters are confined to their home, which is set on a movable platform in the central area of the stage. Surrounded by a large square pool of water, the platform evokes the setting of a small island isolated from the rest of the stage that is strewn with trees, wires, stones and sand – the area where the male characters perform. The water is impassable to the female actors but not to the male ones. Consequently, the marginalization of the female characters is brought to attention:

> Such spatial arrangement placed the coarse conversations and bodily movements of the two tramps very close to the audience; while the noble ladies carried out sad and yet refined conversations, and moved slowly, if no barely, on the platform, keeping both physical and metaphorical distance from the audience.
>
> (Shi 2013: 65)

Lin's production was a challenge to the audience in the 1990s because his feminist patchwork seemed overtly avant-garde to be comprehensible. Yet the significance of portraying passive, constrained and isolated women in contrast to active men who are capable of border-crossing can hardly have been elusive. Commercially, this production was a fiasco: it forced Lin and his business partners to sell their private cars, which were rare personal property in the 1990s, in order to overcome their financial difficulties. After this catastrophe, Lin's *The Three Sisters Waiting for Godot* had to wait for almost twenty years to return to the stage in China's major cities. In more recent times, Lin's work has been well received. After all, with China's increasing globalization in the past two decades, profound economic, social, cultural and educational changes have taken place, and the popularity of Western literature and aesthetics has increased significantly.

While women are subordinate to men in Lin's production, they are the ones who are dominant in two other Beckettian productions well known among China's artistic circles. One is the all-female-cast *Waiting for Godot* (2001) produced by China's first privately owned troupe Hard Man Café Theatre, founded in 2000. As the billboard indicates, actresses Sun Baotong and Zhou Jingjing respectively act as Gogo and Didi. The billboard also shows changes in the names of the other characters: Wang Weiyan as Bozzo, Wang Jun as Lacky and Tang Ren as Nino. As the theatre group's name suggests, the multifunctional place, which epitomizes the new multifunctional structures that mushroomed in China before the new millennium, had a space of 600 square metres, divided into the central performing area, the bar, the auditorium and the VIP area. The rehearsals of *Godot* were made while the bar was open to customers. According to Shi Qingjing, the poster, with a portrait of Beckett, was covered by 'red lip prints all over'. It added 'two layers of meaning to the production: on the one hand it paid tribute to the master; while on the other, it posed a gesture both essentially feminine and markedly seductive in relation to the author and his canonic [sic] position' (2013: 102). While the performance is clearly a tribute to Beckett, the poster has a deeper significance. The point of having red lip-marks on Beckett's stern-looking face – his mouth, right eye and forehead – may suggest that the current adaptation interprets the various aspects of Beckett's *Godot* from the perspective of women, if not feminists. However, since pertinent literature on Hard Man's *Godot* is scarce, it is unclear how the artists changed or localized Beckett's *Godot* to achieve their artistic goals.

What is certain, nonetheless, is their motivation to use the female body to boost business. Co-directed by Zhang Xian and Li Rong, Hard Man's production clearly targeted female customers: its advertisements promised that for each performance there was a chance of winning a small fashionable beaded handbag sponsored by Guesswatchs. An avant-garde dramatist himself, Wang Jingguo, the founder of Hard Man Café Theatre, was thus well aware of the important role women played in his artistic experimentation and in his commercial enterprise. Ironically, however, the all-female-cast *Godot* was unable to save Hard Man Café Theatre, which went bankrupt and had to close two years later.

Another production with women playing the major characters of *Godot* premiered in 2015 at Tianjin Grand Theatre, directed by Feng Yuanzheng, China's famous actor and teacher at the Performance Institute of Beijing Film Academy. Xue Kaiwen and Yuan Wei were the co-directors, and Feng's students played the various characters. As with Hard Man's *Godot*, there is a scarcity of critical material regarding Feng's production so that the theatre group's motivations remain unclear. According to an interview published online, Feng was keenly aware of the crisis faced by Chinese theatre in the wave of pervasive commercialization. As Feng observes, '[T]he institutional reform of China's *Huaju* has pushed many theatrical companies to the market. Having lost opportunities of performing classics, China's *Huaju* is now in its most crucial period' (Zhang 2015).[5] So Feng's motive to help *Huaju* survive its desperate situation may be discernible through performances such as *Godot*, which was popularly well received.

Throughout the aforementioned productions with their various motivations, the central ideas of *Godot* have become a distinctly formative factor in Chinese theatre. In the new millennium, some performances bearing *Godot* in their titles drastically rewrite Beckett's work so that prominent themes like waiting and futility function more as a source of inspiration than the underlying pattern of the play. One such example is *Huaju Godot Comes* (2004), produced by the student drama society Finale at Shanghai International Studies University. According to the writer-director Li Ran, this production is 'rather a deconstruction than an adaptation' of Beckett's *Godot* (cited in Shi 2013: 72). *Godot Comes* opens with the familiar scene of Vladimir and Estragon waiting for Godot, but the performance is soon interrupted by the entry of a female tour guide who announces that Beckett's *Godot* is actually a programme of a theme park to attract tourists. Using meta-theatrical techniques, Li's production turns Beckett's *Godot* into a farce within a play in which the two actors amuse the audience of the theme park with their *Godot*, while also entertaining the actual spectators by ridiculing the characters and people from all walks of life. They also criticize various social phenomena, such as the aggravation of consumerism. Realizing that Godot's intrusion on stage may pose a threat to their business, the actors kill Godot. In the second act, a noble woman, who first claims to be Godot's all-knowing servant, finds out about their crime and threatens to disclose it. She later shows them her card that identifies her both as the CEO of authorized productions of Western absurdist drama in China and, surprisingly, also as Godot. After learning from her that there are numerous types of Godot, the two actors decide to murder her as well. Following the arrivals of the Godots, Samuel Beckett himself appears on the scene. Inspired by the two protagonists' complaints, Beckett decides to name his next oeuvre *Waiting for Godot*. Since Becket's *Godot* is thus treated as a gimmick to boost sales for the theme park, the motif of waiting becomes an old bottle into which new wine is poured, as director Li understands it (Li 2006).

The final production that this chapter considers, *Waiting for–Godot* (2014) directed by Luo Wei, also turns Beckett's trademark motif of waiting into a gimmick. As Luo says in an interview published online, his adaptation is not motivated by Beckett's trademarked act of waiting or by *Godot*; his motivation is 'humanity' because to the contemporary people 'waiting' is no longer an appropriate topic to evoke the sense of crisis (Zhi 2014). In Luo's localization, universalization and anachronism of Beckett there are some noteworthy changes. Luo uses the same technique as Salvador Dali's famous clock that does not refer to any particular time. His characters' names are purposefully chosen to refer to people from different time periods and social systems: for instance, Li Bai, China's ancient poet, and Barrack Obama, the ex-president of the United States of America. While Gogo dwells in a shopping cart, Pozzo is fascinated with the internationally famous brands of luxuries: his whip is manufactured by Prada and Lucky's basket by LV. In Act Two, the tree is replaced by a sculpture on which the Chinese characters 知识就是力量 ('Knowledge is power') appear instead of leaves. In addition to these changes, Luo embeds in his production some faddish elements in contemporary Chinese culture: new words and expressions, network parlance, square dance and the popular song 'Little Apple'. Luo's production was first performed for media personalities in China, but to his disappointment, most journalists in the audience were busy on their mobile phones instead of the performance. Luo regards their attitude as result of unfulfilled expectations of watching an authentic performance of *Godot*. He is thus aware of the importance of fidelity in performing Beckett, but his intention is to subvert the stereotypical understandings of Beckett's *Godot* (Zhi 2014).

As Shi Qingjing tersely sums up, Beckett's dramatic works have been performed 'by theaters at all levels from grass-root amateur groups to large professional theatre companies with governmental support, which secured the author's canonic [*sic*] position on Chinese stage' (2013: 18). The best-received of China's avant-garde productions that bear Beckett's influence, be it overt or subtle, are more than just products of an increasingly commercialized entertainment industry. They bear their own distinct features and characteristics of their time and of Socialist China, reflecting the confusion, perplexity and disillusionment among intellectuals and the general public during critical historical periods. They are, more often than not, the dramatists' serious contemplations about social issues, while also being interventions in the historical process of globalization. The localization and acculturation of these Beckettian performances in mainland China may also be understood as a creative means for Chinese avant-garde artists to interact with the Western canon and challenge its Eurocentric standards.

Notes

1   Each naming was intended to suggest some discontinuity or new direction as with the shift in aesthetics. There was a touch of irony associated with the term 'small theatre' because productions such as Gao Xingjian's *Absolute Signal*, *Bus Stop* and so on were staged by state-run companies often with large audiences. In this essay, 'avant-garde' is used as a relative concept to refer

2   The English titles of the Chinese Beckettian plays are translated according to the meanings of the originals.
3   The date of this online publication is not specified. Please refer to 'Zhao, Yiheng' in the 'Works cited' section.
4   Refer to 'The Irish Production of *Waiting for Godot* Is the Most Faithful to the Original' in the 'Works cited' section. The newspaper article was published anonymously.
5   Written as 话剧, *Huaju* is a common noun in the Chinese language that means modern drama or stage plays.

Works cited

Beckett, S. (1990), *The Complete Dramatic Works*, London: Faber and Faber limited.
Berne, M. (2011), 'Beckett en Chine à Paris: Résonance beckettienne chez Gao Xingjian', *Samuel Beckett Today / Aujourd'hui*, 23: 127–41.
Cao, Xueping (2006), 'Beckett's Centenary: Endgame or Waiting', 29 April. Available online: http://www.china.com.cn/chinese/MATERIAL/1197594.htm (accessed 10 July 2019).
Chen, Jialin (1987), 'Updating Conceptions of Drama, Widening the Domain of the Teaching of Directing: Summary of the Rehearsing and Teaching of the Famous Absurdist Play *Waiting for Godot*', *Theatre Arts*, 2: 66–71.
Crabb, Jerome P. (2006), 'Gao Xingjian', 12 October. Available online: http://www.theatrehistory.com/asian/gao_xingjian.html (accessed 10 June 2019).
Gao, Xingjian (1983), 'Bus Stop', *October*, 3: 119–38.
Gontarski, S. E. (2016), 'Introducing Samuel Beckett', trans. Liu Aiying, in Wu Jian (gen ed), *The Complete Works of Samuel Beckett*, Vol. 1, 9–22, Changsha: Hunan Literature and Art Publishing House.
'The Irish Production of *Waiting for Godot* Is the Most Faithful to the Original' (2004), *Beijing Youth Daily*, 13 May. Available online: http://yule.sohu.com/2004/05/13/41/article220114142.shtml (accessed 15 June 2019).
Jiao, Er (1998), 'Be Loyal, and Then Be Creative: A Criticism on the Small-Theatre *Huaju Waiting for Godot* and Discussion of the Problems in Theatrical Interpretation of Classic Works', *Chinese Theatre*, 1: 11–13.
Li, Ran (2006), 'Words of Li Ran, Playwright and Director of *Huaju Godot Comes*', 11 April. Available online: http://ent.sina.com.cn/x/2006-04-11/18041046299.html (accessed 25 May 2019).
Liang, Fei (2006), 'Meng Jinghui, Pioneer of Experimental Theatre in China', *Canadian Social Science*, 2 (3): 96–9.
Lie, Jianxi, and Mike Ingham (2009), 'The Reception of Samuel Beckett in China', in Mark Nixion and Matthew Feldman (eds.), *The International Reception of Samuel Beckett*, 129–46, New York: Continuum.

Lin, Lidan, and Zhang Helong (2011), 'The Chinese Response to Samuel Beckett (1906–89)', *Irish Studies Review*, 19 (4): 413–25.
Liu, Xiuyu (2013), 'China's Reception of Beckett's Drama', *Literature and Art Forum*, 7: 142–4.
Lo, Irving (1989), '*Waiting for Godot* in the People's Republic of China', *Journal of Beckett Studies*, 11 and 12: 237–9.
Qu, Peihui (2007), '"Waiting" in the Plays of Chekhov and Beckett', *Drama Literature*, 7: 65–8.
Qu, Peihui (2008), 'Lin Zhaohua's *The Three Sisters Waiting for Godot*', *Drama Literature*, 6: 43–5.
Shi, Qingjing (2013), 'Samuel Beckett on Chinese Stage (1964–2011): A Study of Intercultural Performances', PhD diss., School of Foreign Studies, Nanjing University, Nanjing.
Yang, Rongli (1988), '*Waiting for Godot* and *Bus Stop*', *Foreign Literature Studies*, 4: 116–21, 106.
Zhang, Daozheng (2015), 'Feng Yuanzheng: Now Was the Most Crucial Time for China's *Huaju*', 19 July. Available online: http://www.chinanews.com/cul/2015/07-19/7414300.shtml (accessed 16 May 2019).
Zhang, Xiaoping (2009), 'Themes of China's Avant-garde Theatre in the 1980s: In the Case of Gao Xingjian's Work', *Qilu Realm of Arts*, 6: 36–40.
Zhao, Yiheng (date unknown), '*Bus Stop*: Gao Xingjian's "Early Absurdist Drama"'. Available online: http://www.eywedu.org/gaoxingjian/29.htm (accessed 10 June 2019).
Zhi, Wen (2014), 'Luo Wei *Waiting for–Godot*': Ask Whatever Question, but Just Don't Mention Time', 23 December. Available online: https://news.damai.cn/drama/a/20141223/7701.shtml# (accessed 5 June 2019).

PART III

Circulation

11

What goes around comes around: *Godot*'s circularity and world literature

Juan Luis Toribio Vazquez

When *Waiting for Godot* premiered on the evening of 5 January 1953, few could have foreseen that this work would one day be recognized, not only as the most important play in English of the twentieth century (see Lister 1998: n.p.), but as a landmark of world literature.[1] Staged by Roger Blin at the Parisian Théâtre de Babylone, *Godot* sought (or so Martin Esslin claims) to challenge 'the accepted conventions of the theatre of [the] day', and though poorly received at first it soon became 'one of the greatest successes of the post-war theatre' (1968: 39). In an article published less than two decades after its first production, which discusses the play's extensive production history and Beckett's remarkable impact, Anne C. Murch writes that *Godot*'s 'resilience' had confirmed 'its universality', adding that its protagonists 'rapidly left the narrow precincts of art to become [...] part of the collective imagination of our time' (1984: 186–7). Many critics echoed this description, and it was not long before the play became widely acknowledged as a major work of world literature. The question thus becomes: what is it about the play that enables it to be described in this way? Enoch Brater argues that *Godot* 'owes its "wide applicability" to its universalist tendencies and its vagueness about local reference and context' (2003: 156), observations that have become commonplace when discussing the text. So when critics describe the play as a universal work it seems that they are not so much referring to its effective life outside of its culture of origin, as highlighting an alleged inherent potential for this process to unfold.

Although many scholars have emphasized that the term 'world literature' does not aim to refer to a specific canon of literary texts (see Damrosch 2003: 5, 281 or Lawall 2010: 4, etc.), classifying a work in this way inevitably alludes to the possibility of identifying such a canon and, beyond that, to the idea that there are a select number of works bearing a particular set of characteristics that allow them to be described in this way. In other words, when one characterizes a text as a work of world literature the implication seems to be that it has a number of intrinsic qualities that make it universally relevant. Hence, the label 'world literature' does not so much suggest a descriptive use of the term – indicating that a text has circulated beyond its national frontiers, since that would be merely highlighting the fact that literary texts circulate in an unequal system of distribution, from the core to the periphery[2] (see Moretti 2013; Sapiro 2016, etc.) – as that it has an intrinsic potential to be read and understood throughout the world. This is precisely what critics such as Murch and Brater appear to suggest: that *Godot*'s characters have not *become* a part of our collective imagination as a result of the play's extensive circulation and myriad adaptations, but that its heterogeneous production history and transmutability are the result of a prior recognition of its inherent universality; that the play has not gradually turned into a universal work, but was always latently so. Murch says that *Godot* has become a '*stereotype*' (1984: 188), but in branding it a landmark of world literature the implication seems to be that it was already intrinsically *stereotypable*.[3]

Such a claim may certainly be supported by an interpretation of the play in relation to some recent theories of world literature. Franco Moretti's analysis of 'hybrid forms',[4] for instance, may be applied to *Godot* in order to illustrate its status as a text that in some ways belongs at the same time to the periphery and to the core, both in Moretti's Eurocentric sense and in a more general (or idealistic) sense of core as an anti-geographical collective imaginary of literary archetypes. *Godot* belongs to the core as a Parisian text, but also to the periphery since it is a rejection of the core's conventions. Its 'story' (if we can call it that) – an oblique allusion to the monomyth if only because the protagonists appear to find themselves in the midst of a journey – and its themes may arise from the core but they are rendered in a peripheral way. By rejecting the central values of the European theatre of representation, *Godot* also rejects the Western tradition to which it belongs, severing its ties to its specific time and place and speaking in a new dramatic language that establishes the play as a special form of core hybrid. What is more, one could also argue, as Pascale Casanova does, that Beckett is a writer from peripheral Ireland coming to Paris (see 2004: 183). Be that as it may, aside from ostensibly deserving to be studied as a work of world literature given its peculiar bilingual composition and translation history, or because it has transcended national and even continental frontiers (being read, performed, taught and adapted throughout the world), if we consider the play in relation to a more recent system model of world literature such as Alexander Beecroft's we find that it could be described as being intrinsically 'cosmopolitan' since it resists reductive interpretations constricted to a specific ideological stance. Through a process of reduction, Beckett establishes the play's central components as universal signifiers that align his work to an 'ideology of universal rule' (Beecroft 2008: 91), given that it simultaneously accommodates an array of divergent (and often contradictory) readings.

So if *Waiting for Godot* truly conforms to a 'cosmopolitan literary language' (in Beecroft's sense) it is as a result of a process in which Beckett strips its constituent units of their functional (or teleological), cultural or contextual specifications. As Beckett himself writes in his 1931 essay on Proust:

> The only fertile research is excavatory, immersive, a contraction of the spirit, a descent. The artist is active, but negatively, shrinking from the nullity of extracircumferential phenomena, drawn into the core of the eddy.
>
> (1999: 64)

In *Godot*, the result of this excavatory process is a de-familiarizing (innovative or unconventional) rendering of the familiar (universal archetypes or concepts that are integral to the human experience, regardless of sociocultural, political or historical specificities). Stripped of context, action and purpose (*telos*), the play ostensibly becomes universally relatable by presenting life in essence.

Many scholars have recognized this feature of Beckett's writing. Nick Mount, for instance, claims that through his minimalist poetics Beckett, like Chaplin, was able to speak 'about as close to a universal language as it is possible to get [... a] language utterly and completely stripped of ornament' (2009: n.p.) – observations that beg the question of whether cultural specificities and contextual references are mere ornamentation in literary texts and, furthermore, of whether a culturally specific work can be a part of world literature. Beckett spoke through nebulous symbols, global signifiers of vast signifying capacities that, despite certain local references – or given the interchangeability of these (as shown by their diversity in Beckett's own translations) – become universally relatable. This process of reduction has therefore a twofold effect. First, Beckett presents his audience with an unconventional dramatic experience, which renders the familiar in an unfamiliar way, shocking a viewer baffled by the unconventionality of the experience. Second, he forces the spectator to become reacquainted with, and to make sense of, the world rendered alien through the de-familiarizing experience of his anti-play. The excavatory process of de-familiarization demands in turn an excavatory interpretative reading or re-familiarization. It is this twofold effect that is ostensibly responsible for the play's alleged cosmopolitanism, by awarding it with an openness that allows it to accommodate a range of different interpretations.

The most obvious place where we see Beckett's excavatory process unfold in *Godot* is in the removal of a central underlying action motivating the development of the plot. *Godot* is a play about waiting, and waiting is in its mundanity and antithetical nature to action an essentially anti-theatrical theme. This common social activity works greatly towards generating a tension between de-familiarization and familiarity, since it is an ordinary experience of everyday life yet rendered alien both by its anti-dramatic nature and by the unreliability of the protagonists, which encourages us to question whether there truly is a purpose to their waiting. In 'An Anti-Play', Eric Bentley argues that *Godot*'s dialogue is anti-dramatic because Beckett has 'put into a play what "cannot be put into a play"' (cited in Cohn 1987: 23), and the same could be said of the theme of waiting, since it is what bestows the dialogue with an anti-dramatic quality, by exempting it from its conventional dramatic function as the instigator of action. The absence of a central plot also makes the minor events that do take place arrive unjustifiably.[5] Laughter and sorrow emerge circumstantially rather than as a result of key developments in the story, allowing the audience to experience these emotions in isolation and for themselves rather than as the effect of an overarching causal relationship.

The setting becomes a non-space: a non-specific time and place, which acts as an embodiment of both nowhere and anywhere. The road, a universally recognizable symbol of life, change, development or progress is de-familiarized through its status as a path leading nowhere, since the characters fail to go anywhere, or return to it forever, thus undermining the conventional symbolism of this signifier. The same is true of the secondary elements that constitute the play's imagery. Herbert Blau says that 'tree, boot, bowler and black radish seem more human than the people in other plays' (2014: 94), and the reason for this may be that in their reductionist or essentialist rendering (and because of our inherent familiarity with these elements) our ability to accept them, and with them their accompanying semiotic fields, raises them to the status of open signifiers which can be read in different ways yet understood universally. Moreover, the other elements that occupy that space (the rock, moon and sky), which also bear vast symbolic loads – both culturally specific (the tree, for instance, has been identified as the tree of Buddha, of Norse mythology etc.) and universal (as a symbol of strength, vitality or growth) – similarly award the play with a hermeneutic openness through their scarce characterization: the tree is bare, small, weak, perhaps a willow but one that does not weep. Yet it remains, in essence, a tree.

The protagonists also undergo the same excavatory process so that, as Günther Anders observes, they stand as 'abstractions' that seem deprived of memory, identity or real existence (1965: 145). Nevertheless, even as abstractions they remain deeply *human*. Human in its purest essence: 'taken together, [they] portray universal man as he confronts the world we live in' (Cormier and Pallister 1976: 5). Didi and Gogo become universally recognizable by exemplifying human experience at its rawest. As abstractions, they become embodiments of the emotions that underlie their behaviours (love, sadness, friendship, hatred etc.). Their essentialist characterization thus results in a grotesque caricaturing of the experiences of social interaction, which make the protagonists not only human, but also widely relatable.

Yet of all the play's central components its circular narrative structure stands as the paradigmatic example of both a de-familiarizing element (since it is responsible for doing away with the plot) and a cosmopolitan literary feature. *Godot*'s circularity remains cross-culturally familiar as indicative of mythical or ancient time – the cycle of day, year and seasons inscribed in nature's movements (the planets, stars etc.). However, it is also eerie or de-familiarizing in that it stands at odds with linearity as the generally accepted structural model of modernity (and even of many pre-modern societies, as established by the Zoroastrian and Judaeo-Christian monotheistic traditions) as well as of contemporary capitalist societies. The play's circular form not only rejects Aristotelian and representational drama where linearity is inscribed, it also fosters the ambiguation of the play's other elements, such as the theme of waiting or the dialogue (interrelated by means of their reliance on the notions of progress and aim), by denying them their inherent coherence or significance. The rejection of linearity thus allows and encourages Beckett's reductive or excavatory process, since in rejecting a structural model founded on intention, direction and purpose, in clearing the stage from plot, Beckett allows the central elements of his play to stand for themselves, rather than in the service of an overarching aim or *telos*. By doing away with teleology, the value and significance of his drama becomes a perspectivist one in its openness or vast potential for signification. Although, as Graver argues, the cyclical plot encourages the reader to interpret the text in terms of 'something else' (2004: 20), instead of pointing to a single or succinct allegorical interpretation (as linear narratives usually do), the pervasive indeterminacy that is emphasized by the play's circular return points to nothing other than the text itself. Circularity redirects the text onto itself, and in doing so it opens the text by making it resistant to any single interpretation.

Godot's circularity has been discussed extensively by critics, and the play has been explained on account of its structure repeatedly.[6] Collin Duckworth, for instance, describes the action as 'circular and almost static', arguing that the plot is created through 'visual occurrences' that 'succeed one another with an underlying pattern of repetition' (cited in Beckett 1966: lxxxiv). Plot therefore is reduced to the creation of circularity so that it is not so much that the play has a circular plot, as that the plot is nothing but a circle.[7] The elements that make up this pseudo-plot are the same in both acts, precisely to conform its circular structure: one of the protagonists (Estragon in Act I and Vladimir in Act II) standing alone at the opening of the act; an initial reference to the boots; the entering of the other protagonist; the talk of Estragon being beaten during the night; the arrival of Pozzo and Lucky; the appearance of the boy; the sudden falling of night and rising of the moon; and the final comment, 'Let's go', countered by the stage direction '*They do not move*' (Beckett 1966: 85). Thus, as several commentators point out, the famous comment on *Godot* as a play where 'nothing happens, twice' works as an accurate description of its structure.

Additionally, and since the play's 'basic structural unit' is, as Graver maintains, 'a self-contained routine or ritual' (2004: 32), there are also secondary (or ritualistic) internal instances of circularity:

> Vladimir's repetitious pantomime, taking off his hat and knocking out an invisible foreign object; Estragon's repeated fussing with his boots; Lucky's recurrent acts of picking up and putting down the luggage; the hat-exchanging routine; Vladimir's endlessly repeatable round-song [... and] the repeated line 'On attend Godot'.
> (Graver 2004: 32)

To which we may add Didi and Gogo's circular exchanges:

> ESTRAGON: All the dead voices
> VLADIMIR: They make a noise like wings
> ESTRAGON: Like leaves
> VLADIMIR: Like sand
> ESTRAGON: Like leaves.
> (Beckett 1966: 150)

The redoubling replies that close the protagonists' enumerations – thrusting them into what Gordon calls 'the circular miasma of thought-frustration-rationalization' (1999: 63) – follow a circular movement similar to their psychological states which shift constantly from happiness to sorrow in a cyclical fashion, beautifully described by Pozzo at the sight of Gogo's sobbing: 'The tears of the world are a constant quantity. For each one who begins to weep, somewhere else another stops. The same is true of the laugh' (Beckett 1966: 100).

The play's circular structure undermines the little action that does take place, subverting its role as dramatic action and producing an unbearable stasis by eradicating progression and levelling down all action to an eternal moment of waiting. In so doing, the circular structure destroys the plot as plot (depiction of action), generating an anti-plot in which the dialogue is free (not subjected to plot) or anti-functional. The inescapabilty of the characters' situation is intensified by a deterioration (both psychological and physical), which is the only perceptible change between the two acts. Yet this deterioration does not imply an end, since the protagonists even fail to commit suicide. Rather, it intensifies the circular movement, emphasizing their immobility still further. What is more, this stasis results in a highlighting of the present moment, since the removal of progression and purpose revalorizes it as an eternal one. Their daily routine becomes infinite; time ceases to exit, as Pozzo laments after becoming blind. Moreover, this stasis also produces a revalorization of the play's anti-dramatic dialogue as poetry. The protagonists' exchanges acquire a different quality to that of conventional drama, as their thoughts are uttered rhythmically and without an apparent purpose or *telos*.

Speech becomes poetry as the characters' aphoristic interventions fail to lead anywhere, yet constantly allude to an evasive meaning whose expectations are never met. They suggest a concrete sense only to repeatedly undermine it, like a succession of questions accepting no single answer. Uncertainty underlies the very meaning of the utterances as they are spoken, of the references as they are set. The characters are always saying too little and thus saying too much. In this way, every statement becomes an attempt to fill the void with the lyricism of thought – to appreciate or impose beauty upon every single instant by constructing a meaning that collapses immediately within the moment that repeats itself eternally. The dialogue becomes a central aspect of the play not for its performative function, but for its aesthetic value. In drama, where almost all is dialogue, and almost all dialogue is plot, Beckett creates a dialogue that becomes poetic in its rejection of plot. Revalued in this process (through its multi-referentiality), its chief function becomes aesthetic (as opposed to teleological). As a result, the play produces a reversal of the traditional dramatic hierarchy, where the aesthetic is subordinated to plot and mostly expressed through form, setting, costume and gesture. If in conventional drama *what* happens is more important than *how* (content over form), in *Godot* this hierarchy is subverted: form becomes content (*how* becomes *what*).

While some critics have contested the circular nature of Godot's form,[8] its many reappraisals are a clear testament to its importance. Indeed, cyclical structures, images, actions and movements can be found throughout Beckett's oeuvre. In addition to *Godot*, texts such as *Act without Words II* (1956), *Endgame* (1957), *Play* (1963), *Not I* (1972) or *Quad* (1981) all seem to display what Steven Wilmer describes as 'a kind of purgatorial non-space of endless time where the characters are stuck repeating the same phrases and sequences [...] a circular rather than a linear time' (2008: 162). Particularly striking is the case of *Act without Words II*, where Beckett caricatures the monotonous routine of the daily life of two antithetical figures as an unending circular journey. To these we might add works such as *Film* (1965), *Breath* (1969), *Ohio Impromptu* (1981) and *What Where* (1983), where although circularity is not explicitly manifest it is strongly suggested, particularly in the form of meta-representations. Additionally, and like in *Waiting for Godot*, a number of Beckett's other plays (some of which do not have an overall circular structure) also contain secondary or internal ritualistic circular patterns. Duckworth highlights 'Clov's *jeu de scène*, going up and down the ladder [… or] the futility of repeated attempts to reach the water-carafe' in *Act without Words I* (1966: lxxxv), but there are also similar examples in *Krapp's Last Tape* (1958) and *Happy Days* (1961).

Moreover, in what Murch calls one of *Godot*'s most 'radical "tampering[s]"', an adaptation entitled *Ils allaient obscurs sous la nuit solitaire* (1979), while setting, scenography, characters and dialogue all suffered significant variations, '[t]he circular structure of Beckett's play was retained' and 'underlined in powerful visual terms in the finale' (1984: 189). This highlights the crucial significance of this device as one of the work's central components, safeguarded in such a bizarre and eclectic adaptation. Furthermore, among the play's 'sequels' or 'spin-offs' we also find circular texts. Matei Visniec's *Le dernier Godot* (1998), which depicts a conversation between Beckett and Godot himself, also has a circular structure in which the final scene echoes the first: 'it opens with Godot asking Beckett: "Ils t'ont frappé?" [Did they hit you?] and ends with Beckett saying, '"Demande-moi s'ils m'ont cassé la gueule" [Ask me if they beat me up]' (Lecossois 2008: 97).

What is more, in the work of many of those playwrights that Esslin identified as 'absurdist', some of whom have been described as Beckett's direct successors, one finds numerous instances of circularity. In Arrabal's *Fando y Lis* (1955), for instance, it is the stage that becomes a circle, as the homonymous protagonists exit through one end only to remerge from the other end repeatedly in a journey that is to remain dramatically without completion. The couple is unable to reach their desired destination, and, like in *Godot*, the only perceptible transformation they experience throughout the course of the drama is one of degradation. So even if in this case the plot itself is not truly a circular one, since the play ends with the death of one of the protagonists, their repeated entrances and exits from either end of the stage endow the drama with a pervasive sense of stasis and failure through their unrelenting circular movements. Similarly, in Harold Pinter's *A Slight Ache* (1961), the stasis experienced by the protagonists achieves its height when the circular nature of the plot is revealed and the roles of the characters are interchanged. And other circular 'absurdist' texts, to which we may rebate the label of absurdism but not that of circularity, include Arthur Adamov's *All against All* (1953) or Jean Genet's *The Blacks* (1959), to name but two.

As further evidence of circularity's potential as a cosmopolitan literary feature we find myriad reappraisals of *Godot*'s form in a number of later playwrights. Paula Vogel, for instance, has not only avowed Beckett's influence in her work but gone as far as to affirm that *Godot*'s anti-Aristotelian 'circular approach to narrative', which removes linearity's traditional focus 'on the conflict between male characters leading towards a dramatic conclusion', 'opened out theatre to women writers in the 1970s and 80s' (Wilmer 2008: 168). Steven Price identifies David Mamet as another American playwright manifestly influenced by *Godot*'s form in *Glengarry Glen Ross* (1984) (see Kane 2013: 13), and the Spanish playwright Maruxa Villalta's *Esta noche juntos, amandonos tanto* (1970) also appears to be strongly indebted to Beckett, at least structurally. Furthermore, the reappraisal of *Godot*'s circularity has reached as far as Latin America, where we find a number of further examples of circular plays by authors who also seem to be direct successors of Beckett. These include (but are not limited to) the Cubans Virgilio Piñera's *El flaco y el gordo* (1959) and *La niña querida* (1966), Antón Arrufat's *La repetición* (1963) and José Triana's *La noche de los asesinos* (1965); the Argentinian Jorge Diaz's *El cepillo de dientes* (1961); and the Nicaraguan Alberto Ycaza's *Asesinato Frustrado* (1968). These reverberations not only serve as evidence of *Godot*'s status as a work of world literature, they also indicate that structural circularity is a literary device that translates well through different time periods and cultures, possibly owing to its potential in allowing texts to be widely understood or appreciated by way of simultaneously accommodating an array of heterogeneous interpretations.

Nevertheless, and although much evidence has been provided in order to support the claim that *Godot* has several inherent qualities that make it universally relevant (with its circular narrative form being a decisive feature in this respect) it is vital to keep in mind that these observations, like the ones cited at the outset of this chapter (by Murch, Brater, Mount etc.), have been made by a Western scholar and about a Western text, and this fact alone should be reason enough to have some serious reservations about any arguments of this sort. If characterizing a text as a work of world literature is already controversial when the term is used denotatively and not in a purely descriptive fashion – that is, in order to indicate that a work has circulated, has been adapted and translated throughout the world (with the extremely problematic implications that such a description entails) – it is even more so when coming from a Western academic perspective, given the unevenness of the value and impact that certain universities and publishing houses have over others depending on the countries to which they belong. The issue at stake here is thus not only that with these kinds of arguments one is speaking in the name of the world, ostensibly under the assumption that there can be such a thing as a neutral understanding of what may be relevant in another country or culture (or even of what the world itself is – see, for instance, Pheng Cheah's *What Is a World?* (2016)), or that these kinds of arguments mask the unequal system of distribution in which literature circulates and partly legitimizes it by suggesting that texts transcend their national frontiers because of certain alleged intrinsic universal qualities. It is also that the weight of assertions and critical standpoints such as these is uneven depending on the country from which they come.

Any branding of a text as a work of world literature that does not refer to the unequal world system underlying the publication, translation and circulation of literary texts, and that fails to recognize and stress the problematic nature of this system, must be challenged and highlighted as an effort (albeit an inadvertent one) to perpetuate a core-periphery hierarchy – if only by concealing the pragmatic conditions that allow works to have an effective life outside of their culture of origin. What is more, given that the label 'world literature' inevitably implies the existence of certain attributes that make a text universally relevant, it also rests on the assumption that one has the authority to recognize this relevance, and this assumption is especially problematic when coming from the privileged position of a Western academic. Hence, beyond begging the all-too-familiar question of what the term 'world literature' actually denotes, these considerations should also encourage us to think about whether this mode of analysis or 'mode of reading' (Damrosch 2003: 5) is in fact universally desirable. Is it not possible that the study of literature as world literature is itself an inherently imperialist endeavour, a crystallization of the Western strive for world domination, a way of assimilating the works of peripheral literatures into a totalizing paradigm, or an offshoot of global capitalism?

Despite the apparent altruism that originally inspired the idea of *Weltliteratur*, we must not forget that the study of literature as world literature is from its inception a Western discipline so that there is no reason to think that the discipline itself should be of interest in every part of the world. While it may indeed seem that there is enough evidence to support claims such as the ones discussed above, one should keep in mind that there is no such thing as a neutral understanding of international relevance and that the attempt to recognize this potential is conceivably (and paradoxically) a very Western undertaking. Thus, perhaps to read and discuss Beckett as world literature is not so much to comment on the international relevance of his works as to keep these issues in mind and take them up for consideration when doing so; in the same way that to write about world literature is not to take a stance or to provide a definite answer to such questions, as to keep them alive and open.

Notes

1 Chris Ackerley, for instance, opens the Gale Researcher Guide for Samuel Beckett's *Waiting for Godot* by claiming that it is '[w]idely recognized as a

masterpiece of world literature' (2018: 1) and the play has been published as part of Cambridge University Press's Landmark of World Literature series.

2   And only in the opposite direction if they are in line with the tastes of the core (see Masao Miyoshi's *Off Center* (1991) or Lawrence Venuti's *The Scandals of Translation* (1998)).

3   This recalls Beckett's own observation that 'theatre is a spectacle; but not of a place. What goes on in it could go on as well, or as badly, anywhere else – not to mention what is said in it' (2011: 219). It is also similar to what Johnson says about Shakespeare in his Preface to Shakespeare's works.

4   Texts which arise in peripheral literatures containing 'form as struggle between the story that comes from the core and the viewpoint that "receives" it in the periphery' (Moretti 2013: 134).

5   This also results in an undermining of the traditional hierarchical structures implicit in the genres of comedy and tragedy, where the audience is granted a position of superior knowledge in relation to the characters about their impending fate. This subversion, which Mount argues was the reason for the outrage of Godot's first audiences, also paradoxically subjects the spectator to a forced process of familiarization with the protagonists and their environment, since one is obliged to approach them on a 'one to one' level.

6   It has been described as a play where 'plot is eliminated, and a timeless, circular quality emerges' (Kuiper 2011: 166); where 'Like Vladimir's endlessly repeating song at the beginning of Act II [...] much of the repetition [...] is circular [...]' (Taylor-Batty 2008: 29), or where 'in addition to the tension between language and meaning, [...] character and non-character' and 'space and non-space', there is one between time and timelessness so that [b]oth *Waiting for Godot* and *Endgame* play with timelessness in the sense of an infinite or unending time, with actions that endlessly repeat themselves, so that the ends of both plays are not only the end but also the beginning, and so time becomes circular and infinite rather than linear and limited (Wilmer 2008: 161).

7   This is achieved through the repetition of much of Act I in Act II, evincing that the choice of the two-act structure is not arbitrary since, as Duckworth observes, '[t]wo is the magic number denoting continuous repetition [...] in our everyday vocabulary (it went on and on, [...] round and round, [...] for ever and ever)' (1966: xci).

8   Steven Connor argues that there are two forms of repetition in the play: 'on the one hand [a] circular model [...] but on the other a linear [one], whereby some of the repetitions that we perceive [...] seem to indicate not endless reduplication but entropic decline' (1988: 121). Graver points out the divergence of the second act in 'texture, tone, and implication', stating that although Act II is a repetition, it is 'repetition with a difference', since 'within the circle there has been a precipitous decline' (2004: 54). Weller deems it 'an asymptote, with the point of tangency [...] occurring only at infinity' (Weller 2008: 129). Mehta claims that *Godot* (as well as 'all of Beckett's theatre') is not circular but helical, emphasizing that the second act is significantly different to the first, accelerated among other variances and that the repetitions are not exact (the first act being humorous and charming and the second grave and turbulent), proposing a descending spiral model (2010: 372).

Even Duckworth, who clearly identifies the structure of each act as 'circular', defines the overall structure of the play as following a 'gradual downward linear movement [...] towards disintegration' (1966: lxxxv).

Works cited

Ackerley, C. (2018), *Gale Researcher Guide for Samuel Beckett's Waiting for Godot*, Farmington Hills: Gale.

Anders, G. (1965), 'Being without Time: On Beckett's Play *Waiting for Godot*', in M. Esslin (ed.), *Samuel Beckett: A Collection of Critical Essays*, 140–51, Englewood Cliffs: Prentice-Hall.

Beckett, S. (1966), *En Attendant Godot*, ed. C. Duckworth, Paris: Éditions de Minuit.

Beckett, S. (1999), *Proust and Three Dialogues with Georges Duthuit*. London: John Calder Publishers.

Beecroft, A. (2008), 'World Literature without a Hyphen: Towards a Typology of Literary Systems', *New Left Review*, 54: 87–100.

Blau H. (2014), 'Notes from the Underground: *Waiting for Godot* and *Endgame*', in S. E. Gontarski (ed.), *On Beckett: Essays and Criticism*, 189–208, London: Anthem.

Brater, E. (2003), 'The Globalization of Beckett's *Godot*', *Comparative Drama*, 37 (2): 145–58.

Casanova, P. (2004), *The World Republic of Letters*, Cambridge: Harvard University Press.

Cohn, R. (1987), *Samuel Beckett: Waiting for Godot: A Casebook*, London: Macmillan Education Limited.

Connor, S. (1988), *Samuel Beckett: Repetition, Theory, and Text*, Aurora: Davies Group.

Cormier, R., and J. L. Pallister (1976), *'Waiting for Death': The Philosophical Significance of Beckett's 'En Attendant Godot'*, Tuscaloosa: University of Alabama Press.

Damrosch, D. (2003), *What Is World Literature?* Princeton: Princeton University Press.

Graver, L. (2004), *Beckett Waiting for Godot*, Cambridge: Cambridge University Press.

Kane, L. (2013), *David Mamet's Glengarry Glen Ross: Text and Performance*, London: Routledge.

Kuiper, K. (2011), *Poetry and Drama: Literary Terms and Concepts*, New York: Rosen Publishing.

Lawall, S. (2010), *Reading World Literature: Theory, History, Practice*, Austin: University of Texas Press.

Lecossois, H. (2008), 'Samuel Becket, Matéi Visniec: From One Godot to the Last', in P. E. Carvalho and R. C. Homem (eds.), *Plural Beckett Pluriel*, 93–104, Porto: Universidade do Porto.

Lister, D. (1998), '*Waiting for Godot* Voted Best Modern Play in English', *The Independent*, 18 October. Available online: https://www.independent.co.uk/

news/waiting-for-godot-voted-best-modern-play-in-english-1178953.html (accessed 30 September 2019).
Moretti, F. (2013), *Distant Reading*, New York: Verso Books.
Mount, N. (2009), *Big Ideas* [TV programme] TVO, 19 December. Available online: https://www.youtube.com/watch?v=1ddsl5nPfAc (accessed 25 September 2019).
Murch, A. C. (1984), 'Quoting from Godot: Trends in Contemporary French Theatre', *Journal of Beckett Studies*, 9: 113–29.
Sapiro, G. (2016), 'Authorship in Transnational Perspective: World Literature in the Making'. Available online: https://www.youtube.com/watch?v=-3UaLtiaprM (accessed 20 August 2019).
Taylor-Batty, M., and J. Taylor-Batty (2008), *Samuel Beckett's Waiting for Godot*, London: A&C Black.
Wilmer, S. E. (2008), 'Plural Meanings in Beckett', in P. E. Carvalho and R. C. Homem (eds.), *Plural Beckett Pluriel*, 55–72, Porto: Universidade do Porto.
Weller, S. (2008), *Literature, Philosophy, Nihilism: The Uncanniest of Guests*, Basingstoke: Palgrave Macmillan.

12

Unworlding world literature: Or how Godot travels from a country road to the world

Arka Chattopadhyay

This piece will trace Beckett's travel as world literature in two Indian works in Bengali (a play and a film) that are inspired by *Waiting for Godot*. I will discuss how these works introduce an effect of 'unworlding' into Beckett's dramatic 'world' by rendering it opaque and unstable, among other things. When playwright John Arden criticized Samuel Beckett for not writing plays about Algerian crisis, Beckett's American director, Alan Schneider said, all his plays were 'about Algeria' (Gussow 1996: 160). Is it not this unlocatable nature of Beckett's work that makes it open to intercultural translation? The difficulty of attributing a geopolitical name to the 'country road' of *Waiting for Godot* or the 'bare interior' of *Endgame* turns these places into a global everywhere. It will not be enough to say that this makes Beckett's works universal. Logically speaking, we are looking at a specific universal, attained through subtraction and not through inductive generalization. Beckett would subtract place names and cultural details until he exorcized all the 'demented particulars' (Beckett 1936: 12). Apart from his hybrid cultural identity as an Irish Protestant, migrating to Paris and straddling two languages as a bilingual writer, the cultural opacity of his oeuvre makes him an interesting case for world literature. Beckett's world is as Irish as it is French. This makes it no less Bengali or Indian, as we shall see. Deformations of 'world' as a culture-specific notion in Beckett's texts ironically add to their capacity for travelling across national and cultural frontiers.

For David Damrosch, the notion of 'circulation' stands at the centre of the framework of world literature: 'encompass[ing] all literary works that circulate beyond their culture of origin, either in translation or in their original language' (2003: 4). Damrosch theorizes this 'travel' of world literature between its 'source culture' and 'host culture' as a double refraction that works in both directions between the two or more cultures in question. He observes that the work as world literature lives between cultures, connected to both and yet not circumscribed by any one culture (2003: 283). This cultural interstitiality is key to world literature as a practice of reading that highlights difference between and within cultures and worlds:

> Reading and studying world literature [...] is inherently a more detached mode of engagement; it enters into a different kind of dialogue with the work, not one involving identification or mastery but the discipline of distance and of difference. We encounter the work not at the heart of its source culture but in the field of force generated among works that may come from very different cultures and eras.
>
> (2003: 300)

If we take world literature to be a differential reading practice, it seizes a text in its moment of passage between worlds where it opens its pathways to a multiplicity of cultures. It is not located in one world or culture at that moment but spreads its wings across many. Such readings destabilize cultural borders of different worlds and put pressure on any monolithic notion of the global. World literature is a theoretical construction that results from economic and cultural globalization, as J. Hillis Miller suggests (see 2016: 147). But this construction may also be used to interrogate any simplistic idea of cultural homogenization in one uniform global village. It places a marked stress on circulation that produces difference, rather than homogeneity. Ranjan Ghosh in his formulation of 'more than global' is aware of this gap between the local and the global:

> On the surface, the local and the global have their usual separateness and rupture; but, in what I argue is more than global, such ruptures often become a kind of provocation to question the promise and latency of a dialogue between the two. Diffractive refigurings produce the more than global phenomenon that acknowledges how globality becomes the 'enclosure in the undifferentiated sphere of a unitotality' and is suppressive, as Jean-Luc Nancy points out, of 'all world-forming of the world'.
>
> (2016: 113)

For Ghosh, this 'more than global' dimension resists the literary globalization, underlying world literature, through a radically immanent taking place of the text. The text as event ruptures the local and the global and effectuates what I would call 'unworlding'. Though I share the critical spirit behind Pheng Cheah's use of 'unworlding' to highlight temporality and counter the overemphasis on spatiality in the 'world' of world literature, I will not limit 'world' or 'unworlding' to space or time. For me, 'unworlding' exposes the shakiness behind any solid construction of 'worlding' through ideas, tropes, language and culture at large. Unworlding is thus a complex cultural experience in which one world does not translate into another and creates differences. When the local and the global aspects of a text are radically severed, its 'world' is split in its very substance. What Ghosh calls the 'intra-active transculturality' of a given text is similar to the culturally opaque character of Beckettian text. Beckett's text turns the 'trans' of 'transcultural' into an intra-textual possibility. In this way, *Godot* is an intrinsically 'transcultural' text in an 'intra-active' sense. Beckett's twice-born play is an obvious example of this 'intra-active transculturality' as it travels between French and English cultures in its split ontology. I will examine instances of *Godot*'s travel to India in Nabhendu Sen's 1968 Bengali play, *Nayan Kabirer Pala*, Supriya Kundu's 2012 play script, *Tepantor* and Ashish Avikunthak's 2015 film, *Kalkimanthankatha* (*The Churning of Kalki*). The innate cultural doubling of Beckett's play is further problematized when it becomes an inspiration for another play, *Nayan Kabirer Pala*, which is then fused with *Godot* to produce a third text, *Tepantor*. This triangulation, due to the addition of textual worlds, leads to a more complex and still more radical 'unworlding'. In *Kalkimanthankatha*, the film, Beckett's text is echoed but only to be diffracted by the presence of another text in the form of a book (Mao's *Little Red Book*), read out loud by the protagonists – another technique of 'unworlding'. We shall see how Beckett's *Godot*, in these three instances of cross-cultural travels, enacts a radical deformation of any solid notion of the world. The 'worlding' of *Godot* as world literature reveals this point of 'unworlding' where worlds come together only to fall asunder.

Tepantor fuses *Godot* with *Nayan Kabirer Pala* for good reasons. Sen's play is written in the wake of *Godot* and consistently echoes Beckett. Let me chart the transition from allusion to intertextuality in *Nayan Kabirer Pala*, focusing on the cultural intermeshing of multiple worlds in *Nayan Kabirer Pala* and *Tepantor*. In a culturally attentive Bengali translation of Beckett's text, *Tepantor*, Kundu creates an encounter between Vladimir and Estragon and Nabhendu Sen's clowns when they enter Beckett's world in place of Lucky and Pozzo. As we shall see, the *gap* between these two textual worlds is at the heart of the problematic of search and waiting in *Tepantor*. From this I will move into *Kalkimanthankatha* where we find Vladimir and Estragon, waiting for Vishnu's tenth and final avatar Kalki at the MahaKumbh in India.

As the unnameable country road becomes the holy spot of Hindu pilgrimage (i.e. MahaKumbh), the spatial mode of a text's cultural travel as world literature opens up. The intercultural religiosity of this re-localization is undercut by the contrapuntal use of Mao Zedong's *The Little Red Book* in the second half of the film where Vladimir and Estragon read out from the controversial political treatise to prepare for an enigmatic guerrilla warfare. Politicization of the religious setting opens up the history of ultra-Left movements in the form of 'people's war' in the Indian subcontinent and indicates another way *Godot* travels as world literature. The Maoist intertext is inherently transnational in the Indian context. It creates an alternative political reference frame for *Godot* by supplementing the muted context of the European world wars.

Nabhendu Sen's play uses the native, rural Indian theatrical form of 'pala'. 'Pala' as a non-urban form of folk theatre becomes the transcultural filter to situate the figure of the 'tramp' in Beckett's *country* road. We witness two clowns ('*bhanr*'), Nayan and Kabir, waiting for the van that would carry away props after a production. They pass the time by performing to themselves without a text. Waiting as a theme is flagged from the outset: 'There is excitement in this waiting. Nobody is around and it feels as if the entire stage has suddenly slipped into our clenched fingers' (Sen 2012: 21).[1] They feel that the era of Bengali stage clowns is eclipsed by heroism in theatre. They wait for their missing audience. They also declare that they would not perform anything 'serious', i.e. any specific performance of a preordained text, composed by an other – the author. The two are waiting for their own text. As clowns, they have fallen out of vogue. Dramatists have stopped writing roles for them. Bereft of any text, they 'play' with time alone, on an empty stage. The metaphorical thread connects time with stage space, if we relate the following with the previous citation: 'as if someone has thrown into our clenched fingers, a time as round as a ripe apple' (Sen 2012: 23). They have been thrown onto the stage. Time has been thrown into their clenched fingers, to play with. Both time and stage are ripe for their own autonomous performance without the authority of any external author figure. This absent author as well as authority figure is one incarnation of Godot in Sen's play.

Similarity between *Nayan Kabirer Pala* and *Godot* is obvious and themes of 'anti-story', lack of 'action', so-called irrationality, failed narration, absence of theatrical text and audience, cross-culturally travel into this text. Kabir calls his life nothing but 'anti-story'. Whenever Nayan gets into a descriptive mode, Kabir derides him and asks him to tell the story without description. As the two clowns try to make their own impromptu script, Nayan gets concerned about the overabundance of dialogue and lack of action in it. Kabir on the other hand demands more action. Even after framing a narrative that goes nowhere, Nayan regrets that '[t]here are no events in our lives. All that happens, happens in thoughts or dreams. We rearrange a story time and again and yet it doesn't end' (Sen 2012: 47).

In one of the failed storytelling acts, Nayan narrates:

The boy didn't get a job but the girl did and thus ran their family. The boy didn't get a job but their expenses increased and they had to borrow money. The boy didn't get a job but the debts increased; so they lost their dignity. The boy didn't become a father but the girl became a mother; so they repaid their debt. [...] They ate well with all the money and committed suicide by jumping into the lake.

(Sen 2012: 26)

This comically compressed storytelling in a circuitous style is similar to the recursive narrative dead ends of Didi and Gogo. We may recall Estragon's story about the Englishman in the brothel and Vladimir's story about the Evangelists and thieves. The principal narrative, fashioned by Nayan and Kabir, is also centred on failed rationality. It revolves around a mysterious man who suddenly turns up one day and declares himself to be the protagonist's father. Not only do they fashion this story but they also rehearse it on stage. If the paternal authority figure in this story is taken to be a Godot-like entity, his arrival is put under question by the protagonist as he does not recognize him. Just as Didi and Gogo's waiting leads to the arrival of Lucky and Pozzo, but not Godot, in Nayan's story, someone arrives but we cannot tell if he is the awaited figure.

Clowns apprehend directorial imposition and this absurd story is turned into sentimental melodrama when the protagonist kills the person claiming to be his father, in his sleep. The protagonist thinks that the imposter has a mission of making him mad. Murder becomes his way of protecting his sanity. This trope of madness speaks to the famous aphorism in *Godot*: 'We are all born mad. Some remain so' (Beckett 2003: 75). *Godot* does not develop the madness trope. It quietly nestles there, as a cultural assumption, tied to the tramp figure, as the tramp is often socially construed as a 'madman'. Sen's play builds on this motif and connects it integrally to the narrative, generated by the clowns. The obsession with 'sane' narrative-making underlines social judgement on madness as the failure of reason. Both *Godot* and *Nayan Kabirer Pala* mark this rationalist exceptionalism with irony.

A love letter breaks into Nayan and Kabir's narrative as a trace of the real when they realize how both have been pursuing the same girl. The protagonists stop their play-acting here to settle personal scores. As their dialogue proceeds, we come to understand that the woman they refer to is not an individual in flesh and blood but a romantic feminine ideal. Their words become poetry as prose turns to metrical verse. The gradual abstraction of the feminine figure climaxes in a sense of nothingness with metaphors of deception, auction and void. Nayan and Kabir conclude that 'today, tomorrow or the day after', their 'meeting with Mani or Ramala will certainly take place' just as 'today, tomorrow or the day after', their 'conflict with the playwrights will definitely come to an end' (Sen 2012: 48). *Nayan*

Kabirer Pala pushes the Godot figure towards a culturally mediated image of heterosexual love as Godot becomes a symbol of the beloved – an object of romantic desire. This romantic gendering of Godot as a feminine archetype is the most significant cultural shift in Sen's play. *Godot* hardly thematizes amorous love beyond Didi and Gogo's latent homoeroticism as a male pseudo-couple. Hence, this intercultural move towards romantic idealism produces a deformation of Beckett's world in Sen's play. From *Godot* to *Nayan Kabirer Pala*, cultural translation works as a way of 'unworlding' the 'world' of the source text.

Tepantor fuses *Godot* with *Nayan Kabirer Pala* and radicalizes this trajectory of cultural translation as 'unworlding' by introducing another world into the play text. 'Tepantor' is a Bengali word, oft-used in fairy tales and children's literature. It refers to a vast open field where strange encounters take place. The transformation from 'country road' to 'tepantor' is a cultural translation that preserves the unlocatable nature of the setting but renders it across cultures with intra-cultural sensibility. 'Tepantor' embodies an appropriative translation that attempts to find an analogue to the source world of Beckett's play *within* the Bengali host-cultural idiom. 'Tepantor' is not a specific place: though uninhabited, it is pregnant with the promise of magical sightings. This makes it a perfect setting for *Godot*. The play script is true to its title in transplanting stories like that of the Englishman in the brothel with archetypal Indian fairy tales about kings and flying horses. 'Mamu' – the name, replacing 'Godot' – removes the obvious association with 'God' but the derogatory colloquial synonym for 'uncle' maintains Beckett's vaudeville humour. 'Mamu' makes the mysteriously absent figure mundane and earthy. It suggests his susceptibility to being deceived by the tramps, Ela and Bhola.[2] This hints at a role reversal. Godot on whom Didi and Gogo's destiny depends is potentially made deceivable to them.

There is no Lucky or Pozzo in *Tepantor*. They are replaced by Sen's clowns who are renamed as Nimai (Nayan) and Kadir (Kabir). The referential point of contact between *Tepantor* and *Nayan Kabirer Pala* hinges on the shared theme of failed causality. Before Nimai and Kadir appear on the scene, Ela and Bhola echo the same maxims that Nayan and Kabir had evoked, while fashioning their impromptu narrative on problematic causal directions. These two maxims are 'In mother's house, the cow gave birth and in aunt's house, the bird died' and 'The goat entered the garden and the loose-wired wife was lost' (Sen 2012: 34). These maxims point to contingent convergence of events that have no causality. In both proverbial cases, temporal convergence leads to speculative implications of causality but there is no such relation. These examples of arbitrary events in a random world find their way from *Nayan Kabirer Pala* to *Tepantor*. Let us remember that *Tepantor* is not an adaptation of *Nayan Kabirer Pala*. It is an adaptation of *Godot* that combines Beckett with Sen. The aforementioned maxims are the intertextual bridges for *Tepantor* to invoke Sen's play. This echoes the trans-cultural passage of Beckett's global image as an absurdist. With Nimai and Kadir's entries, the situational similarity with Sen's play becomes clearer. They are searching for the boy who has left with the props in his van.

While in *Nayan Kabirer Pala*, the van driver who is supposed to carry away the props has not arrived, in *Tepantor* he seems to have lost his way with the props or is playing truant. A list of props and scenography like 'the garden of the selfish giant', 'Job Charnock's shoes' and 'Derozio's blackboard', as detailed by Nimai and Kadir, reinforces the folkloric trope. The intra-cultural but transnational nature of these references is noteworthy. To look at the three references in their order, Oscar Wilde's fable about the selfish giant is popular to the point of being appropriated into Indian folklore. Job Charnock was the British founder of the colonial capital of Calcutta. He is thus another famous transnational but intra-cultural name in India. Henry Vivian Derozio, the revolutionary teacher of what is now Presidency University in Kolkata, is another iconic figure in the context of the Indian struggle for freedom. All three references thus evoke a transnationalism, folded within the Indian intra-cultural rubric.

As substitutes of Lucky and Pozzo, Nimai and Kadir are attached to movement. This counterpoints Ela and Bhola's inclination for stasis. In *Godot*, Pozzo's first word, 'On' is representative of his commitment to movement. His famous speech on the abrupt and imperceptible fall of darkness at dusk bespeaks an anxiety regarding sudden acceleration of time. *Tepantor* crystallizes this dialectic of stasis and movement by juxtaposition. Bhola tells Kadir that they are waiting for someone and they cannot leave without meeting him. Kadir contrasts this with his answer that someone is waiting for them and without meeting him, they cannot stop. There is no explicit master-slave relation in *Tepantor* and no equivalent of Lucky's famous unpunctuated thinking. Nimai and Kadir reappear in the second act to announce that their van driver has lost his way. They emphasize that anyone who spots him should help him find them. They insist that without the missing props and scenography, their performance would be underwhelming.

The intersection between *Godot* and *Nayan Kabirer Pala* in *Tepantor* underscores the gap between the two dramatic worlds that come into mutual contact. On the one hand, when Nimai and Kadir enter the scene, the implication is that they enter from the world of another text. Their inability to find their van driver suggests this passage from one world to another. In other words, the protagonists are looking for him in the wrong world. On the other hand, we do not know if Ela and Bhola are also looking for their 'Mamu' in a world where he does not exist. Ela and Bhola do not travel into Sen's world, like Nimai and Kadir who come from *Nayan Kabirer Pala*. Nimai and Kadir, as trans-textual characters, have unwittingly changed worlds. They are now unable to finish their action in this markedly different world. This makes the intertextual dialogue disjunctive rather than synthetic. It shows a radical deformation of worlds as they come in touch with one another. In this layering of porous parallel worlds, if figures from one enter into another, it does not necessarily translate into a synthesis of worlds, unlike what the myth of globalization would have us believe. This trans-worldly passage, instead, highlights the fissure between the two worlds. 'Inter-worlding' reveals a point of 'unworlding' here. Nimai and Kadir are lost in a different textual world which has 'unworlded' their own. The insight into this disjunctive multiplicity of worlds suggests a re-reading of Beckett's play in turn. It opens up the possibility that there are multiple parallel worlds in *Godot*. Didi and Gogo are perhaps after someone who belongs in another world. Adaptive appropriations and intertextual echoes open up a complex string of encountering worlds. The way they encounter one another is a work of chance. It is this contingency that tilts the possibility of synthetic 'inter-worlding' towards a differential de-familiarization of 'unworlding'. Instead of a smooth and logical inter-world passage, we stare at an asymptotic encounter of worlds where one creates a sense of unfamiliar uncanniness for another.

This encounter of worlds assumes a patent intercultural dimension in Ashish Avikunthak's film, *Kalkimanthankatha*, when the culturally opaque country road of *Godot* is displaced onto MahaKumbh. This is the site of a Hindu religious festival that happens after every twelve years and Hindus make a pilgrimage to bathe in the sacred river. MahaKumbh happens after twelve Kumbh festivals, i.e. after a cycle of 144 years. This trans-human timescape extends the waiting act and gives the occasion an aura of singularity. The Didi- and Gogo-like figures declare that they have come to MahaKumbh in order to search for Kalki, Vishnu's tenth and final avatar who would come one day to mark a return to *Satya Yuga* (the age of truth) from the prevailing *Kali Yuga* (the age of demon). 'Kalki' means 'destroyer of filth'. This avatar is supposed to act as a saviour of humanity by purging their sins and reviving the reign of truth. Avikunthak gives a strong Hindu religious slant to *Godot* as it literally travels in a geopolitical sense to arrive at MahaKumbh. The shift from Godot to Kalki consolidates the divine symbolism, glimpsed in the signifier 'Godot' and developed with interpretive seductiveness, in the various theological references in Beckett's text.

The film's overt religious ambience is dialectically pressurized by a political subtext that slowly develops. Grainy images of pilgrims, walking in single file, in a dense fog, suggest refugee crisis. For Indian and Bengali viewers, these shots are reminiscent of numerous images of famished processions, during the 1947 partition of British India or the 1971 war that led to the birth of the independent nation of Bangladesh. A transnational viewer might understand these sequences in the contemporary context of the world crisis of refugees and the 'precariat'. These are cultural associations enabled by

Godot's travel into India. They inflect Franco Moretti's idea of 'distant reading' where one culture responds to a text from another culture through its own intra-cultural frames of reference. The film explicitly politicizes the religious setting when Kumbh becomes a virtual battleground. The two unnamed Didi- and Gogo-like figures prepare for a nameless guerrilla warfare by doing rigorous physical exercises and reading Mao Zedong's *The Little Red Book*. Details of this war are never disclosed. This contextlessness returns us to the Beckettian opacity we had started with.

Lack of context increases universal identifiability of the situation. Despite the absence of context, what the political subtext opens up is the history of the radical left, especially the Maoist 'people's war' and 'cultural revolution' movements in India and Bengal. For the regional viewers, Mao Zedong's name is inextricably attached to the 1960s and 1970s Naxalbari upsurge, an armed peasant movement that took place in West Bengal. The urban youth and students in Kolkata supported the movement. Chairman Mao became the transnational torchbearer of this protest with slogans like 'The chairman of China is our chairman'. The film plays provocatively with this local cultural memory without explicit references. The anonymous war motif remains an analogue to the similarly muted context of the world wars in *Godot*. This lack of referencing is not apolitical but ethico-political in a deep sense. Vladimir and Estragon's aforementioned stasis undercuts Lucky's obsessive march of imperial mastery. If the imperialist myth of war emphasizes triumphalist action, Didi and Gogo's stagnation has an ethico-political note of critical passivity. This ethical aspect underwrites 'unworlding' as a process that complicates simplistic inter-world mobility. Worlds encounter one another by chance. The movement that makes them come together also uncouples them from one another.

There is no Lucky or Pozzo in the film. The two nameless figures do not encounter anyone apart from fleeting, wordless meetings with the 'Bahurupi' (chameleon) performers in the festival. The void of Lucky and Pozzo is filled up by the readings of Mao's text. This would remind regional viewers of the ideological teaching sessions that once animated the circles of the Communist Party of India Marxist-Leninist (CPIML). The act of reading from the book introduces a different order of intertextuality. As the end credits clarify, lines from *Godot* and *The Little Red Book* are used but these two usages are different. While Beckett's lines are not *quoted* by the characters, Mao's sentences are *read* from a text. These two modalities refine the trans-textual, polymorphic 'travel' that happens in this cinematic text. Beckett's play is not an external text for the couple in the film. They are in its world and find themselves identified with it. They have internalized Beckett's text. In contrast, Mao's text is external and has a political pedagogic value. It is a text that they learn to prepare for the impending war. The performance of this act of reading triggers a reflection on how books and ideas travel across national borders to become world literature. This pedagogic emphasis is historically faithful to the Naxalite context and its present-day continuation in the 'people's war,' conducted by the Communist Party of India-Maoist.

Mao's text shows how worlds come together through political pedagogy. The trans-cultural is folded back within the intra-cultural at the level of travel and reception. More than its original Chinese context, Indian and especially Bengali viewers of *Kalkimanthankatha* would identify with the 'intra-cultural' context of Naxalism. Beckett's text becomes the dialectical Other of Mao's in this trans-cultural, transnational appropriation of texts, ideas, discourses, each of which are worlds in themselves. MahaKumbh and Naxalism operate as 'intra-cultural' markers. They contextualize Beckett and Mao for the Indian audiences while maintaining a distant appeal to the global. *Godot* and *The Little Red Book* form a counter-intuitive textual pseudo-couple that cuts across cultures. Their worlds are mutually remote and what alienates them further is the Indian context. The encounter of worlds insists more on distance than homology here. It underwrites an experience of 'unworlding'. World literature is our critical lens to think through these transnational formations and deformations of the intercultural and the intra-cultural. The Marxist emphasis on the international is not far from this. Marx and Engels' *The Communist Manifesto* (1848) was famously one of the first texts to articulate a notion of world literature as part of the communist project of abolishing private cultural properties of nations:

> The intellectual creations of individual nations become common property. National one-sidedness and narrow-mindedness become more and more impossible, and from the numerous national and local literatures, there arises a world literature.
>
> (2017: 16)

For Marx and Engels, world literature is a concomitant of world revolution. Just as revolution crosses national borders, literature as a reflection of the revolutionary society transcends national boundaries to become world literature. The reading of Mao's book in *Kalkimanthankatha* is symptomatic of this worldwide class struggle of literature when it has trans-cultural circulation. As the film progresses, the two tramps name Bukharin, Trotsky, Kamenev and Ceaușescu (Soviet and Romanian political leaders) alongside Kalki, among the ten avatars of Vishnu. As opposed to the right-wing mobilization of Hinduism as a religion in contemporary India, in Avikunthak, we find a left-inflected Hindu mythology. This politicization of Hindu mythology deflects the religious symbolism of Kalki as Godot in a strategically similar manner to the way *Godot* evokes religious symbolism but only to frustrate it with increasing ambiguities. It is the missing masses that metaphorically assume the role of Kalki or Godot in *Kalkimanthankatha*. In a radical democratic context, people themselves acquire political agency. The excerpts from Mao, quoted by the tramps, depict people (*demos*) as the driving force of the revolutionary party. The missing populace in the film thus becomes a parallel to the missing audience in both *Godot* and *Nayan Kabirer Pala*.

In the film, the two tramps meet at various places: from under a huge tree (as in Beckett's play) to upturned boats. They move from ruins to rail bridges, from mobile phone towers to highways and, on occasions, suddenly disappear to reappear at a different spot. The spatial stagnation of Didi and Gogo in *Godot* is thus replaced not only by displacement but also by sudden and magical disappearance and reappearance. This plays on the cinematic memory of local viewers. The sudden comings and goings are similar to Satyajit Ray's 1969 Bengali cult fantasy film, *Goopy Gyne Bagha Byne*. In Ray's film, we see two tramps get boons from the king of ghosts. They acquire the power of disappearing from one place and reappearing at another by clapping and saying magical words when they wear their gifted boots.

The echo of Ray's film works as an intra-cultural intertext for *Kalkimanthankatha*. This buried reference shows another severance between the global and the local receptions of the work. A distant Western reading might disregard the intertextual echo of the Indian vernacular film, but for a local viewer, this popular children's fantasy film would be a near-obvious reference frame. This uncoupling of the local and the global implies 'unworlding'. From the first half of the film where the tramps say lines from *Godot* to the second half in which they read Mao's text, a dialectical structure is developed. In the first part of this dialectic, the religious backdrop 'unworlds' Beckett's text by alienating it into a very different world. In the second, the political subtext creates another world to envelop the rest of the film. These two worlds have a mutual tension. One forces the source text with an overt religiosity and the other interpolates it with radical politics. This adaptive appropriation therefore deploys two dialectically interlocking worlds to 'unworld' Beckett's play.

To conclude, I have used the term 'unworlding' in an ethical spirit, similar to that of Emily Apter who mobilizes 'untranslatability' to critique world literature (see 2013: 1–27). While Apter uses 'translation' and untranslatability in a linguistic sense, the problematic of 'unworlding' has to do with ontological as well as cultural 'untranslatability' of one world into the other(s). When a work travels as world literature, its textual world comes in contact with a new world in the 'host culture'. The three travels of Samuel Beckett's *Waiting for Godot* exemplify how this encounter of worlds leads to radical difference between them. One world never translates into another in an unproblematic way. Translation of one into another yields what is untranslatable in this passage. Encounter of worlds adds alienating filters and produces a de-familiarized insight into 'unworlding'.

'Unworlding' exposes the separation of local and global receptions. If there are pores that permit mobility from one world to another, there are also irreducible gaps that do not allow them to be entirely translatable.

Beckett's *Godot* is part of a triangular constellation in *Tepantor* and *Kalkimanthankatha*. In the former, it interacts with Sen's play and Kundu's culturally translated world of the play script. But this triangulation leads to an *aporetic* point when personages from one world are literally lost in another. Worlds are not just spatio-temporal; these are ontological, cultural and discursive worlds. They touch each other to alienate each other and produce differences in the experience of 'unworlding'. The play thus allegorizes 'unworlding' as the alienating interpellation of one world by another. In Avikunthak's film, Mao and Beckett textually alienate one another, and MahaKumbh as a culturally transplanted world of waiting adds another layer of 'unworlding' to Beckett's play. The 'inter-cultural' (e.g. Beckett and Mao) is often contextualized by the 'intra-cultural' (e.g. MahaKumbh, Naxalism) to the point that the latter overwrites the former. The 'intra-cultural' also alienates the 'inter-cultural'. This happens particularly when the intra-cultural is intuitively available to local reception but not to global audiences (e.g. the echo of Ray's film). This chasm between the intercultural and the intra-cultural characterizes 'unworlding'. World literature as a critical practice of reading must become ethically sensitive to this 'unworlding' of untranslatable worlds.

Notes

1 Throughout this article, quotes from *Nayan Kabirer Pala*, *Tepantor* and *Kalkimanthankatha* are reproduced in my English translations.
2 To make someone a 'mamu' is to deceive them. The names 'Ela' and 'Bhola' are Bengali equivalents of Tom, Dick and Harry and underline their social insignificance as tramps.

Works cited

Apter, E. (2013), *Against World Literature: On the Politics of Untranslatability*, London and New York: Verso.
Beckett, S. (1936), *Murphy*, London: Calder.
Beckett, S. (2003), *The Complete Dramatic Works*, London: Faber.
Cheah, P. (2016), *What Is a World? On Postcolonial as World Literature*, Duke: Duke University Press.
Damrosch, D. (2003), *What Is World Literature?* Princeton: Princeton University Press.
Ghosh, R., and J. H. Miller (2016), *Thinking Literature across Continents*, Durham: Duke University Press.
Gussow, M. (1996), *Conversations with and about Beckett*, New York: Grove.
Kalkimanthankatha (2015), [Film] Dir. Ashish Avikunthak, India and Germany.

Kundu, S. (n.d.), *Tepantor*, unpublished play script emailed by the author.
Marx, K., and F. Engels (2017), *The Communist Manifesto*. Available online: https://www.marxists.org/archive/marx/works/download/pdf/Manifesto.pdf (accessed 16 April 2017).
Miller, J. H. (2016), *Literature Matters*, London: Open Humanities Press.
Ray, S. (Dir.) (1969), *Goopy Gyne Bagha Byne*, [Film] India: Purnima Pictures.
Sen, N. (2012), *Natyashangraha. Collected Plays: Part One*, Kolkata: Dey's Publications.

13

Godot's arrivals: Beckettian and anti-Beckettian discourses in Bulatović's *Godot Has Arrived* and Komanin's *Godot Has Arrived to Collect His Dues*

Snežana Kalinić

In his influential work *What Is World Literature?* (2003) David Damrosch offers a new interpretation of the old term, defining it as a mode of circulation and interpretation of literary texts. According to Damrosch, a literary work becomes a part of world literature 'whenever, and wherever, it is actively present within a literary system beyond that of its original culture' (2003: 4). In his analysis of such literary works, Damrosch notes that the *'effective* life' of a work of world literature inspires different translations, interpretations, stagings and adaptations, because of which it *'manifests* differently abroad than it does at home' (2003: 4, 6). As a result, a work of world literature becomes not only enriched by its worldwide circulation but also reframed and even changed sometimes. Hence, Damrosch emphasizes 'the variability of a work of word literature' as 'one of its constitutive features – one of its greatest strengths when the work is well presented and read well, and its greatest vulnerability when it is mishandled or misappropriated by its foreign friends' (2003: 5).

Samuel Beckett's *Waiting for Godot* has had a highly '*effective* life' all over the world. Burkman argues that its worldwide circulation has 'actually created a modern myth': the 'nonarriving Godot has taken his place beside Sisyphus, Prometheus, and other mythological figures of old' (2008: 33–4). In addition, Beckett's famous tragicomedy has also displayed an immense 'variability' by inspiring different philosophical, theological, psychological and other interpretations, numerous theatrical, cinematic and television performances and rewritings – enabling the work to live on and gain alternative identities. This chapter discusses *Waiting for Godot*'s circulation in Serbia and other parts of the former Yugoslavia, where its '*effective* life' extended beyond different translations, interpretations and performances, inspiring two Serbian playwrights of Montenegrin descent to rewrite the text. Both Miodrag Bulatović's *Godot Has Arrived* (*Godo je došao*; *Godot ist gekommen*) (1965)[1] and Žarko Komanin's *Godot Has Arrived to Collect His Dues* (*Godo je došao po svoje*) (2002) present the arrival of the long-awaited title character and the subsequent creation of a dystopian society. However, while Bulatović's play presents the arrival of a Christ-like Godot, embodied in the figure of a baker who is derided for attempting to act as the liberator of the oppressed, Komanin's rewrite presents the arrival of an antichrist-like Godot, embodied in the figure of a weapons merchant who profits from the misfortunes of those who are indebted to him.

The theoretical framework for this comparative study is not only provided by Damrosch's interpretation of world literature but also by Lubomir Doležel's investigation of fictional worlds because it offers a detailed explanation and useful typology of 'postmodernist rewrites of classic works' (Doležel 1998: 206). In his seminal work *Heterocosmica: Fiction and Possible Worlds* (1998), Doležel explains that postmodernist rewrites 'come into existence because every fictional world, however canonical, however authoritative, however habitualized, can be changed' and 'displaced by an alternative world' (1998: 222). In addition, he notes that postmodernist rewrites affirm the value and relevance of the established literary canon but also have the power to 'question' and 'confront' it (1998: 206). Depending on the kind and the extent of the canonical work's transformations, Doležel distinguishes three types of postmodernist rewrites: *transposition, expansion* and *displacement*. While *displacement* radically changes the canonical text by 'reinventing its story', *transposition* 'preserves [...] the main story of the protoworld but locates' it 'in a different temporal or spatial setting' (Doležel 1998: 206–7). *Expansion*, on the other hand, aims neither to replace nor to repeat the original story but to 'extend the scope of the protoworld, by filling its gaps' and 'constructing a prehistory or posthistory' (Doležel 1998: 207).

At first glance, both Serbian rewrites of Beckett's *Godot* could be classified as its radical *displacements* and criticized as impertinent ways of what Damrosch calls misappropriating and mishandling a work of world literature (see 2003: 5). In both cases, the nonarriving Godot not only arrives but has a very active stage life, which makes both rewrites look like prime examples of 'manipulation and even deformation' of Beckett's masterpiece (2003: 24). On the other hand, these two rewrites could be classified as its *expansions* because they both present the outcome of Godot's arrival. By highlighting not only the obvious anti-Beckettian discourses in Bulatović's and Komanin's plays but also the less apparent similarities between Beckett's tragicomedy and its rewrites, this comparative study attempts to show that *Godot* has not been subjected to 'manipulation and even deformation' in the Serbian cultural context but protected by its 'cultural prestige' and enriched by these two Serbian *expansions* (2003: 24).

*

Serbia did not have to wait much for *Waiting for Godot*: its Belgrade premiere took place as early as in 1954; however, this performance was only a semi-public rehearsal. The official premiere was banned after a respected Croatian and Yugoslav writer Miroslav Krleža found the play somewhat 'nihilistic' (Todorović 2013: 473). Since cynicism and nihilism were not welcome in Tito's communist Yugoslavia, only the employees of the Belgrade Drama Theatre were allowed to watch this first performance (Todorović 2013: 473). A small number of outsiders who managed to sneak in had to remain hidden. A Serbian writer, Antonije Isaković, was 'kicked out' by 'a cleaning lady' with 'a broomstick', and *Godot*'s first Serbian director, Vasilije Popović, was fired shortly after the performance (Todorović 2013: 473–4). This, however, turned out to be a fortunate event for Popović, who continued his directorial work, but eventually became more focused on writing (under the pseudonym of Pavle Ugrinov) and soon became a respected author.

Another secret performance of Popović's staging of *Godot* was soon held in the atelier of an acclaimed Serbian painter Mića Popović. 'Chalk' was used to draw 'the stage borders', and a plain 'broomstick' served as the tree from Beckett's play (Todorović 2013: 475). This performance eventually led to the opening of a new 'avant-garde theatre in Belgrade, Atelje 212', where the official Belgrade premiere of Popović's staging of *Godot* finally took place in 1956 (Todorović 2013: 475–6). Later on, Beckett's *Godot* prompted different stagings in other theatres of the former Yugoslavia.

Aiming to finally end Beckett's waiting game, Bulatović's *Godot Has Arrived* and Komanin's play *Godot Has Arrived to Collect His Dues* 'expand' (in Doležel's sense) Beckett's minimalistic world, which fed its characters' ever-weakening faith with nothing but carrots and turnips or 'vague and unfulfilled promises' (Duckworth 2000: 139), by describing the consequences of Godot's arrival. However, these texts also display some of the features of the most radical type of postmodernist rewrites, which Doležel names *displacement*, because they seem to confront Beckett's world view and 'create *polemical* antiworlds, which undermine or negate the legitimacy of the canonical protoworld' (1998: 207). In Bulatović's play, Godot has an intense sexual relationship with a post office girl. In Komanin's rewrite, Vladimir's companion is not named Estragon but Josip, like Josip Broz Tito himself, even though the play does not deal with titocracy but with Vladimir's and Josip's financial problems and the arranged marriage between Vladimir's son and Josip's daughter. By transforming the old characters and adding new ones, Bulatović and Komanin attempt to weaken and subvert what Burkman calls 'the Godot myth', i.e. 'Beckett's refusal to offer solutions, to tell us whether Godot exists, who he is, or whether he will ever arrive' (2008: 50).

The general critical tendency when discussing *Godot* has been to argue that Beckett wrote a play about waiting because he was aware that the arrival of any Godot would be 'either an anti-climax or a shattering disillusion' (Zilliacus 1970: 9) and to read the text as 'an essentially metaphysical tragicomedy with a Judeo-Christian background' (Rhodes 1963: 261), in which 'God shows himself to be absent' more than in any other Beckett's work (Duckworth 2000: 135). Due to Godot's 'active absence' or 'passive non-revelation', Beckett's characters get the impression that God is 'playing on their hopes and expectations' by exposing them to the dullness of waiting, the hardship of hoping and suspense of expecting (Duckworth 2000: 135-6). The repeated frustrations and constant deprivation that Vladimir and Estragon endure impelled Bulatović and Komanin to investigate whether it is really 'better to wait, even with diminishing hope, [...] than to have the certainty of the worst' (Duckworth 2000: 136-7). Hence, they both present dystopian visions of Godot's arrival by depicting societies that are 'considerably worse' than the ones they lived in (Sargent 1994: 9). Komanin's antichrist-like Godot is terrifyingly evil, while Bulatović's Christ-like Godot is ridiculously benevolent, but neither of them offers any hope. In spite of certain religious overtones, the focus of these rewrites is not on 'chiliastic certainties' of hope or despair but on the issues raised by utopian and dystopian fictional worlds, which display human (in)ability to create a better world 'without transcendental support or intervention', as Bloch emphasizes (1959: 607).

*

Miodrag Bulatović claims to have written *Godot Has Arrived* in order to correct Beckett's 'genius, cynical and utterly unjust formula' which 'condemned mankind to lifelong waiting' (2003: 6). In the first act of his play, the Boy joyfully declares that Godot has arrived. He also claims that Godot is in the post office, sexually involved with the post office girl, who is mesmerized by him. The sounds of aeroplanes, tanks, livestock-transporting freight trains and squeaking beds are heard just before Godot's arrival. Yet, in spite of these expectations, Godot turns out to be an ordinary man – a middle-aged baker, completely covered in flour. When he finally enters the stage in the second act, he gets trapped in the doorway because of the heavy bags he carries, and the gifts he bears are plain bread and white flour, not the miracles performed by the saviour. As a virile man, he brings lust instead of love. Thus, utterly disappointed, Vladimir and Estragon greet him with unhidden mistrust, which prompts him to admit that they expected a saint but ended up with a baker. Realizing that although they awaited a saviour with 'at least one aureole' (2003: 74),[2] they have received a foe, a fornicator and a maniac, the other characters deride Bulatović's Godot by calling him Flour Man – an ironic allusion to the Golden Man (El Dorado) and, by extension, to utopian fiction. Instead of welcoming the Golden Man, Bulatović's characters have to settle with the Flour Man – an incompetent and lustful baker, who has been repeatedly fired from his job because of his laziness.

Even as a Chaplinesque Flour Man, Bulatović's Godot has, as Zilliacus notes, 'the makings of a Christ as the radical theologians would have him: he is [...] carrying meal and bread to a starving humanity' (1970: 9). The bread imagery calls forth Christ's miracles, the Last Supper and the ritual of Eucharist. In addition, Bulatović's Godot attempts to act as the liberator of the oppressed; he sets Lucky free and tries to liberate Pozzo as well, when Lucky seizes power and enslaves him. The baker is also endowed with other Christ-like virtues. He is the healer who helps the wounded by covering their open wounds with pastry, and, eager to sacrifice himself, he offers his heart to the Boy, who is a half-hearted messenger in Bulatović's play.

Bulatović's Godot also recalls Christ when he is subjected to the other character's judgements, mocking and tortures. He is put on trial and sentenced to death, corresponding to Christ's crucifixion. However, the trial is a travesty. Godot is accused of intruding into the other characters' lives, bothering them with his flour and acting against the United Nations. Pozzo acts as the judge and claims that Godot is a scoundrel and poisoner, Lucky accuses him of being a hypocrite, Vladimir declares him to be an enemy of the people and Estragon orders him to go away. Yet Bulatović's Godot remains Christ-like and forgives his accusers, and although he is not actually executed after the trial, the others declare him to be non-existent.

Bulatović's Godot is also Christ-like in his eagerness to spread the message of love. He is full of tenderness, compassion and forgiveness. However, his message of love is presented in a grotesque manner. He practises corporeal instead of spiritual love with the post office girl. Likewise, the bread he bakes has little to do with the rite of Eucharist; it is offered to the others as plain bread, devoid of spiritual meaning, as if their hunger is merely corporeal. As a result, Christ's message of love is debased, the spiritual is transmuted into corporeal, salvation is reduced to bare survival, and purity and innocence are transformed into debauchery and sin.

Burdened with his own vices and sins, Bulatović's Godot is incapable of bringing forth the expected utopian social order. His gifts of bread and love, as well as his well-intended actions, are rejected by the other characters as naive altruism and perverse sexuality. They also reproach him for offering bare survival instead of salvation, and for his vision of universal freedom, which they disagree with. While Godot is determined to provide freedom for all, even for people like Pozzo and Lucky, who tend to abuse it by abusing each other, the other characters are convinced that freedom is not for everyone. They are aware that Lucky's salvation is futile because the oppressed eventually become the oppressors and vice versa, while oppression itself is never abandoned. After enslaving Pozzo, Lucky himself explains the inevitability of slavery and the impossibility of universal freedom: 'The rope *must* be wrapped around somebody's neck. Freedom exists only in books' (Bulatović 2003: 84). Godot, however, fails to recognize Pozzo and Lucky as the 'tragicomic pair of the eternally unequal' and disregards the volatile and circular nature of power and oppression (Đurić 2011: 366).

Like many other utopian thinkers, Bulatović's Godot is unable to transgress the limits of his own knowledge and prejudices. As a result, the other characters increasingly perceive him as a naive idealist and a demagogue, who promises inviting but unrealistic projects of ideal social order. Aware of the paradox inherent in Godot's idea of universal freedom, Pozzo perceives him as an ignorant tyrant who is unable to respect the individual's right to be different. He accuses Godot of being 'a torturer more than a liberator' and warns him that freedom cannot be imposed; 'even the Holy Bible' claims 'that freedom is not for everyone' (Bulatović 2003: 62). Pozzo's harsh words reflect Bulatović's claim that his play has more to do with the lack of freedom than the abundance of bread (see Bulatović 2003: 7). Pozzo's accusations emphasize the aggressiveness of uniformity implicit in utopian ideas about the shared needs, values and desires of the entire humankind. This disregard of individual differences lurks behind all utopias and causes, as Đergović-Joksimović points out, 'one man's utopia' to eventually become 'another man's dystopia' (2009: 18).

Godot's importunacy and intolerance prompt Vladimir and Estragon to reject his gift of white flour. Instead of feeding the poor, the Flour Man feeds mice and rats because 'flour is followed by mice. Mice are followed by rats. And rats might be followed by people again' (Bulatović 2003: 72). Godot's intrusiveness impels the other characters to start thinking about revolutions, uprisings and places of bloodshed such as the Bastille or Waterloo (Bulatović 2003: 63, 68). Their dark aspirations reveal that people who are compelled to wait are not necessarily passive, as they have been portrayed in Beckett's play. After a period of passive waiting, they can become hyperactive and start thinking about another French Revolution or 'even a Latin American putsch' (Bulatović 2003: 61). As a result, *Godot Has Arrived* differs radically from Beckett's original text. Its plot is full of actions: everything happens 'very fast, without a single pause, almost in panic' (Bulatović 2003: 5). It transforms what Pervić calls Beckett's 'poetry of deep deprivation' (Pervić 2002: 85) into a satire of shallow disillusion that presents human history as a pile of books made from 'human skin' and full of bad memories (Bulatović 2003: 68).

Bulatović reaches the conclusion that mankind is never satisfied and that the present world is much worse than it was in Beckett's tragicomedy: not only is it 'paradoxical and ridiculous', but also 'evil and pestiferous' (Bulatović 2003: 12). And yet his rewrite is not entirely different from Beckett's original. In fact, it looks like a simple variation on one of Beckett's favourite subjects, what Gontarski describes as 'heaven's hellishness': 'the conflict between the traditional blissful notion of heaven and its potential horror, its changelessness, its eternity, its blandness' (1985: 72). Bulatović himself pointed to the presence of something infernal in his play when he mentioned that there are 'phosphorus' emissions hidden inside this text (2003: 5).

*

Komanin's *Godot Has Arrived to Collect His Dues* presents an even darker vision of the human condition than Bulatović's play. As mentioned above, in Komanin's rewrite, Godot is not the epitome of futile goodness but the embodiment of effective evil. He is a devil-like weapons merchant who punishes those who are indebted to him and abducts the bride of Vladimir's son. All the characters of Komanin's play depict him as the most vicious villain: a bloodthirsty imposter and ultimate destroyer. Some of them perceive him as the devil himself because Komanin's Godot, just like the devil, inevitably comes to collect his dues. In this play Vladimir and his companion, Josip, are not waiting for Godot's arrival; rather, they are praying for the very opposite. As a result, Komanin's rewrite of Beckett's tragicomedy is less devoted to the elusiveness of a desired future than to the inevitable arrival of an unwanted one.

Komanin's protagonists are shameless imposters and corrupt businessmen, so much indebted to Godot that they are willing to sacrifice their own children in order to pay their debts. Josip has arranged a marriage between his daughter, Juliette (Julija), and Vladimir's son, Aleksandar, because both Josip and Vladimir secretly hope that one of them is wealthy enough to pay off the debt. As a result, the plot of Komanin's play resembles the plot of Balzac's satirical comedy *Mercadet* (1851) much more than that of Beckett's tragicomedy. In Balzac's comedy, an indebted stock exchange speculator named Mercadet is prepared to sacrifice his daughter by giving her to a man who merely appears to be wealthy. Fortunately for Mercadet, Balzac's

Godeau arrives and saves the indebted family. Contrary to that 'fairy-tale' ending (Rhodes 1963: 262), Komanin's Godot comes not to bring salvation but to collect the money and abduct the beautiful bride of Vladimir's son. One of Vladimir's cousins explains: 'Rapacity costs money' (Komanin 2002: 13). Vladimir and Josip try in vain to postpone the payback time by attempting to deceive the deceiver and trick the trickster.

Komanin's *Godot* is thus a tragicomedy about deceived deceivers. As Vladimir's son Aleksandar explains to his father: 'Godot deceives you. You deceive Godot. You deceive me. I deceive Juliette. All of us deceive. All of us are deceivers' (Komanin 2002: 64). Aleksandar feels betrayed and accuses his father: 'You have sold me to Godot for thirty pieces of silver!' (Komanin 2002: 72). In addition to referring to Judas's betrayal of Christ, Aleksandar articulates all the unpleasant truths about human rapacity, selfishness and weakness. He portrays the hero of his times as a diabolical creature who would 'kill the Father, the Son and the Holy Spirit' for the sake of 'his own interest' (Komanin 2002: 72). In Komanin's money-oriented world, which is not unlike the one depicted in Balzac's works, authentic beauty is a precious rarity. The only embodiment of beauty and virtue is Josip's daughter Juliette, who attempts to resist the power of Godot's money. Well aware of her innocence, Vladimir's son, echoing Hamlet, warns her that the world they live in is a corrupt one and that all men, himself included, are dishonest creatures. By adding such a female character to the male pseudo-couples of the 'Godot myth', Komanin associates Beckett's *Godot* not only with Shakespeare's *Hamlet*, but also with *Romeo and Juliette* and *The Merchant of Venice*. As Pervić argues, 'if Komanin's Juliette calls forth Ophelia, then his Godot has the makings of a modern-day Shylock' (2002: 100). In so doing, Komanin adds new dimensions to the well-known allusions to Shakespeare and the Bible in Beckett's *Godot*. He widens the scope of the 'Godot myth', which seemed to be undermined by the initial changes to Beckett's original plot and protagonists.

*

Aiming to challenge Beckett's world view and to confront the apparent uneventfulness of *Waiting for Godot*, Bulatović and Komanin present dynamic rewritings of this tragicomedy. Insolent *displacements* and mishandlings at first sight, these rewrites are in fact radical *expansions* of the original text because they reveal the pathos of disillusionment and other consequences of Godot's arrival and thus create what Doležel calls a 'posthistory' of the canonical story (1998: 207). Even though they present Godot's arrivals, they resemble Beckett's tragicomedy about 'hope deferred' (Beckett 2006: 12) inasmuch as they also present certain delays – that of awaited satisfaction and of unavoidable sufferance. Accordingly, both rewrites postulate that wishful thinking always remains unfulfilled. Awaited or unwanted, Godot may arrive, but he cannot make a wish come true. The arrivals of both Godots turn out to be highly disappointing, just as Beckett suggested that *any* Godot's arrival would be. In Bulatović's play, the Christ-like Godot fails to meet Vladimir's and Estragon's expectations and to fulfil their wishes. His gift of bread does not satisfy their hunger, and his gift of freedom is something Vladimir and Estragon wilfully sacrifice for the sake of progress. In Komanin's play, Vladimir's wish that the antichrist-like Godot would not come also remains unfulfilled. Consequently, the Serbian Godots not only complement Beckett's original story but also somewhat resemble each other. Moreover, it seems that Beckett's original and its rewrites, as different as they are in content and in form, eventually reach the same conclusion – that wishes can never be fulfilled without bringing their own fulfilment into question.

As a result, while the Serbian *expansions* of Beckett's metaphysical tragicomedy seem to utterly undermine 'the Godot myth' (Burkman 2008: 50), in reality, they magnify the meaning and importance of the very myth they seem to subvert. They begin challenging Beckett's world view but end up by reaffirming it. In so doing, Bulatović and Komanin underline one of Beckett's old insights: it is the utopian Godot who never comes; the dystopian one never fails to arrive.

In this way, these two Serbian playwrights of Montenegrin decent have drawn out *Godot*'s propensities for being one of the masterpieces of world literature, while *Godot* itself has confirmed its own 'variability' to be 'one of its greatest strengths', rather than 'its greatest vulnerability' (Damrosch 2003: 5). Even though, as Damrosch insightfully notes, the 'worlds of world literature are often worlds in collision' (2003: 14), Bulatović's and Komanin's texts demonstrate that this collision is often a fruitful one. And yet in spite of their attempts to finally end the waiting game by presenting its inevitably dystopian outcome, the wait for a future utopia seems to have no end.

Notes

1   Bulatović's play *Godot ist gekommen* was first performed on 28 May 1966 at the Düsseldorf Schauspielhaus.
2   All the English translations of quotes from Bulatović's and Komanin's plays are mine.

Works cited

Beckett, S. (2006), *The Complete Dramatic Works*, London: Faber and Faber.
Bloch, E. (1959), *Das Prinzip Hoffnung*, Frankfurt: Suhrkamp.

Bulatović, M. (2003), *Godo je došao*, Beograd: SKZ.
Burkman, K. H. (2008), 'The Nonarrival of Godot: Initiation into the Sacred Void', in H. Bloom (ed.), *Bloom's Modern Critical Interpretations: Samuel Beckett's 'Waiting for Godot' – New Edition*, 33–53, New York: Bloom's Literary Criticism.
Damrosch, D. (2003), *What Is World Literature?* Princeton and Oxford: Oxford University Press.
Doležel, L. (1998), *Heterocosmica: Fiction and Possible Worlds*, Baltimore and London: Johns Hopkins University Press.
Duckworth, C. (2000), 'Beckett and the Missing Sharer', in M. Buning, et al. (eds.), *Samuel Beckett Today/Aujourd'hui*, Vol. 9, *Beckett and Religion: Beckett/Aesthetics/Politics/Beckett et la religion: Beckett/l'esthétique/la politique*, 133–44, Amsterdam–Atlanta: Rodopi.
Đergović-Joksimović, Z. (2009), *Utopija: alternativna istorija*, Beograd: Geopoetika.
Đurić, K. S. (2011), 'Problem apsurda u delima Miodraga Bulatovića (*Đavoli dolaze, Crveni petao leti prema nebu, Godo je došao*)', *Zbornik Matice srpske za književnost i jezik*, 59 (2): 349–75.
Gontarski, S. E. (1985), *The Intent of Undoing in Samuel Beckett's Dramatic Texts*, Bloomington: Indiana University Press.
Komanin, Ž. (2002), *Godo je došao po svoje*, Beograd: SKZ.
Pervić M. (2002), 'Godo po treći put među Srbima', in Ž. Komanin (ed.), *Godo je došao po svoje*, 81–103, Beograd: SKZ.
Rhodes, S. A. (1963), 'From Godeau to Godot', *The French Review*, 36 (3) (January): 260–5.
Sargent, L. T. (1994), 'The Three Faces of Utopianism Revisited', *Utopian Studies*, 5 (1): 1–37.
Todorović, P. (2013), 'Beket u Beogradu', *Književna istorija*, 45 (150): 467–82.
Zilliacus, C. (1970), 'Three Times "Godot": Beckett, Brecht, Bulatovic', *Comparative Drama*, 4 (1) (Spring): 3–17.

14

Waiting for the arrivant: Godot in two poems by Nizār Qabbānī

Hania A. M. Nashef

Introduction

And when the critics started to argue about the absurdist identity of Godot, you did not understand what the fuss was all about. You were smarter than all the critics and even Beckett himself, for he who has waited twenty years knows Godot.

(Darwish 2010: 99)

The late Palestinian writer Mahmoud Darwish is surprised about the critics who are still debating the identity of Godot. A Palestinian, who has waited endlessly for a political solution, knows Godot well. In this instance, the wait implied by Darwish encompasses more than one, and in its fold exist many expectations. A priori, it is the wait for a homeland to come into being. It is also an end to being humiliated for not having a homeland, not recognized as a human being who is entitled to one and being marginalized by those in power. In this absence, the Palestinian can only wait. His or her wait is for a saviour who will come with a solution to one's woes. The humiliation of the Palestinian is one that is shared by many Arabs, as it reminds them of their failures, specifically their crushing defeats in the 1948, 1967 and 1973 wars. The Beckettian wait is an action that Arab poets and playwrights, such as the Egyptian Tawfiq al-Hakim, the Lebanese Roger Assaf, the Syrians Saadallah Wannous and Walid Kowatli, and the Moroccan At-Tayib As-

Siddiqi, have not only long identified with but also incorporated in their work. The wait has evolved to define the condition of the human being in a number of Arab countries, including Algeria, Iraq, Jordan, Lebanon, Syria and the Palestinian territories. As with Beckett's characters, the passage of time signals a life with diminished prospects. If movement is to be had, it is likely to be for the worst. In this chapter, I will discuss two poems by the late Syrian diplomat and poet Nizār Qabbānī based on the theme of waiting.[1] The verses in both poems, 'Waiting for Godot' from his short collection of poems *No* (1999)[2] and 'A Television Interview with an Arab Godot' from his anthology *A Match in My Hand, And Your Petty Paper Nations* (1990), describe an arduous and a ceaseless wait, echoing the despair experienced by a great part of the Arab world, due to failed economies and dictatorships since gaining independence. Like Darwish, Qabbānī imagines he knows Godot as he searches for a saviour who will rescue the Arab nations from political and social malaise, and paralysis.

Godot, the awaited Arab saviour

The mythical 'Arab' Godot embodies the only hope available to generations of Arabs since colonial times, as they continue to wait in desperate circumstances, imprisoned by their inability to effect change, even though the wait itself borders on futility. According to Harold Schweizer, the act of waiting 'extends across barren mental and emotional planes' and 'those who wander [...] through it find themselves in an exemplary existential predicament, having time without wanting it' (2008: 2). This is the situation that the citizens in Qabbānī's poems find themselves in. In the poem, 'Waiting for Godot', Qabbānī urges Godot to appear, and the wait in this case is in anticipation of a messiah who will lift the people from their desolate existence. The poem begins with a collective wait for a train from which the imagined hero will emerge from the annals of history. The citizens' inactivity during the wait renders them prisoners in a barren landscape.

Qabbānī has often been criticized for his use of simple language and banal imagery.[3] Similarly, Szafraniec notes that 'Beckett has been repeatedly seen as an author who exploits the commonplace and the banal' to convey 'its own emptiness' (2007: 90). This emptiness is felt in both of Qabbānī's works and manifests itself in the situation of those who wait. The pronoun 'we' in 'Waiting for Godot' points to the Arab masses that continue to suffer. Even though the speaker wants Godot to emerge from certain proud historic moments, such as the battle victories of Badr, Yarmouk or Hittin, recent history is compared to a train station that suffocates those who have been waiting for deliverance from its clutches since the 1920s – a date that coincides with the fall of the Ottoman Empire and the beginning of colonial and mandate rule by Western nations in the Arab region. Their saviour could come in the image of Saladin who defeated the crusaders.

Godot, this anticipated saviour, will appear in the form of a messiah out of the dead voices, echoes of the past and centuries of history that permeate the poem. Beckett writes, 'Yesterday is not a milestone that has been passed, but a daystone on the beaten track of the years, and irremediably part of us, within us, heavy and dangerous' (1931: 3). The Syrian poet regards recent Arab history as a double-edged sword; it has shaped the Arab persona and deformed the individual. At the same time, he longs for historic moments from a brighter era. Yet he wants the human being to be free from the clutches of outdated practices and habits. This dilemma is also felt in the poet's attempt at understanding the Godot persona. Likewise, the past is not dead in Beckett's *Waiting for Godot*: 'a myriad of voices, [which include] the "dead voices," [is] beckon[ing] to be heard' (Watt 2006: 177). The voices of the dead and the living cannot be silenced; instead they will 'talk about their lives' as to 'have lived is not enough for them' (Beckett 1979: 40). For both writers, the past continues to haunt and paralyses the individual through an endless wait.

Daniel Watt argues that a wait that is characterized both by interruption and repetition often results in a continual deferral of discourse in the dialogues of Beckett's characters, awaiting another's revelation or another's call (see 2006: 177). The same holds true for the citizens in Qabbānī's poem. Their discourse will come to light once the awaited Godot arrives. At the same time, in a footnote to both poems, Qabbānī not only acknowledges that Godot is a direct borrowing from Beckett's play but also remains perplexed as to the nature of this appropriated persona (see 1999: n.p.). He ponders over this borrowed character: 'Is he the saviour, or the healer, or the one who will turn a dream into reality? [...] Is he hope, bliss, happiness? Is he death, emptiness, pointlessness?' (1999). Qabbānī reflects upon the identity of Godot, asking if this awaited entity will bring relief and whether he will be capable of rescuing the individual from the debilitation of time or whether this anticipated arrival of a saviour brings more destruction and calamity. Yet, until such a time, everything is deferred.

According to Joseph Anderton, the words of Vladimir and Estragon anticipate an authoritative and superior body to validate them, ahead of Godot's promises (see 2016: 104). Anderton argues that Godot remains both a prospect and a possibility that is deferred (2016: 105). For Derrida, everything begins with a wait for an apparition of a spectre (see 1994: 2). This spectral moment 'no longer belongs to time', as this apparition links the 'modalized presents (past present, actual present: "now", future present)' (1994: xix). Thus, everything begins with the initial appearance and then the wait for this apparition to re-emerge. Derrida adds, 'The anticipation is at once impatient, anxious, and fascinated: this, the thing ("this thing") will end up coming. The revenant is going to come. It won't be long. But how long it is taking' (1994: 2). The pertinent question lies with expectation, as without the knowledge of the arrival of the spectre, it will only paralyse those who continue to wait. The very experience of waiting predicates that time and space expand tediously into a dreary dimension (see Schweizer 2008: 8). Yet physically the space imprisons and confines. In Qabbānī's 'Waiting for Godot' there is both impatience and urgency, even though the wait symbolically transcends various epochs. Godot has to appear to relieve them from stagnation and humiliation. Godot becomes their only hope, the one entity that could free them from political and societal ills. But with this kind of wait, the waiting itself could only amount to the thing itself (see Schweizer 2008: 12). The Syrian poet describes scenes in which historic events and promises made by those in power have resulted in disappointments, resulting in this endless wait:

Fifty days – perhaps – the train is late…	خمسين يوما ـ ربما ـ تأخر القطار…
Fifty years – perhaps – the train is late…	خمسين عاما ـ ربما ـ تأخر القطار…
Fifty centuries – perhaps – the train is late…	خمسين قرنا ـ ربما ـ تأخر القطار…
[...]	[...]
The flesh on our backs…	وصار لحم ظهرنا…
Plastered to the walls…	جزءا من الجدار
	(Qabbānī 1999: n.p.)

Abdullah Al-Shahham argues that for Qabbānī, Godot could provide a rebellion against state corruption that renders people impotent (see 1989: 254). The poet is in effect calling for a revolution marked by the arrival of the spectre in the person of Godot. The arrivant will help the citizens revolt against stagnant societal practices and corrupt dictators, who are often portrayed in the forms of a ruler, a caliph or a sultan representing, in Mohja Kahf's words, 'the oppressive political and social Establishment' (2000: 45). Thus, as Derrida notes, the return of the spectre may be revolutionary, inciting change, but its appearance may testify to a past that is not over rather than to a future that is yet to be lived (see 1994: 99). In essence, it may fail to deliver. In all likelihood, Qabbānī's Godot can only testify to a lived past.

Not having any knowledge of the spectre[4] allows the person to attribute various qualities to it. In the poem, Qabbānī admits that they have never seen the awaited Godot, but those who claim to have seen him ascribe magical and god-like qualities to him. The arrivant is an awaited messiah whose radiant face will not only baffle those who see it but whose actions would provide sustenance for the poor, cure the sick and raise the dead (see Qabbānī 1993: 289). Qabbānī's Godot assumes god-like qualities, as with his arrival comes the promise of paradise underneath which rivers flow, a sentence that is a direct borrowing from the Quran. In Derrida's words, the citizens in the poem wait in a 'desert-like messianism (without content and without identifiable messiah), of this also *abyssal* desert, "desert in the desert"', waiting for the 'coming of the other' (1994: 28). Qabbānī's citizens wait in this desert-like locale with optimism, ignorant of the messianic, because they hope that 'the coming of the other, the absolute and unpredictable singularity of the arrivant [is] justice' (1994: 33). The spectre or arrivant, as per Derrida, indicates a certain visibility of the invisible (see 1994: 100). The citizens in the poem have never encountered Godot, yet they continue to wait. By being invisible Godot paralyses, and this invisible presence may fail to bring forthwith justice. Derrida writes that the spectre is also what we visualize and an imaginary screen on which we project our wishes (1994: 125). The fifty years' wait of the Arab citizens may not deliver the intended, for they are projecting what they wish to see on the screen. Nonetheless, they persevere in their wait, as they are unable to leave; they remain at the mercy of someone who in all likelihood will not come. Similarly, Schweizer notes that waiting in Beckett's play is in all probability a wait for Godot who will not come, but one is forced to invoke him to sustain the wait (see 2008: 11).

In Qabbānī's poem, however, the waiting becomes the only option for the citizens to free themselves from the constraints of the past and the cruelty of the present. In the station, which evolves into a metaphor for their lives, they are constricted in their movement, their lives are postponed and time stands still. The poet writes:

We wait for the train	ننتظر القطار
The clock has been broken since we arrived	مكسورة ـ ـ منذ أتينا ـ ساعة الزمان
Time is stagnant...	و الوقت لا يمر..
There are no hands to mark the seconds	والثواني ما لها سيقان
The loudspeakers crush us...	تعلكنا..
Suppress us...	تنهشنا..
With their grinding teeth...	مكبرات الصوت بالأسنان..
Take heed!...	إنتبهوا !..
Take heed!...	إنتبهوا !..
No one can leave the place	لا أحد يقدر أن يغادر المكان
To buy a newspaper...	ليشتري جريدة
Or a bread roll...	أو كعكة

(Qabbānī 1999: n.p.)

Time is suspended, and in this deferred time no one is able or even allowed to leave. Moreover, because of the uncertainty of arrival, time must be endured and felt rather than traversed and thought (see Schweizer 2008: 2). They are at the mercy of this deadening silence in an arid desert – and the desert has often been presented as the void that would invite a certain divine power. Asja Szafraniec suggests that it is also the final image of renunciation and self-denial, 'which by its negative aspect paved the way to the direct intimation of God' (2007: 164). The assumption being that absolute lack can only invite change. The deserted space of Beckett's stage may similarly reflect a climate of renunciation (2007). But by invoking a renunciation, one could potentially also be invoking its opposite. In *Waiting for Godot*, Estragon complains of this desert-like existence: 'Nothing happens, nobody comes, nobody goes, it's awful!' (Beckett 1979: 27). This expanse must be filled with words.

In a desert-like locale, there remains a possibility of an arrival. Meanwhile, time itself is irrelevant as it is always deferred. Time will only become relevant when the spectre in the form of Godot appears. In the meantime, the only markers of time point to a deteriorating situation; a radish turns into a turnip and boots no longer fit. This is also the condition of the citizens who wait in Qabbānī's poem. Godot will always come tomorrow, and in his absence, there is nothing but decline and stagnation. Qabbānī urges Godot to appear to help incite change. He will help those who wait to revolt against merciless regimes. However, Derrida argues that the 'messianic, including its revolutionary forms (and the messianic is always revolutionary, it has to be), would be urgency, imminence but, irreducible paradox, a waiting without horizon of expectation' (1994: 211). This despairing messianism has a curious 'taste of death' (1994: 212). It reeks of a finality that will not arrive.

As I have mentioned earlier, in his footnote to the poem, Qabbānī is apprehensive that this awaited saviour may cause more destruction, carrying death within its folds. The citizens' wait is a silent one, as their wishes are echoed through the words of the poet. Conversely, Vladimir and Estragon are more vocal. In the case of Beckett's tramps, Anderton notes that the 'ideal for Vladimir and Estragon is a figure of meaning for their future and the charade that Godot embodies provides a suitable distraction from their abandoned state' (2016: 108). They need a validation that they exist. With Qabbānī, the anticipated validation is a deliverance from pain and a freeing from enslavement rather than a proof of existence.

Ultimately, the arrival of Godot is immaterial. In the play, the lives of Vladimir and Estragon are disrupted and marked by the wait. Their life evolves into a suspended wait, and with it comes uncertainty. If there is to be activity, it is often composed of repetitive acts that maintain the circuitousness of existence, the inability to arrive anywhere. The actions are robotic, evolving from mere repetitions. As Ulrika Maude argues:

The paradox of habit therefore resides in its diminution of consciousness and will, conventionally associated with ideas of self, but also in its simultaneous suggestion that any sense of self resides precisely in and emerges out of these mechanical, near-automated actions.

(2012: 480)

These repetitive actions become the part of the self that is accessible. Eventually, the wait and these repeated actions develop into the only possible existence.

The Arab Godot, humanity's saviour

As previously discussed, in his introduction to the poems Qabbānī endeavoured to define Godot. Both poems draw on centuries of Arab history and cultural symbols, and Godot becomes the persona that is invited by the poet to emerge from and form part of this history. Godot embodies one component of a lost humanity, and his arrival will help restore part of this human dignity to the citizens. With Beckett, meanwhile, what remains of a person's identity is humanity itself, and this is signified through the wounds, which depict the 'universality of pain' (Levy 2001: 624). In *Waiting for Godot* Vladimir tells Estragon, 'But at this place, at this moment of time, all mankind is us, whether we like it or not' (Beckett 1979: 51). This collective pain is also present in both of Qabbānī's poems. The wait becomes the shared destiny of the citizens. In 'A Television Interview with an Arab Godot', however, the communal pain disintegrates to become the poet's pain; the collective pronoun is replaced by the first-person pronoun in the opening stanza, and the wait becomes more desperate:

I am waiting for the train to depart	مُنْتَظِرٌ أَن يَرْحَلَ القِطَارْ
Any train...	أَيُّ قِطَارٍ كانَ ...
[...]	[...].
I am like Godot...	أنا كغودو ..
[...]	[...]
I waited in the queue for a million years.	وقفتُ في الطّابورِ مليونَ سَنَةْ

(Qabbānī 1990: 61–2)

The speaker becomes all of humanity and his only companion now is a crawling cockroach on his suitcase (Qabbānī 1990: 64). In an imagined dialogue between the two, the cockroach identifies himself as an immigrant who is also waiting for the train (Qabbānī 1990: 64). As with the poet, the cockroach is wearing a hat and a coat, a direct allusion to Beckett's characters.

It is also a metaphor for a diminished existence. Exasperated by the wait, the poet begins to identify himself as Godot. And this new Godot evolves to personify the Arab person, who has been denied entry into the world:

I am Godot...	... غودو أنا
Stranger in every city	وليسَ في العالمِ من مدينةٍ
in this world.	يَعْرِفُني فيها أحدٌ.
All the lights of the stations I seek	كلُّ المحطاتِ التي أقْصِدُها
Are turned off.	مُطْفَأَةُ الأنوارِ
	(Qabbānī 1990: 65)

The poet questions whether the passing trains that leave him behind are his destiny or whether they are announcing the arrivant that personifies death. The death-like wait marks eternity; the citizens will remain in limbo waiting helplessly in this endless time.

Even though Qabbānī, representing the Arab individual, embraces the character of Godot, he also remains waiting for a saviour who will free him from the clutches and cruelty of history and the oppression of society. He remains optimistic that one day the arrivant will deliver and one day a green shrub will sprout from the barren landscape:

And I am still searching in between the sand, for some green shrubs	لم أزلْ أبحثُ فوق الرَمْل ، عن بقية اخْضرارٍ
[...]	[...]
And I am still a believer in poetry that will emerge like a rose from the ruins.	ولم أزلْ أوْمِنُ بالشعرِ الذي يَطْلُعُ كالوردة من خاصرةِ الدمارِ
	(Qabbānī 1990: 69)

His hope of finding salvation lies with the female figure of Fatima, who bears messianic qualities.[5] The poet tells us that she is the only person who could protect them from the Mongol invasion.[6] Fatima and the speaker have exchanged roles; she becomes the Godot-like figure who will bring about change, while the speaker only assumes the name Godot. The reference to Fatima points to another deferral, as the speaker gives her the attributes of Zarqa'a al-Yamama, who was able to foresee the future.[7] The Godot-poet figure, meanwhile, continues in his million-year wait, donning his coat, carrying his bags, as he hopes to invent the train to leave this desolate state behind (Qabbānī 1990: 70). If in *Waiting for Godot*, Beckett offers us the space 'in which we must pause, breaking from the categories of presence and absence – of life and death, speech and silence into a ghostly environment of waiting for the night' (Watt 2006: 177), Qabbānī, on the other hand, leaves us in an eerie station consumed by voices from the past awaiting a saviour. In his poetry, there is always a glimpse of hope, but hope for Qabbānī tends to come through the next generation; hence it is forever deferred (see Litvin 2011: 119).[8]

Temporality is also irrelevant in this poem; the present is always pointing to an event that is yet to happen or to a past event that has already happened. The present is suspended in time and subjugated to another juncture. In *Waiting for Godot*, the markers of time abound, but a fixed temporal landmark is lacking (see Ionescu 2013: 73). When Vladimir says that they have a date with Godot on Saturday, Estragon replies, 'But what Saturday? And is it Saturday? Is it not rather Sunday? (Pause.) Or Monday? (Pause.) Or Friday?' (Beckett 1979: 11). Similarly, in Qabbānī's poems, in spite of the many references to time, it exists elsewhere, beyond the present. The speaker tells us that their watches have stopped (Qabbānī 1990: 63 and 1993: 285) and that he has been waiting a million years, a thousand years (Qabbānī 1990: 53, 60), from the 1920s to 1970s, and fifty days (Qabbānī 1993: 285, 286). One will never know when or if the arrivant will appear. Time is irrelevant, as the anticipated arrival can compress or extend it. Time can only exist as a reference if lives are set according to clocks or synchronized with watches (see Schweizer 2008: 3). In this instance, the clocks have stopped, and time is chaotic.

Conclusion

Both of Qabbānī's poems end as they have begun, with waiting. The last stanza of 'Waiting for Godot' emphasizes the barrenness and helplessness of the people's situation, and the one exit from this paralysis lies with the anticipated arrival (see Qabbānī 1993: 296). In 'A Television Interview with an Arab Godot', it is the speaker in the person of Godot who waits, convinced that in the distant horizon a station awaits him, and if he wills it, he can create a train to reach his destination (see Qabbānī 1990: 70). In spite of the unlikeliness that salvation will arrive in the form of Godot, both poems end in the same spirit as Beckett's play, with an inability to move:

VLADIMIR: Well? Shall we go?
ESTRAGON: Yes, let's go.
        They do not move. (Beckett 1979: 60)

Like Vladimir and Estragon, the speaker ends by saying that if he decrees, a train will arrive, the assumption being that the decision is his. Yet he remains seated in this barren place, waiting for a train that will never materialize; he will never arrive at a station that would free him from the clutches of time. Beckett's characters and the citizens of Qabbānī's poems find themselves with a useless currency, time; because their time of waiting cannot be exchanged (see Schweizer 2008: 6). They are unable to leave and can only wait silently for an unlikely arrival.

Swedish stage director Jan Jönson, who directed Beckett's plays in both San Quentin State Prison in California and Kumla Prison in Sweden, once told Beckett in Paris that what attracted him to the plays was the silence (see Knowlson and Knowlson 2014: 279). He added that the prisoners understood Godot. The agonizing and muted wait of the Arab citizens is what pervades the lines of Qabbānī's Godot poems. Like San Quentin's actors, these citizens who waited endlessly for salvation also understood who Godot is.

Notes

1. 'Nizār Qabbānī (born 21 March 1923, Damascus, Syria – died 30 April 1998, London, Eng.), Syrian diplomat and poet whose subject matter, at first strictly erotic and romantic, grew to embrace political issues as well. Written in simple but eloquent language, his verses, some of which were set to music, won the hearts of countless Arabic speakers throughout the Middle East and Africa. Qabbānī, who was born into a middle-class merchant family, was also the grandnephew of the pioneering Arab playwright Abū Khalīl Qabbānī. He studied law at the University of Damascus (LLB, 1945) and then began his varied career as a diplomat. He served in the Syrian embassies in Egypt, Turkey, Lebanon, Britain, China and Spain before retiring in 1966 and moving to Beirut, Lebanon, where he founded the Manshurāt Nizār Qabbānī, a publishing company' (Britannica 2016). According to Z. Gabay, some of Qabbāni's poetry was influenced by 'Western poetry and especially by Baudelaire, Verlaine, Mallarme, Prevert and also by the symbolist Arabic poets. Some of his poems are dedicated to Baudelaire and other French poets' (1973: 220).
2. The poem was also published in a collection of political poems, and as part of an anthology of Qabbānī's poetry, *Al 'amaal assiyasiya alkamila* by Manshuraat Nizār Qabbānī in Beirut.
3. For more details, please refer to Ali Ahmed Mohammed Al-Arood's book, *Jidaliyyat Nizār Qabbānī fi el-Naqd el 'Arabi el-Hadeeth* (Al-Arood). In addition, according to Gabay, 'Qabbani, perhaps more than any other poet of his range and calibre has suffered spiritually because of his sensitivity, sincerity and moral courage. He has been accused of treason or reaction by those ruling his society because he has tried "to lift the veil" that covers corruption and

backwardness in the life of the Arabs' (1973: 211). While in contrast, Salma al-Khadra al-Jayyusi considered the writings of the Syrian poet an important social document (1957: 1029).

4   Derrida writes regarding the spectrer: 'one does not know what it is ... It is something that one does not know ... and one does not know if precisely it is, if it exists, if it responds to a name and corresponds to an essence. One does not know: not out of ignorance, but because this non-object, this non-present present, this being-there of an absent or departed one no longer belongs to knowledge ... One does not know if it is living or if it is dead' (1994: 6).

5   Although the poet is here referring to Fatima, one of Prophet Mohammed's daughters, the name itself has been used extensively in Arabic literature to personify the patient and enduring Arab female who can stand against all adversity.

6   The Mongols sacked and destroyed Baghdad, the capital of the Abbasid Caliphate, and destroyed other Arab cities such as Aleppo in northern Syria. The invasion was led by Hulagu Khan in 1258.

7   Zarqa'a al-Yamama warned her people that their enemies will arrive camouflaged behind trees; initially, her people did not believe her, and when the omen came true, they plucked out her eyes.

8   In his poetry, Qabbānī has often defended the young: 'He brought to the fore the crucial personal problems of the Arab youth, who were rebelling against their fathers' ways' (Loya 1975: 483). The Syrian poet was able to read and expound on the Arab political malaise and failures because of his long years serving as a diplomat (Kamel 2011).

Works cited

Al-Arood, Ali Ahmed Mohammed (2007), *Jidaliyyat Nizār Qabbānī fi el-Naqd el 'Arabi el-Hadeeth*, Irbid: Dar al Kitab al Thaqafi.

al-Jayyusi, Salma al-Khadra (1957), 'The Poetry of Nizar Qabbānī: An Important Social Document', *al-Adaab*, 11: 1027–111.

Al-Shahham, Abdullah A. M. A. (1989), 'The Political Poetry of Nizar Qabbani: A Critical Study and Translation', PhD diss., University of Edinburgh, Edinburgh.

Anderton, J. (2016), *Beckett's Creatures: Art of Failure after the Holocaust*, New York: Bloomsbury Methuen Drama.

Beckett, S. (1931), *Proust*, New York: Grove Press.

Beckett, S. (1979), *Waiting for Godot*, New York: Grove Press.

Britannica, The Editors of Encyclopædia (2016), 'Britannica.com', *Encyclopædia Britannica*, 3 December 2017 Available online: https://www.britannica.com/biography/Nizar-Qabbani (7 April 2016).

Darwish, M. (2010), *Journal of an Ordinary Grief*, trans. Ibrahim Muhawi, New York: Archipelago Books.

Derrida, J. (1994), *Specters of Marx: The State of the Debt, The Work of Mourning & The New International*, trans. Peggy Kamuf, New York: Routledge.

Gabay, Z. (1973), 'Nizār Qabbānī, the Poet and His Poetry', *Middle Eastern Studies*, 9 (2): 207–22.

Ionescu, A. (2013), 'Waiting for Blanchot: A Third Act for Beckett's Play', *Partial Answers*, 11 (1): 71–86.

Kahf, M. (2000), 'Politics and Erotics in Nizar Kabbani's Poetry: From the Sultan's Wife to the Lady Friend', *World Literature Today*, 74 (1): 44–52.

Kamel, Mohammad Hassan (2011), 'Nizar Qabbānī: bayn Matraqit al-Naqd wa Sindan al Hadatha', *Ittihad al-Kuttab wal Muthaqafeen al-Arab*. Available online: http://www.alexandrie3009.com/vb/archive/index.php/t-1232.html (accessed 26 April 2019).

Knowlson, James and Elizabeth Knowlson, eds. (2014), *Beckett Remembering/ Remembering Beckett*, New York: Arcade Publishing.

Levy, Eric P. (2001), 'The Beckettian Mimesis of Seeing Nothing', *University of Toronto Quarterly*, 70 (2): 620–32.

Litvin, M. (2011), *Hamlet's Arab Journey Book Subtitle: Shakespeare's Prince and Nasser's Ghost*, New Jersey: Princeton University Press.

Loya, A. (1975), 'Poetry as a Social Document: The Social Position of the Arab Woman as Reflected in the Poetry of Nizar Qabbani', *International Journal of Middle East Studies*, 6 (4): 481–94.

Maude, U. (2012), 'Beckett and the Laws of Habit', *Modernism/Modernity*, 18 (4): 813–21.

Qabbānī, N. (1990), *A Match in My Hand, and Your Petty Paper Nations (Al-Kabrit fi yadi ... wa Diwailatukum min Waraq)*, 2nd ed., Beirut: Manshuraat Nizār Qabbānī.

Qabbānī, N. (1993), *Al 'amaal assiyasiya alkamila. 5*, Vol. 3. Beirut: Manshuraat Nizār Qabbānī.

Qabbānī, N. (1999), *No*, 13th ed., Beirut: Manshūrāt Nizār Qabbānī.

Schweizer, H. (2008), *On Waiting*, New York: Routledge.

Szafraniec, A. (2007), *Beckett, Derrida, and the Event of Literature*, Redwood City: Stanford University Press.

Watt, D. (2006), '"It's a Joke, I Do Not Accept": Derrida's Demanding Call and Other Dead Voices', *Journal for Cultural Research*, 10 (2): 173–83.

15

Forgetfulness of the past as revealed in Minoru Betsuyaku's *Godot Has Come:* A play inspired by *Waiting for Godot*

Mariko Hori Tanaka

As James Berger writes, 'The Baudrillardian, postmodern post-apocalypse is the site of "post-history"' (1999: 9); terms such as 'post-modernity', 'post-apocalypse' and 'post-history' have become concepts that refer to the inhuman mass destruction in atrocities such as the Holocaust and Hiroshima. Jean-Luc Nancy relates Fukushima's nuclear catastrophe, which happened after the March 2011 earthquake in north-east Japan, to such calamities in order to highlight that 'What Fukushima adds to Hiroshima is the threat of apocalypse that opens onto nothing, onto the negation of an apocalypse itself, a threat that depends not just on military use of the atom and perhaps not even on the sole use of the atom in general' (2015: 21). If the very meaning of apocalypse is threatened by today's irreparable catastrophes, history will also become impossible because history 'is the first manifestation of catastrophe: procedure, growth, plan, then progress', and today 'there is no indication of what should be substituted for the destroyed or disappeared' (2015: 58).

After the Second World War, many French and Japanese survivors, as if trying to ward off their uneasiness of having assisted the Germans or of having been driven to a losing battle, were desperately striving to get through the confusion of the immediate post-war era by turning a blind eye to the aftermath of the war. The most vulnerable and powerless were left suffering both from the physical and psychological pain endured during the conflict, in Nazi concentration camps or cities destroyed by air raids. Many invalided soldiers were met with scornful indifference at their return from the war. In a surge of patriotism to rebuild countries, the victims were hidden, foreigners were discriminated against and perpetrators were often acquitted of charges for their cooperation with wartime authorities. Such deliberate forgetfulness regarding the atrocities of war prevailed throughout many post-war societies, demonstrating how, as E. Ann Kaplan states, '[i]ndividuals and cultures [...] perform forgetting as a way of protecting themselves from the horrors of what one (or the culture) has done or what has been done to oneself or others in one's society' (Kaplan 2005: 74). Resisting such mechanism of forgetting, Beckett's work illuminates those who are victimized, discriminated against, marginalized in society, and those who die in silence. Beckett sought to give a voice to those that remained and had been ruined, whose voiceless voices are affluent in today's post-apocalyptic and post-historical world.

Slavoj Žižek describes *Waiting for Godot* as the 'prototype of a modernist text', for we all know that Godot will not arrive and that he is 'just a name for nothingness, for a central absence' (1992: 145). Besides, one may imagine that Godot would be a fearful character if he was to come, but the modernist text evades his arrival in any case. Žižek, however, argues that, in a post-modernist version of the text, Godot would appear in front of us:

> [H]e would be someone exactly like us, someone who lives the same futile, boring life that we do, who enjoys the same stupid pleasures. The only difference would be that, not knowing it himself, he has found himself by chance at the place of the Thing; he would be the incarnation of the Thing whose arrival was awaited.
>
> (1992: 145)

As Žižek adds, 'the Thing' here means 'a strange body in its very centre' encircled by its antagonists (1992: 169). In other words, the Thing is the Other who is distanced, dismissed, forgotten, ignored and victimized, a victim that is alive but does not exist for most of the people in society.

Minoru Betsuyaku, a Japanese playwright strongly influenced by Beckett, depicted such a postmodern Godot as Žižek describes, in his rewriting of *Waiting for Godot*, entitled *Godot Has Come* (2010). In this play, Godot appears as 'someone exactly like us' but Vladimir and Estragon (who are waiting for him) do not understand the significance of his arrival.[1] Betsuyaku explains the mechanism of 'waiting' in his comparative analysis of *Waiting for Godot* and 'Waiting in Vain [Machiboke]', a popular Japanese song based on a Manchu legend:[2]

While a farmer in 'Waiting in Vain' would not mistake what he waits for, Vladimir and Estragon, who are exhausted from waiting for so long, no longer interested in what they wait for but in 'waiting' itself, would mistake what they wait for.

That is why Vladimir and Estragon are not so interested in who Godot is. Therefore, even if Godot appears in the name of Godot, instead of Pozzo or Lucky, they would never be able to meet Godot.

When Godot appears and says 'I am Godot', Vladimir and Estragon would say to him, 'No, we are waiting for Godot' [...].

No one would deny that such an exchange can be born out of the structure of *Waiting for Godot*. The despair of the two tramps' waiting for Godot is structured in this way.

(2012: 309–10)

Betsuyaku, therefore, sees in the structure of *Waiting for Godot* the lost incentive of Vladimir and Estragon's waiting, which induces their state of oblivion regarding what they are waiting for. Naturally, Betsuyaku was motivated by this observation to write *Godot Has Come*. The remainder of this chapter will discuss *Godot Has Come* and some of Betsuyaku's earlier works in the light of these insights, as well as in relation to Japan's global and local situation.

*

It goes without saying that *Waiting for Godot* was written when Europe was still in ruins and that the play is studded with dialogue and metaphors that Beckett observed during the war. The scarcity of food and lodging in the stable that is mentioned in the play might have been based on Beckett's own experience, particularly from his conversation with Suzanne during their escape from Paris to Roussillon, as James Knowlson points out (see 1996: 379). The play's barren landscape recalls a land ravaged by air raids; it could be Saint-Lô, for instance, where Beckett committed himself to the rehabilitation of the city and its people. Moreover, the protagonists also seem to allude repeatedly to the aftermath of the war, though in a tacit manner:

Estragon: The best thing would be to kill me, like the other.
Vladimir: What other? [*Pause.*] What other?
Estragon: Like billions of others.
Vladimir: [*Sententious.*] To every man his little cross. [*He sighs.*] Till he dies. [*Afterthought.*] And is forgotten.

(Beckett 1986: 58)

Estragon and Vladimir have this conversation just before they refer to 'the dead voices' (Beckett 1986: 58). How many people have died and been forgotten in the course of human history? Do political leaders bear in mind all those who died in war and calamity? Despite the absence of specific references that clarify the couple's dialogue, such rhetorical questions seem to pierce through their exchanges.

Waiting for Godot influenced many young Japanese artists in the 1960s who were frustrated by the government's settlement of the war that promoted a forgetting of the past and encouraged thinking ahead for future prosperity. Some had difficulty expunging their feelings of guilt towards those killed in the war and thought of themselves as losers. Young people were especially sensitive and discontented with the government's lukewarm performance in post-war recovery. Their criticism became heightened when Japan was due to renew the US-Japan Mutual Security Treaty, but their voices would not be heard. Artists and writers such as Betsuyaku and Tadashi Suzuki,[3] who constituted the so-called first generation of the Little Theatre Movement in the 1960s, felt great frustration and despair and sought to express it in the theatre. The language of failure expressed by Beckett gave them the impetus to experiment with their own theatrical voice.

Responding to Beckett, Betsuyaku wrote several plays that could well be characterized as belonging to the Theatre of the Absurd. Clearly inspired by Beckett, his post-apocalyptic *The Elephant* (1962), like *Endgame*, 'crystallized the dilemma of human survival in the nuclear age, an age in which the threat of imminent mass death makes a mockery of all human action' (Goodman 1994: 191). The main focus of this play is the psychological dilemma that the *hibakusha*, A-bomb victims, experienced in post-war Japanese society. In it, the Invalid, one of the victims confined to a hospital, wishes to show his keloid scar to other people, while his nephew, also a *hibakusha*, tries to stop his uncle from doing so, believing that it is better for the *hibakusha* to accept the meaninglessness of their lives and die silently. In those days, without proper scientific information, the *hibakusha* were discriminated against by rumours that they suffered from contagious diseases or might give birth to handicapped offspring, and as a result many faced difficulty in getting married or securing jobs. Although the play could be read as a criticism of society's rejection of the *hibakusha* and how it forced them to accept lives of passive resignation, 'the central issue of the play', writes David G. Goodman, 'whether to accept or reject the devaluation of experience – comes directly from the 1960 demonstrations and has specific political implications' (Goodman 1994:). Defeated in their struggle against the government, many young Japanese were faced with the decision of whether to continue their futile struggle or to abandon it.

Another play by Betsuyaku, *A Corpse of a Marine under Water* (1978),[4] was born from his plan to adapt *Endgame*, although replacing the latter's background of unknown catastrophe with the war Japan had fought and lost. The main characters are two wounded soldiers: one suffers from a psychic trauma triggered by the death of his fellow soldier, who did not know the war was over and committed hara-kiri (self-disembowelment), while the other, like Clov, takes care of the former. The first soldier wishes to be forgiven both by the Emperor and the State because he did not go to the front line, as well as by his comrade who died unavailingly. Feeling like he is no longer alive and yearning to do so, he strives to experience bodily pain. And so, he first restrains himself from emptying his bowels, then asks the second soldier to strangle him and cut his wrist, and finally strangles himself and dies. As he dies, he gasps: 'I'll live, I'll keep living' (Betsuyaku 1979).

The feeling of loss experienced by first soldier recalls that of those who, having worshipped the God-Emperor in the pre-war period, had suddenly lost Him with the State after the war. Betsuyaku replaced the death that was nothing but a void for Hamm in *Endgame* with the Emperor and the State, which, however, 'are something ungraspable in life' so that the invalided soldier can only try 'to understand them through his feeling of pain' (Betsuyaku 1991: 248). If Hamm cannot grasp death or the void, the soldier cannot understand the Emperor and the State that deprived him of the feeling that he is alive. Both Hamm and the soldier suffer from a feeling of loss, unaware of why they feel it, but while Hamm bears his futility in life the soldier puts an end to it, believing that he has found its meaning.

While Beckett wrote plays about the pain of disaster victims, in many cases purposely obscuring the cause of their calamity, Betsuyaku often localized his works, focusing, for instance, on the pain of those who survived the Pacific War (such as in the early plays discussed above). However, in 2007, responding to more recent global catastrophes, but also to the repeated mechanism of forgetting, Betsuyaku wrote *Godot Has Come*, his most recent play that has been inspired by Beckett's work. The play received two prestigious theatre awards in Japan – the Tsuruya Nanboku Play Award and the Asahi Award. Like Beckett's original text, *Godot Has Come* begins with Estragon's attempt to take off his boot. It also includes Pozzo, Lucky and the boy who bears a message from Godot but introduces four new unnamed women along with the homonymous protagonist, making Betsuyaku's play take a different course from the original.

Unlike in *Waiting for Godot* and Betsuyaku's earlier plays, the Vladimir and Estragon in *Godot Has Come* do not speak much about their pain – physical or psychological. They also seem less jaded than Beckett's tramps, although they too kill time: Vladimir plays a trumpet to express what he wants to say; Estragon attempts to fish a carrot out of a bucket with a fishing rod. The protagonists even forget that they are waiting for Godot, hence, when he arrives they do not seem to care. It is then that the other characters appear and Woman 1 suggests that they have the boy beat them so that they might realize that Godot has arrived. However, violence is unable to make Vladimir and Estragon recognize the real meaning of Godot's arrival. It turns out to be a futile attempt, and as a result the play ends as a slapstick comedy. Physical pain, as in the case of the invalided soldier in *A Corpse of a Marine under Water*, is of no use here, because those living in twenty-first-century Japan no longer feel pain or have any understanding of what Godot represents. The traumatic feeling of guilt and remorse that caused the pain of the war survivors is long lost.

In Beckett's play Godot may be a sort of 'Thanatos' who brings death to the two tramps. In fact, Beckett once said in his letter to the director of the West German premiere production of *Warten auf Godot* that while '[e]ach person is free to put a face on him' and the 'more fortunate, will see in him Thanatos', he forbids interpreting any character, including Godot, as 'emblems' or 'symbols' (2011: 391). Beckett also says that 'Godot himself is not a different species from those he cannot or will not help' (2011: 391). Beckett's Godot is another 'Unnamable' and as a result neither Vladimir nor Estragon can approach him. In Betsuyaku's play, however, Godot is just a strange man in whom the tramps are not interested. This is in line with Žižek's definition of Godot: he is someone like us but regarded as the Other. The key event in Betsuyaku's play is thus not Godot's arrival, but the fact that the tramps have completely forgotten the significance of his arrival.

*

The forgetfulness of an immediate past is shown in *Waiting for Godot* through Estragon's inability to tell what his own boots are like, whether or not he met Lucky, whose bone he ate, or even what day of the week it is. In *Godot Has Come*, the uncertainty is not limited to such simple memories. It is expressed in the uncertainty about missing family members. Woman 4, who pushes a pram carrying her sister's child, is looking for the child's father named Vladimir, so when she meets Vladimir she makes the child call him 'Daddy', while Woman 1 claims that Estragon is her son. However, Vladimir denies being the child's father and Estragon is confused by the woman's assertion. And yet they do not seem to care about whether they have actually found the person they were looking for. As Wonde argues, 'Das Warten und Suchen bzw. das Philosophieren über die Suche ist ihnen lieber als wirklich etwas zu tun. Das Finden interessiert schon nicht mehr' (The characters are absorbed in arguing about the idea of seeking, rather than just waiting or seeking. They are no longer interested in finding) (2012: n.p.). By envisioning their lost family members in strangers, these characters are trying to cope with their loneliness in the absence of their loved ones. But while Beckett's tramps seek to bond with anyone who passes by, Betsuyaku's couple evade involvement with strangers. With the theme of broken families Betsuyaku relates the text directly to a major social issue in post-war Japan.

Betsuyaku often uses a bus stop in his works as a meeting point for strangers. He explains why as follows:

If I sit on a bench at a bus stop, no passers-by will doubt that I am waiting for a bus. Even if I am not waiting for a bus, if I just sit on a bench there, people will just pass me by, thinking that I am just waiting for a bus. Therefore, if I want to tell the passers-by that I am not waiting for a bus, I have to stand up and stop him to tell him that I am not waiting for a bus but just sitting on a bench. But even so, he will say 'So what?' and leave without seeing my face. What I want to say is that the human relationship based on unimaginable suspicions is one caused by the fact that people are always watching other people in doubt, even if they behave as they look. The community we used to have in the old days was always like that. My love and hate towards the so-called 'community' always start from that.

(Betsuyaku 1991: 145)

Betsuyaku suggests here that mistrust is a precondition to communicating with strangers. Such suspicion is also seen in *Waiting for Godot*, e.g. when the two tramps and Pozzo meet. Marjorie Perloff contends that it reflects the situation that Beckett experienced when he was hiding in Rousillon, where 'there was no sure way of differentiating between friend and enemy. Collaborator and Resistance fighter, after all, looked alike' (2005: 81). Whether it is in wartime or in peace, both Beckett and Betsuyaku seem to suggest that such doubt always underlies any human encounter. If there appears to be no such doubt in the encounters of *Godot Has Come*, it is only to reflect that in today's Japan people keep away from the encounter itself.

The characters in the play are all more or less criminals and outcasts or vagabonds. Jean Baudrillard calls this merging of roles a sign of our being 'all simultaneously victims, murderers and accomplices' of today's 'forms of violence' (1998: 67). The Other, who used to fight for his/her freedom and rights in the 1960s, has lost his/her ideals. 'No longer having either object or objective' (1998: 66) to change society or to create new systems, he/she turns his/her anger of being an outcast towards society.

Those who commit meaningless crimes in Betsuyaku's play are misfits in society. Betsuyaku once referred to the similarities between the 'incomprehensibility' of today's crimes and 'pain':

The crime analysts in the media temporarily soothe our anxiety affected by the 'incomprehensibility' of crimes but the roots of the crimes can never be cured with their analyses, just like injecting morphine to momentarily ease a patient's pain of an unknown origin. Pain is a kind of warning. The 'incomprehensibility' of crimes is also a kind of warning [...]. The reason why the media reports news of crimes is to keep us responding to the news with our healthy feeling of life and to remove our anxiety to be left in a huge building without any warning devices.

(1981: 7–8)

Hence, Betsuyaku believes that crimes are essential to our 'healthy' lives, just as pain is necessary for us, because it warns us when there is something wrong with our bodies. But he also deplores that crimes today, having become more incomprehensible than ever, 'do not work as crimes healthily' (1981: 16). This is not unrelated to the lack of love and care in the family system that used to support healthy human relationships in Japanese society referenced in the play.

A society where such 'forms of violence' pervade cannot properly deal with illness and death either. In Betsuyaku's *Godot Has Come*, Pozzo, who suffers from an unknown illness, is in wheelchair and on an IV drip. It is clear that this is a critical allusion to the system of hospitalization in today's Japan. With the development of healthcare, people in terminal diseases are often kept at the hospital until they die, rather than spending their last days at homes. Betsuyaku once wrote that 'entering a hospital resembles imprisonment' (2001: 55), an incarceration that deprives the individual from a dignified death.

Betsuyaku also uses funeral homes often as a setting for his plays. In *Godot Has Come*, an empty coffin is prepared for a dead person, but there is no one to be put in it. A funeral reception desk is set, but there is no funeral to be performed. In Japan, the names of attendees at a funeral must be registered at the funeral reception as a record for the host, who usually sends offerings in return to those who have made offerings at the funeral. This is perhaps a uniqueness of Japanese funerals. Receptionists are appointed to record the names of condolers. Anyone can attend the ceremony, even passers-by. Therefore, Godot, a stranger and a passer-by, is welcomed to register his name in the reception book. In fact, he is forced to register by two women, as if caught in a trap. But by whom he is deceived is unknown, for the funeral has no dead person. If in *Waiting for Godot* it is Godot who is absent, in this case it is death. Nevertheless, and regardless of this absence, the ceremony takes place.

*

The collective memory of the dead in war or disaster is often publicly preserved in the form of memorials, but this kind of remembrance can also be replaced by mass forgetting. Baudrillard warns about such mechanism of forgetting in the name of 'archives', which can be exemplified in Hiroshima today:

> Now, it's true that Hiroshima is a city reborn, but this new Hiroshima is also a part of its being definitively wiped out. The traumatic event has been whitewashed. All archives are whitewashing devices. The event is distanced from us once and for all by the very means available to us

for remembering it. This is a form of fatality. But who are we to make responsible for it? We're all party to it.

(1998: 30)

Baudrillard's lament must have been a part of Betsuyaku's motive for writing *Godot Has Come*. The ability to recognize Godot, and the importance of remembering the atrocities experienced in the Pacific War and Hiroshima (and now Fukushima), disappears from the Japanese collective consciousness. The pain that the elders suffered during the war, or the fact that people living today have lost their homes in Fukushima, does not seem to evoke empathy in the majority of people in today's Japan. Betsuyaku's play alerts us to such a state of oblivion that pervades contemporary Japanese society. As Baudrillard observes:

> With the construction of a parallel, virtual world substituted for our own, we're no longer in the world. Being in the world has become an improbable eventuality.... Being in the world isn't being present in the world, nor being identical to oneself. It's playing on complicity, absence, illusion, distance from the world.
>
> (1998: 32)

Such a 'distance' is clearly apparent in Betsuyaku's characters, who seem too afraid to face reality and choose, instead, to remain in the comfort of a 'virtual world'. This loss of reality is a consequence of the forgetfulness of historical pain or trauma. Despite the fact that Godot has finally arrived, he has become an 'otherness' of which we have forgotten the significance: something unapproachable and fearful that is repressed in our everyday life, but that might break into it at any time.

Notes

1 Rewritings of *Waiting for Godot* are often seen in Japanese theatre. *Godot Has Come* is not the first adaptation in Japan in which Godot appears. In 1974, Kohei Tsuka wrote a play called *Matsugaura Godot no Imashime* (*A Lesson from the Matsugaura Godot*), in which Godot is named 'Absurd Man', rides on a motorcycle and dressed like Superman, appearing as a saviour to provide a cure for the corruption of society, but ironically, looking weak and powerless. In 1992, Seikou Ito also wrote a kind of backstage play of *Waiting for Godot*, entitled *Godot wa Matarenagara* (*Godot Being Waited For*). It is a cleverly written monologue by Godot who painfully regrets letting Vladimir and Estragon wait for him. In Ito's play, Godot is thus a man who suffers from his feeling of guilt due to failing to keep his promise to them, but he, too, is

victimized by the loss of human communication. For the reception history of Beckett in Japan, see Hori Tanaka (1996), and Tajiri and Hori Tanaka (2009).
2 'Waiting in Vain' is a story about a farmer who, having once caught a rabbit that ran into a tree stump, thought that he might be able to catch game if he just waited for it. The farmer decided to stop cultivating his land and wait for a rabbit instead, but no rabbit appears and, in the end, the land he had stopped ploughing became seriously neglected.
3 Betsuyaku founded the Free Stage Company in 1961 (reorganized five years later as Waseda Small Theatre Company) with director Tadashi Suzuki. Their collaboration continued until Betsuyaku left the company in 1967.
4 For more detailed discussions on *The Elephant* and *A Corpse of a Marine under Water* (see Hori Tanaka 2003).

Works cited

Baudrillard, J. (1998), *Paroxysm: Interviews with Philippe Petit*, trans. Chris Turner, London and New York: Verso.
Beckett, S. (1986), *Complete Dramatic Works*, London: Faber and Faber.
Beckett, S. (2011), *The Letters of Samuel Beckett 1941–1956*, eds. George Craig, Martha Dow Fehsenfeld, Dan Gunn and Lois More Overbeck, Cambridge: Cambridge University Press.
Berger, J. (1999), *After the End: Representations of Post-Apocalypse*, Minnesota: University of Minnesota Press.
Betsuyaku, M. (1979), *A Corpse of a Marine under Water [Umi Yukaba Mizuku Kabane]*, Tokyo: San'ichi Shobo.
Betsuyaku, M. (1981), *The Criminal Syndrome [Hanzai Shokogun]*, Tokyo: Sanseido.
Betsuyaku, M. (1991), *Scenery from Plays [Serifu no Fukei]*, Tokyo: Hakusuisha.
Betsuyaku, M. (1994), *A Sketch of Crimes [Hanzai no Mitorizu]*, Tokyo: Okokusha.
Betsuyaku, M. (2001), *A Life in Contentment [Michitarita Jinsei]*, Tokyo: Hakusuisha.
Betsuyaku, M. (2010), *Godot Has Come [Yattekita Godot]*, Tokyo: Ronsosha.
Betsuyaku, M. (2012), *How to Create Words [Kotoba no Tsukaikata]*, Tokyo: Ronsosha.
Goodman, D. G. (1994), *After Apocalypse: Four Japanese Plays of Hiroshima and Nagasaki*, New York: Cornell University's East Asia Program.
Hori Tanaka, M. (1996), 'Special Features of Beckett Performances in Japan', in L. Oppenheim and M. Buning (eds.), *Beckett On and On …*, 226–39, London: Associated University Presses.
Hori Tanaka, M. (2003), 'The Legacy of Beckett in the Contemporary Japanese Theatre', in L. Ben-Zvi (ed.), *Drawing on Beckett: Portraits, Performances, and Cultural Contexts*, 47–59, Tel Aviv: Assaph Book Series.
Hori Tanaka, M., and M. Menish, trans (n.d.), *Godot Has Come* (English), for overseas productions. Dialogues from the play cited in this essay are based on this translation. Other citations from works in Japanese are all my translation.

Kaplan, E. A. (2005), *Trauma Culture: The Politics of Terror and Loss in Media and Literature*, New Brunswick: Rutgers University Press.
Knowlson, J. (1996), *Damned to Fame: The Life of Samuel Beckett*, London: Bloomsbury.
LaCapra, D. (2001), *Writing History, Writing Trauma*, Baltimore: The Johns Hopkins University Press.
Nancy, Jean-Luc (2015), *After Fukushima: The Equivalence of Catastrophes*, trans. C. Mandell, New York: Fordham University Press.
Perloff, M. (2005), '"In Love with Hiding": Samuel Beckett's War', *Iowa Review*, 35 (1): 76–103.
Tajiri, Y., and M. Hori Tanaka (2009), 'The Reception of Samuel Beckett in Japan', in Mark Nixon and Matthew Feldman (eds.), *The International Reception of Samuel Beckett*, 147–62, London: Continuum.
Wonde, B. (2012), 'Yatte Kita Godot im Deutschen Theater – tsurezure naru mama ni', Stellv. Leiterin der Mori-Ôgai-Gedenksätte, Berlin, written on 22 December.
Žižek, S. (1992), *Looking Awry: An Introduction to Jacques Lacan through Popular Culture*, Cambridge: MIT Press.

INDEX

... *but the clouds* ... 52

absurd 24, 53, 77, 125, 127, 171, 173, 191
academic 109
Africa 36, 200
Absurdism/ Theatre of the Absurd 8–9, 138–40, 142, 146, 148, 160, 206
academia 3–4, 11, 49, 99–100, 142, 161–2
Act without Words I 115–16, 118–20, 160
Act without Words II 118, 159
Adorno, Theodor 2, 6, 86, 88, 112
affect 59–68
Algeria 167, 192
Al-Hakim, Tawfiq 191
alienation/ unbelonging 30, 40
alterity 100
   the Other 100, 204–5, 208
amplitude 65–6, 68
An Anthology of Mexican Poetry/ Mexican Poetry: An Anthology 4, 19, 45, 50–2
Andaházy, Margit 128
Anglicism 37, 75, 77
Apollinaire, Guillaume 18, 50
Apter, Emily 5–6, 46–7, 85–6, 177
Arabic/ Arab world 9, 11, 191–200
Aristotle 93, 157, 161
Arrabal, Fernando 160
arrivant 194–5, 198–9
Asmus, Walter 140
Assaf, Roger 191
As-Siddiqi, At-Tayib 191–2
Attridge, Derek 59, 61, 66–7
Auerbach, Eric 4–5, 65
authenticity (impossibility of) 78

Avant-garde 77, 94, 111, 137–8, 140, 142–5, 147
Avikunthak, Ashish 11, 169, 174, 176, 178

Balzac, Honoré de 105, 187–8
Baudrillard, Jean 203, 209–11
Beckett Digital Manuscript Project, (BDMP) 30–41
Beckett on Film 10, 87
Beckett, Samuel,
   as director 61–2, 65–6, 87–9, 158
   as poet 18, 46–7, 50, 52, 79, 159
   as self-translator 5, 8–10, 20–6, 29–30, 45, 52–5, 72, 75–7, 86–90, 93–5, 155
   as translator 4–6, 9–10, 17–22, 45–7, 50–2, 55–6, 76–7
Beckford, William 20
Beebee, Thomas 47
Beecroft, Alexander 155
Bentley, Eric 156
Bérczes, László 130–2, 135
Berger, James 203
Betsuyaku, Minoru 203–12
   The Elephant 206, 212
beverages 35
bi-culturalism 38
bilingualism 9, 17–26, 31, 40–1, 45–6, 48, 50, 154, 167
Blau, Herbert 156
Blin, Roger 21, 26, 54, 133, 153
Bloom, Harold 54
Body 62–3, 72–4, 92, 104, 119, 121, 143, 145
Bourdet, Gilas 66
Bowles, Patrick 30, 36–7, 39
brand,

INDEX

Axminster 35
baume Bengué 35
Beauty of Bath 35
Eintopf 39–40
Iodex 35
Irish stew 40
Thermogène 35–6
Wilton 35
Wintergreen 35
Brater, Enoch 61–2, 88, 153–4
Bray (Ireland) 31
Brazil 10, 109–22
Breath 118–19, 160
Breton, André, 18
Buddhism 74, 77
Bulatović, Miodrag 11, 181–9

canon 3–5, 7, 54–5, 77, 85, 100–1,
    108, 110, 145, 147, 154, 182
capitalism 49, 86, 128, 157, 162
Cappiello, Leonetto 36
Carrickmines 31
Casanova, Pascale 5–6, 48–9, 154
Catastrophe 7, 90
Céline, Louis-Ferdinand 25
Chabert, Pierre 92
Chaplin, Charles 155
    Chaplinesque 185
Cheah, Pheng 161, 169
China 10, 71–81, 137–47, 175
Christianity 52, 157, 184
circularity/ circular narrative structure
    10, 104, 112, 153–63
Colbert, Jean-Baptiste 33
Colgan, Michael 89
Collection Merlin 36
Come and Go 52
comedy 74, 76–7, 80, 127, 131, 141,
    187, 207
Commonwealth 36
communism 49, 134, 175–6, 183
Company 117
Connor, Steven 88, 163
Conrad, Joseph 24
Cooppan, Vilashini 41
core-periphery 154, 162–3
A Corpse of a Marine under Water
    206, 207–8, 212

cosmopolitanism 4, 9, 10–11, 45, 81,
    90, 155–7, 160
Crevel, René 18
crime 209–10
cultural affinities 29–41
currency 34

Dalkey (Ireland) 31
Damrosch, David 3, 5, 29, 41, 49, 53,
    78, 162, 168, 181–3, 189
Darwish, Mahmoud 191–2
de Biasi, Pierre-Marc 30
de Valera, Éamon 33
de-familiarization 155–7, 174, 177
Deleuze, Gilles 62–3
delocalization 33, 41
Derrida, Jacques 51, 66–7, 79–80,
    101–2, 193–6
destabilization 10, 33–5, 37, 168
Devlin, Denis 90
Devon 35
Dimock, Wai Chee 51
dish,
    Eintopf 39–40
    Irish stew 40
displacement 31, 40, 66, 88, 174, 177,
    182, 184, 188
Doležel, Lubomir 182–4, 188
domestication 77
Dream of Fair to Middling Women 1,
    99, 103, 108
Dublin 1–2, 17, 24, 26, 29, 31, 85,
    87–9, 91–5, 112
Duckworth, Colin 157, 160, 163, 164,
    183–4
Duve, Thierry de 94

Eagleton, Terry 3
Echo's Bones 99–100, 103, 105–6, 110
Eisenstein, Sergei 90
Eleutheria/ Éleuthéria 19, 111
Éluard, Paul 18, 50
Endgame/ Fin de Partie 10, 66, 86,
    104, 110–14, 125–34, 159, 163,
    167, 206–7
England 1, 29, 34, 48, 53
English/ British/ Anglo-Saxon 2, 4–6, 8,
    10, 17–26, 29–32, 34–41, 45–7,

48–9, 50–6, 72–5, 77, 86, 87, 153, 169, 173–4
Eriksson, Göran O. 66
Esslin, Martin 9, 24, 153, 160
ethics 61, 67–9, 175, 177–8
Europe/ European 2, 4, 26, 33–4, 46–7, 49–50, 60, 74, 77, 91, 154, 170, 205
Eurocentrism 41, 49, 147, 154
existentialism 77, 192

Faber and Faber 18, 54, 72
failure (aesthetic) 7–9, 11, 46, 55, 74, 87, 94, 160, 206
Fatima 198, 201
Feldman, Matthew 60
field (literary) 9, 30, (linguistic) 5, 45, (semiotic), 156
field of memory 91–2
Film 160
film 2, 5–6, 8, 11, 87–9, 91–5, 142, 167, 169–70, 174–8
'First Love' 115, 117
Footfalls 61–3, 66–8, 118, 119
forgetfulness 95, 203–4, 206–8, 210–11
France 1, 8, 20, 22, 26, 29, 30–1, 33, 35–6, 40, 48–9, 53–5.
Franzen, Erich 39
Freud, Sigmund 41, 104

Garton Ash, Timothy 68
genetic criticism/ critique génétique 10, 29–41
German 4, 19, 29, 31, 39–41, 46–7, 55, 77, 87, 208
German Diaries 39–40
Germany 1, 8, 29, 39, 48, 68
Girodias, Maurice 36
global/ globalized/ globalization 3–4, 8–9, 11, 32, 36, 40–1, 49, 51–2, 55, 59–61, 63, 67–8, 81, 86–7, 92–3, 99, 107, 110, 145, 147, 155, 162, 167–9, 173–4, 176–8, 205, 207
Godot Has Come 203–11
Goethe, Johann Wolfgang von 3–4

Gontarski, Stanley E. 60, 66–8, 87, 91, 117, 121, 138, 187
Gregg, Melissa and Gregory J. Seigworth 63–4
Grove Press 36, 54, 72
Guattari, Felix 62
guilt 206, 208, 211
Gyárfás, Miklós 126–31, 134

Happy Days 160
Hall, Peter 79–80
Hayot, Eric 60, 64–5, 68–9
Hebrew 38
Helfand, William H. 36
Hiberno-English 30, 37–8, 74
Hill, Leslie 30, 41
Hinduism 169, 174, 176
Hiroshima 203, 210–11
Hitler, Adolf 39, 47
holocaust 203
Hungary 9, 125–37
Huszár, László 131
hybrid forms 154
hybridity 30, 40, 79, 88, 167

Iglódi, István 128
impotence 7, 8, 11, 46, 78, 194
India 9, 11, 167, 169–70, 172–7
Inke, László 128
interculturalism/ internationalism 72, 90
inter-subjectivity/ subjectivity 64, 74–5, 78
Iraq 192
Ireland/ Eireann (Anglo-)Irish/ Gaelic 2–3, 5, 8–9, 18, 24, 26, 29–41, 48, 77, 87, 154
  Irish culture 24
  Irish nationalism 40
Irish Free State 32–3, 40
Islam 201
Italy/ Italian 4, 18–19, 29, 36, 46–7, 55

Japan 8, 9, 203–11
Jordan 192
Joyce, James 2, 5, 17–18, 24, 47–8, 54, 90, 102–3

Kalkimanthankatha 11, 169, 174, 176–8
Karmitz, Marin 92
Kazimir, Károly 127
Kéry, László 130
Kittler, Friedrich 95
Klein, Robert 133
Klemperer, Victor 40
Knowlson, James 2, 7, 30, 47, 50, 55, 78, 102, 105, 200, 205
Komanin, Žarko 181–4, 187–9
Kőmíves, Sándor 128
Kowatli, Walid 191
Krapp's Last Tape 101, 115, 160
Krauss, Rosalind 88–91, 94–5
Kumla Prison 200
Kundu, Supriya 169, 178
Kurtág, György 125, 132–5

L'Innommable/ The Unnamable 21, 30, 55
Lake Como 113–14, 128
Latin-America 50, 75, 161, 186
Lebanon 192, 200
lessness 86, 90, 92
Lindon, Jerôme 7, 85, 111
Lloyd, David 64
The Lost Ones 121
Louis XIV 33
Lowery, Bruce 20
Lucas, Cyril 37
Lucky's speech 71–8, 80

Malone Dies/ Malone meurt 21, 26, 30, 40
A Match in My Hand, and Your Petty Paper Nations 192
McGowran, Jack 115
McNaughton, James 39
measurements / metric system / imperial system 33–35
Metha, Rohit 64
Molière 30, 114
Molloy 3, 10, 23, 25, 29–41, 110, 115–16
Moloney, Alan 91–3
Monomyth 154
Mooney, Sinéad 30, 37, 40

More Pricks than Kicks 1, 24, 30, 99–100, 105, 108
Moretti, Franco 8, 49–50, 154, 175
Morin, Emilie 30, 32, 34, 37, 40, 77
Mount, Nick 155, 161, 163
Murphy 1, 3, 20–2, 24, 30–2, 47, 55
musicality 73–4, 76, 77, 79–80

Nagyvilág (journal), 127, 130
Nancy, Jean-Luc 86, 91–2, 168, 202
nationalism/ nationality/ patriotism/ patriotic 9, 26, 32, 40–1, 54, 78, 87, 204
Nayan Kabirer Pala 11, 169–73, 177
Nazism 39–40, 47, 53, 55, 204
Neary, J. Peter 22, 33
Nixon, Mark 40, 60
Nobel Prize 6–8, 19, 85, 138
Not I 79, 81, 85, 89, 104, 115, 144, 159

O'Donnell, Damien 91–3
Ó Gráda, Cormac 33
Occupation 20, 24
Ohio Impromptu 99–108, 113–14, 118–19, 160
Olympia Press 36
orientalism 20, 50

Paál, István 125, 130–2
pain 35, 196–7, 204, 207–11
Palestine 191–2
Pályi, András 128–9
Paris/ Parisian 2, 17, 20, 22, 26, 29–30, 33, 36, 45, 47–50, 54–5, 72, 74, 85, 92, 101, 112, 118, 133, 143, 153–4, 167, 200, 205
Paz, Octavio 4, 45, 50–2
performative reading 71–81
Perloff, Marjorie 8, 112, 209
Péron, Alfred 17–18, 20, 47
Philology 4, 50
Pinter, Harold 11, 160
politics 2–4, 7–9, 40, 45, 49, 51, 55, 90, 93–5, 103, 109, 111, 130, 131, 139, 141–2, 155, 167, 170, 174–7, 191–2, 194, 206

post-apocalypse 205
post-medium condition (Krauss) 88–90, 94–5
Postmodern/ Postmodernism 6, 9, 11, 86, 89–90, 141, 182, 184, 203–4
poverty 33, 186, 195
Proust (essay) 1, 24, 71–2, 75–6, 155
Puchner, Martin 93

Qabbānī, Nizār ('Waiting for Godot', 'A television interview with an Arab Godot') 191–200
Quad I & II 88, 118–21, 159

Ray, Satyajit 177–8
reception 2, 6, 10–11, 60, 76, 85, 87, 109–10, 118, 121, 122
regime 47, 55, 132, 196
religion 2, 77, 103, 170, 174–7, 184
representation 61, 64–6, 76, 93, 118, 154, 157, 160
resistance 24, 47, 74, 76, 86, 88–9, 93–4, 119, 209
rewrite 146, 182–4, 187–9
Rimbaud, Arthur ('The Drunken Boat') 5, 46–8, 50
river 2, 17, 50, 102–3, 106–8, 174, 195
Rivoallan, Anatole 48
Rosset, Barney 36–7
Rough for Radio II 90
Roundelay 133

Salzburg Opera Festival 133
San Quentin State Prison 2, 200
Sapiro, Gisèle 49, 154
Scanlan, Robert 66
Schneider, Alan 89, 167
Scott, Walter 38
Second World War 1, 10, 30, 45–7, 55, 131, 203
Sen, Nabhendu 170–2
Serbia 11, 182–3, 189
Shelley, Percy Bysshe 46
Shenker, Israel 20, 24
setting 30–1, 34–5, 89, 91, 93, 101–3, 106, 111–12, 114, 117, 121, 143–4, 156, 159–60, 170, 172, 175, 182, 210

singularity 61, 67, 174, 195
Spain/ Spanish 8–9, 19, 46, 50–1, 55, 161, 68, 200
spectre 102, 104, 193–6, 201
Steiner, George 52
Suzuki, Tadashi 206, 212
Sweden 6, 66, 200
Swift, Jonathan 33, 38
synchronicity 92, 199
Syria 191–4, 201
Szigligeti Theatre 125, 130

teleology 87, 116, 155, 157, 159
Tepantor 169, 172–3, 178
'Texts for Nothing' 25
Thália Theatre 125, 130
That Time 90
Théâtre de Babylone 153
Theatre of affect 59–68
Teatro alla Scala 132–3
Three Dialogues 54
Tompa, Gábor 132
traduttore traditore/ Transtraitor 19, 47, 55
tragicomedy 3, 52, 182–4, 186–9
translation 2, 4–6, 8–11, 17–69, 71–81, 85, 86–95, 100–1, 109, 114, 118, 121, 125–6, 134, 138, 139, 154–5, 161–2, 167–9, 172, 174, 177–8, 181–2
transnationalism 9, 170, 173–6
travel 22, 26, 29, 132, 168

UNESCO 4, 10, 19, 45, 49–51, 55
Unites States of America/ American 4, 20, 31, 34, 36–7, 39, 41, 49, 110–11, 147, 161, 167
unity 35, 40, 105
universality 6, 11, 85, 99, 131, 143, 147, 153–7, 161–2, 167, 175, 186, 197
untranslatability 5, 9–10, 45–7, 64, 66–7, 75, 77, 85–6, 92–3, 109, 177–8
unworlding 167, 169, 172–8

Váncsa, István 131–2
Vaucluse 20

Venuti, Lawrence 47, 54, 76–7, 81, 163
violence 33, 47–8, 76–80, 109, 114, 129, 141, 207, 209–10
Voigts-Virchow, Eckhart 92

waiting 52, 103, 105, 125, 138–9, 143, 146, 156–8, 169–71, 173–4, 178, 183–4, 186–7, 189, 192–200, 204–5, 207–9
Waiting for Godot/ En Attendant Godot 2, 3, 8–11, 19, 21, 25–6, 36, 45, 48, 52–5, 60, 71–5, 79–81, 111, 125, 127–8, 130, 132–3, 137–47, 153–62, 167, 169–78, 181–9, 191–200, 203–11
Wannous, Saadallah 191

Watt 20, 24, 38–9, 47, 193, 199
Weller, Shane 5, 41, 163
Western 8, 41, 49–50, 52, 54, 74, 122, 131, 137–9, 142, 145–7, 154, 161–2, 177, 193
What Where 10, 86–95, 160
Wiltshire 35
Winstanley, Adam 33
The World Republic of Letters 48
worldedness 61, 64–5, 68
worlding/ unworlding/ inter-worlding 167, 169, 172, 174–8
Worstward Ho 3, 8, 117
Wundt, Wilhelm 39

Žižek, Slavoj 2, 204, 208
Zsámbéki, Gábor 125–30

www.ingramcontent.com/pod-product-compliance
Lightning Source LLC
Chambersburg PA
CBHW072231290426
44111CB00012B/2042